A READER
IN EARLY
FRANCISCAN
THEOLOGY

MEDIEVAL PHILOSOPHY
Texts and Studies

Gyula Klima, *Fordham University*
series editor

Richard Cross
Brian Davies
Peter King
Brian Leftow
John Marenbon
Robert Pasnau
Giorgio Pini
Richard Taylor
Jack Zupko
editorial board

A READER IN EARLY FRANCISCAN THEOLOGY

The *Summa Halensis*

EDITED AND TRANSLATED BY
LYDIA SCHUMACHER AND OLEG BYCHKOV

FORDHAM UNIVERSITY PRESS

New York   2022

This work is licensed under a Creative Commons AttributionNonCommercial-NoDerivatives 4.0 International License.

This project has received funding from the European Research Council (ERC) under the European Union's Horizon 2020 research and innovation programme (grant agreement No714427).

Copyright © 2022 Fordham University Press

All rights reserved. No part of this publication may be reproduced, stored in a retrieval system, or transmitted in any form or by any means—electronic, mechanical, photocopy, recording, or any other—except for brief quotations in printed reviews, without the prior permission of the publisher.

Fordham University Press has no responsibility for the persistence or accuracy of URLs for external or third-party Internet websites referred to in this publication and does not guarantee that any content on such websites is, or will remain, accurate or appropriate.

Fordham University Press also publishes its books in a variety of electronic formats. Some content that appears in print may not be available in electronic books.

Visit us online at www.fordhampress.com.

Library of Congress Cataloging-in-Publication Data available online at https://catalog.loc.gov.

Printed in the United States of America

24 23 22   5 4 3 2 1

First edition

CONTENTS

A Guide to Citing the *Summa Halensis* / ix

Introduction / 1

1. The Science of Theology / 55
2. The Knowledge of God in This Life / 80
3. The Necessary Existence of God / 110
4. The Divine Nature / 120
5. The Transcendentals / 138
6. The Trinity / 172
7. Christology / 200
8. Free Choice / 228
9. Moral Theology / 248

A GUIDE TO CITING THE *SUMMA HALENSIS*
Prepared by Lydia Schumacher and Simon Maria Kopf

When citing the Quaracchi edition of the Franciscan Fathers, we suggest and use in this volume the following form as a standardized way of citing the *Summa Halensis*:

Alexander of Hales, *Doctoris irrefragabilis Alexandri de Hales Ordinis minorum Summa theologica* (*SH*), 4 vols. (Quaracchi: Collegium S. Bonaventurae, 1924–48), Vol. 3, In2, Tr2, S2, Q1, Ti1, C7, Ar3, Pr1, Pa2 (n. 162), Solutio, 179.

The second instance of citation should read as follows (including all relevant text divisions):

SH 3, In2, Tr2, S2, Q1, Ti1, C7, Ar3, Pr1, Pa2, Solutio, 179.

The relevant text divisions of the Quaracchi edition include, in the following order:

Vol.—Volume (*liber*)
P—Part (*pars*)
In—Inquiry (*inquisitio*)
Tr—Tract (*tractatus*)
S—Section (*sectio*)
Q—Question (*quaestio*)
Ti—Title (*titulus*)
D—Distinction (*distinctio*)
M—Member (*membrum*)
C—Chapter (*caput*)
Ar—Article (*articulus*)
Pr—Problem (*problema*)
Pa—Particle (*particula*)

Within the question, one may find the following:

[arg.]—Objections
Respondeo/Solutio—Response/solution
(Sed) Contra—On the Contrary
Ad obiecta—Replies to Objections

A READER
IN EARLY
FRANCISCAN
THEOLOGY

INTRODUCTION

The Franciscan intellectual tradition as it developed before Bonaventure, and above all, Duns Scotus, has so far garnered relatively little scholarly attention.[1] By most accounts, Bonaventure's forebears, and even Bonaventure himself, worked primarily to systematize the intellectual tradition of Augustine that had prevailed for most of the earlier Middle Ages.[2] In contrast, Scotus is supposed to have broken with the precedent set by earlier Franciscans in order to develop innovative philosophical and theological positions that anticipated the rise of modern thought.[3]

The passages selected for this reader contribute to making the case for the innovativeness of early Franciscan thought and its fundamental significance to the further development of the Franciscan intellectual tradition. The passages have been excerpted from the so-called *Summa Halensis*, a massive text that was collaboratively authored by the founding members of the Franciscan school at Paris between 1236 and 1245, with some final additions in 1255–56. For a long time, the text was attributed solely to Alexander of Hales, the first master of the school, who had joined the order in 1236 after

---

1. There are a number of articles and books on select topics in the *Summa Halensis* (SH), which will be cited at appropriate places in what follows. For an overview of the major theological topics covered in the *Summa* and in this reader, see Lydia Schumacher, *Early Franciscan Theology: Between Authority and Innovation* (Cambridge: Cambridge University Press, 2019). See also Lydia Schumacher, ed., *The Summa Halensis: Sources and Context* (Berlin: De Gruyter, 2020); *The Summa Halensis: Doctrines and Debates* (Berlin: De Gruyter, 2020); and *The Legacy of Early Franciscan Thought* (Berlin: De Gruyter, 2021).

2. See, for example, Ignatius Brady, "The *Summa Theologica* of Alexander of Hales (1924–1948)," *Archivum Franciscanum Historicum* 70 (1977): 437–47; Etienne Gilson, *The Philosophy of St. Bonaventure* (Chicago: Franciscan Press, 1965). See also A-M. Hamelin, "L'école franciscaine de ses débuts jusqu'a l'occamisme," *Analecta medievalia Namurcensia* (Louvain: Nauwelaerts,1961), and Christopher Cullen, *Bonaventure* (Oxford: Oxford University Press, 2006).

3. Olivier Boulnois, *Être et representation: Une généalogie de la métaphysique moderne à l'époque de Duns Scot* (Paris: Presses Universitaires de France, 1999). Ludger Honnefelder, *Scientia transcendens: Die formale Bestimmung der Seiendheit und Realität in der Metaphysik des Mittelalters und der Neuzeit* (Hamburg: Felix Meiner, 1990).

a long career in the University of Paris, where he was one of the most sophisticated and influential masters of his generation.[4]

As is well established, Alexander championed the effort to give a central place in the theology curriculum to lectures on Lombard's *Sentences*, which was a collection of authoritative quotations from scripture and the church fathers. In fact, he composed one of the earliest commentaries on the *Sentences* and established this practice as the prerequisite for obtaining the license to teach theology in the university—the modern equivalent of the doctoral degree.[5] Although he certainly oversaw the work on the *Summa* and contributed a great deal to it, whether indirectly or directly, the editors of the third volume eventually established that other Franciscans were involved in its composition as well.[6] The first and third volumes were likely authored primarily by Alexander's chief collaborator, John of La Rochelle, who had plans to prepare a *Summa* of his own before Alexander entered the order and his services became otherwise enlisted. Most probably, volumes 2.1 and 2.2 were prepared by a third redactor, who worked on the basis of John and Alexander's authentic works but did not always follow them exactly.[7]

---

4. Keenan B. Osborne, "Alexander of Hales," in *The History of Franciscan Theology* (St. Bonaventure, NY: The Franciscan Institute, 2007).

5. Philipp W. Rosemann, *The Story of a Great Medieval Book: Peter Lombard's Sentences* (Toronto: University of Toronto Press, 2007).

6. Victorin Doucet, "Prolegomena in librum III necnon in libros I et II Summae Fratris Alexandri," in *Alexandri de Hales Summa Theologica* (Quaracchi: Collegii S Bonaventurae, 1948); "The History of the Problem of the Summa," *Franciscan Studies* 7 (1947): 26–41, 274–312.

7. For details of the manuscripts of the *Summa Halensis* and their circulation, see Doucet, "Prolegomena," and the more recent and up-to-date studies by Riccardo Saccenti, "The Reception of the *Summa Halensis* in the Manuscript Tradition before 1450," in *The Legacy of Early Franciscan Thought*, ed. Lydia Schumacher (Berlin: De Gruyter, 2021), 353–73, and "The Manuscripts and Printed Editions of Book IV of the *Summa fratris Alexandri*," *Archivum Franciscanum Historicum* 114 (2021): 3–46. A survey of the manuscript tradition shows that already in the 1250s and 1260s, the *Summa* circulated in the *pecia* system, which saw its wide diffusion among students at the University of Paris and especially among the masters. The evidence derived from the manuscript tradition, combined with the witnesses concerning the influence of the text ascribed to Alexander of Hales, including the words of Roger Bacon, support the idea that the *Summa* quickly became a major text not only within the university milieu in Paris or Oxford but also inside the education system of the Franciscans.

The multiple authorship has been one reason for the *Summa*'s neglect, since modern scholars have tended to focus on single-authored works by a known author who could presumably guarantee the coherence of his work. However, the *Summa* is far from a compilation of relatively disjoined sections by different contributors. The coherence of the work is confirmed by manuscript evidence, which illustrates that the first three volumes were received as a whole following the deaths of John and Alexander in 1245.[8] Only two small additions and no major corrections were made to these volumes in 1255, when Pope Alexander IV ordered William of Melitona, then head of the Franciscan school at Paris, to enlist any help he needed to complete the fourth volume on the sacraments, which was not composed by Alexander and John and has yet to be prepared in a modern critical edition.[9] Thus, the *Summa Halensis* is significant precisely because it represents the "collective mind" of the founders of the Franciscan intellectual tradition at Paris and their attempt to articulate the contours of this tradition for the very first time.[10]

Another major reason for the neglect of the *Summa* is the aforementioned assumption that Franciscan thought before and including Bonaventure was primarily aimed at defending Augustine's longstanding intellectual tradition against the rising tide of Aristotelianism.[11] Even the editor of the *Summa*

---

8. Doucet, "The History of the Problem of the Summa," 296–302. See also Palémon Glorieux, "Les années 1242-1247 à la Faculté de Théologie de Paris," *Recherches de théologie ancienne et médiévale* 29 (1962), 234–49.

9. Robert Prentice, O.F.M., "The *De fontibus paradisi* of Alexander IV on the *Summa Theologica* of Alexander of Hales," *Franciscan Studies* 5 (1945): 350–51. The additions include SH 1, *De missione visibili*, 514–18; 2.1: *De corpore humano*, 501–630; *De coniuncto humano*, 631–784.

10. Etienne Gilson, *History of Christian Philosophy in the Middle Ages* (London: Sheed and Ward, 1955), 327–31.

11. Franz Ehrle, *Grundsätzliches zur Charakteristik der neueren und neuesten Scholastik* (Freiburg im Breisgau: Herder, 1918) was among the first to label early Franciscans "neo-Augustinians." Etienne Gilson followed suit in his voluminous works, including his *History of Christian Philosophy in the Middle Ages* (New York: Random House, 1955), as did other leading medievalists like Bernard Vogt, in "Der Ursprung und die Entwicklung der Franziskanerschule," *Franziskanische Studien* 9 (1922): 137–57, and Maurice de Wulf, *Medieval Philosophy: Illustrated from the System of Thomas Aquinas* (Cambridge, MA: Harvard University Press, 1922). The reading of Bonaventure and early Franciscans as "Augustinians" and relatively unoriginal systematizers of past authorities is indeed ubiquitous in the scholarly

Halensis articulated this opinion: "The significance of the *Summa Halensis* consists in this, namely, that all the elements of this Augustinian tradition, both theological and philosophical, are gathered, arranged, and defended in it, even though Aristotle was on the rise. Thus, it is universally and rightly seen as the foundation of the Augustinian-Franciscan school in the thirteenth century."[12]

Admittedly, there is an exceptional number of quotations from Augustine in the *Summa*. The work contains a total of 4,814 explicit and 1,372 implicit references to Augustine, which amounts to more than one quarter of the sources cited in the text. At the time, however, this pattern of quotation was not unusual: many scholastic authors gave disproportional weight to Augustine's authority, including Peter Lombard in his *Sentences*. The emphasis on Augustine was attributable to his status as the fountainhead of the Western Christian tradition and thus the "authority of authorities." To quote him was to situate one's own work on the right side of theological history.

Although appeals to Augustine sometimes involved simply repeating or defending his viewpoints, more often than not, the reason for quoting Augustine was to enlist his endorsement for whatever opinion an author himself wanted to develop.[13] As Mary Carruthers has noted, works of authorities like

---

literature. See also Artur Michael Landgraf, *Introduction à l'histoire de la littérature théologique de la scolastique naissante*, ed. A. M. Landry, trans. L. B. Geiger (Paris: Vrin, 1973); Jaroslav Pelikan, *The Christian Tradition: A History of the Development of Doctrine* (Chicago: University of Chicago Press, 1991).

12. Doucet, "Prolegomena in librum III necnon in libros I et II *Summae Fratris Alexandri*," lxxxviii: *Sed momentum, ni fallimur, Summae Halensianae in hoc consistit, quod omnia elementa, theologica scilicet et philosophica, huius traditionis augustinianae in ea colliguntur, ordinantur atque defenduntur Aristotele licet iam invadente. Quare et merito fundamentum Scholae augustino-franciscanae saec. XIII communiter salutatur.*

13. Marcia L. Colish, "The Sentence Collection and the Education of Professional Theologians in the Twelfth Century," in *The Intellectual Climate of the Early University: Essays in Honor of Otto Grundler*, ed. Nancy Van Deusen (Kalamazoo: Western Michigan University, 1997), 1–26, at 11; Marcia L. Colish, "Authority and Interpretation in Scholastic Theology," in *Studies in Scholasticism* (Aldershot: Ashgate, 2006), 1–16, at 5; Jacques Bougerol, "The Church Fathers and *Auctoritates*," in *The Reception of the Church Fathers in the West: From the Carolingians to the Maurists*, ed. Irena Backus (Leiden: Brill, 1997), 1:289–335, at 334. As Bougerol has written, this was a period when "everyone could use the tradition as he chose." See also Bert Roest, "Franciscan Augustinianism: Musings about Labels and Late

Augustine were considered authoritative precisely because and to the extent that they gave rise to new interpretations and meanings.[14] The liberal readings of Augustine that resulted were facilitated considerably by the wide circulation of spurious works that were often attributed to the bishop in the Middle Ages.

The most popular of these works among Franciscans included the *De fide ad Petrum* (On Faith, to Peter), *De ecclesiasticis dogmatibus* (The Dogmas of the Church), and, above all, *De spiritu et anima* (The Spirit and the Soul), a twelfth-century text produced in Cistercian circles before 1170, which the *Summa*'s immediate predecessors and contemporaries such as Philip the Chancellor and Albert the Great had already declared inauthentic.[15] This work contained an array of intellectual schemata that made it possible to associate practically any psychological theory with Augustine.

In this regard, it eased the incorporation of the works of natural philosophy that had recently become available to Latin thinkers through the translation movement of the twelfth century. Most famously, this movement saw the major works of Aristotle translated into Latin. However, the massive *Book of the Cure* of the Islamic scholar Avicenna also became available during this time and was actually more popular than Aristotle in the period of the *Summa*'s authorship. There are numerous reasons for this, one being that Aristotle's works were introduced in a gradual and sporadic fashion, with some like the *Metaphysics* and *Nicomachean Ethics* circulating only in partial forms into the early thirteenth century.

Medieval School Formation," in *Franciscan Learning, Preaching and Mission c. 1220–1650* (Leiden: Brill, 2015), 111–31. Francois-Xavier Putallaz also queries the validity of the "Augustinian" label for Bonaventure and later Franciscans in his *Figures franciscaines de Bonaventure à Duns Scot* (Paris: Cerf, 1997).

14. As Mary Carruthers has observed in *The Book of Memory: A Study of Memory in Medieval Culture* (Cambridge: Cambridge University Press, 1990), 262, authorities in this period were not authors but texts, and texts were not static entities but resources to be interpreted in new and creative ways. In turn, these interpretations became part of and indeed expanded the perceived meaning of the text, "which was in a continual process of being understood, its plenitude of meaning being perfected and completed."

15. Bernard McGinn, "Introduction," in *Three Treatises on Man: A Cistercian Anthropology* (Kalamazoo, MI: Cistercian Publishers, 1977), 67, 71; G. Théry, "L'authenticité du *De spiritu et anima* dans Saint Thomas et Albert le Grand," *Revue des sciences philosophiques et théologiques* 10 (1921): 373–77, at 376.

Another problem concerned the quality of the translations from Greek into Latin, which was perceived as quite poor by comparison to the translations from Arabic into Latin. Although Avicenna's work contained treatises on all the main topics Aristotle covered—metaphysics, physics, logic, and the soul—he was not a mere commentator on Aristotle. This is evidenced by the fact that his works do not appear in the manuscript tradition together with Aristotle's, as is the case with the works of Averroes on Aristotle, which only became available around 1230, though their actual incorporation apparently took longer.[16]

By contrast to "the commentator," who followed Aristotle's text closely, Avicenna offered highly original insights on broadly Aristotelian *topoi* that nonetheless integrated many key facets of Neoplatonism. The reconciliation of Aristotle and Platonism along these lines was not perceived as extraordinary at the time given that Aristotle himself was regarded in both the Greek and Arabic commentary traditions as a kind of Neoplatonist, whose mature theological views were supposedly presented in the spurious *Theology of Aristotle*, which was in fact a compilation based on the *Enneads* of Plotinus.[17]

Though this work was not translated into Latin until the Renaissance, a similar work called the *Liber de causis* was extremely popular in the Middle Ages and was attributed to Aristotle until 1268, when Thomas Aquinas identified Proclus as one of its major sources. Around this same time, new and improved translations of Aristotle were also produced. These along with the genuine commentaries of Averroes, which garnered more interest following the production of new translations of Aristotle, encouraged the more direct and faithful reading of Aristotle. Until the mid-thirteenth century, however, Latin thinkers generally operated on the assumption that Aristotle could be read in conversation with Christian Platonic sources—above all, Augustine—interpreting both in line with Avicenna, who offered the most sophisticated resource available at the time for grappling with Greek natural philosophy.[18]

---

16. Dag N. Hasse, *Avicenna's De Anima in the Latin West* (London: Warburg Institute, 2000), 226.

17. See Lydia Schumacher, "Christian Platonism in the Medieval West," in *Christian Platonism: A History*, ed. John Kenney and Alexander Hampton (Cambridge: Cambridge University Press, 2020), 183–206.

18. Amos Bertolacci, "On the Latin Reception of Avicenna's Metaphysics before Albertus Magnus: An Attempt at Periodization," in *The Arabic, Hebrew and Latin*

While the Franciscans were by no means exceptional in making use of Avicenna during this period, they were by far the most predominant school of thought to do so. Moreover, their incorporation of Avicennian themes was far more extensive than that of many of their contemporaries. In the case of the Franciscans particularly, there appears to have been a sort of "happy coincidence" between the Avicennian materials that were available and popular at the time and what was well suited to articulating a distinctly Franciscan form of thought.[19] As noted already, a major reason for the very production of the *Summa* was to give expression to a way of thinking theologically and philosophically that was presumably consistent with the vision and values of Francis of Assisi, who had passed away only ten years before work on the *Summa* began in 1236.

Although the *Summa* genre did not lend itself to speculation on motives for writing, the need for this initial statement of Franciscan thought was presumably urgent for a number of reasons. In the first place, the rapid growth of the order—from twelve members in 1209 to as many as twenty thousand by 1250—called for a means by which to induct learned friars who were rapidly accumulating in the order into the Franciscan way of life. In fact, the *Summa Halensis* formed the basis for the education of friar-scholars at least through the time of Duns Scotus.[20] Bonaventure, for one, credits everything he learned to his "master and father" Alexander of Hales, which is scarcely an exaggeration.[21]

Another reason for the *Summa*'s production was certainly to establish the place of the Franciscans in the University of Paris, which was founded around 1200 and served as the center for theological study at the time. Although Francis did not originally envisage a role for his friars in the university, higher

---

Reception of Avicenna's Metaphysics, ed. Dag Nikolaus Hasse and Amos Bertolacci (Berlin: De Gruyter, 2012), 197–223, at 204.

19. This was noted some time ago by Étienne Gilson, who mistakenly believed that "Avicennizing Augustinianism" was an authentic representation of Augustine. Gilson, "Les sources gréco-arabes de l'augustinisme avicennisant," *Archives d'histoire doctrinale et littéraire du moyen âge* 4 (1929): 5–107; "Pourquoi saint Thomas a critiqué saint Augustin," *Archives d'histoire doctrinale et littéraire du moyen âge* 1 (1926–27): 5–127.

20. Bert Roest, *A History of Franciscan Education* (Leiden: Brill, 2000), 126.

21. Bonaventure, *Commentaria in quattuor libros Sententiarum Magistri Petri Lombardi: in librum II* (Turnhout: Brepols, 2011), Prologue, Lib II, d 23, a 2, q e (II, 547).

education quickly became the precondition for religious and spiritual authority in the period and thus for the very survival of the order.[22] Nevertheless, there was considerable controversy both within and outside the order as to whether the friars minor should be engaged in university affairs. Inside the order, for example, lay friars, some of whom had known Francis, protested that the pursuit of higher education and academic esteem undermined the founder's fundamental principles of poverty, humility, and simplicity.

Within the wider university, the secular masters, or masters who were not part of a religious order, saw the friars as a threat to their own jobs, student enrollment numbers, and therefore salaries. Under the circumstances, the growing body of learned friars—led by none other than Alexander and John—faced enormous pressure to establish a distinctly Franciscan form of thinking that would resonate with and uphold the principles of their founder, at a level of sophistication that would prove their worth as academics and their right to remain and even dominate in the university context.

The *Summa Halensis* was evidently the solution to this problem—and a highly successful one at that. Not only was it the first major theological treatise extensively to incorporate the new natural philosophy, but it also delved into more recently recovered theological sources, in addition to all the traditional patristic sources that were popular and available at the time and that had been invoked by Peter Lombard. These newer works included John of Damascus, whom Lombard had only begun to incorporate in a provisional way; Anselm of Canterbury, whose works had largely been neglected before Alexander of Hales; and Hugh and Richard of St. Victor and Bernard of Clairvaux.[23]

In addition to mastering all available sources, the *Summa Halensis* far outstripped other texts of the period in terms of the size and scope of its inquiry. That is not to deny that there were other great works that preceded it, including many commentaries on Lombard's *Sentences* and early *summae* like the *Summa aurea* of William of Auxerre and the *Summa de bono* of Philip the Chancellor, which also comprise major conversation partners for the *Summa Halensis*. However, the text that is by far the largest among these earlier works, namely, the *Summa aurea*, contains only 818 questions for

---

22. Neslihan Senocak, *The Poor and the Perfect: The Rise of Learning in the Franciscan Order 1209–1310* (Ithaca, NY: Cornell University Press, 2012).
23. McGinn, "Introduction," 67.

discussion by comparison to the 3,408 of the *Summa Halensis*, as Ayelet Even-Ezra has shown.[24] There is virtually no comparison in size between the *Summa* and earlier scholastic sources.

In this regard, the *Summa* served as a sort of "first installment" in the *summa* genre for which university scholasticism would quickly become famous, and a prototype for later and perhaps more well-known *Summae* like that of Thomas Aquinas. The Dominican master clearly had the *Summa* to hand when he began work on his magisterial *Summa Theologiae*, a full twenty years after the *Summa Halensis* itself was completed. As a comparison of these two *summae* confirms, Aquinas adopted many topics that had first been introduced in the Franciscan *Summa*, including his famous "Five Ways" to prove God's existence, his treatment of natural and eternal law, and the structure and key aspects of his account of the soul.[25] While he situated these topics within his own frame of reference, with a view to bolstering his own doctrinal positions, his reliance on the Franciscan precedent in formal terms is often very apparent.[26]

Even before Aquinas, Albert the Great had borrowed extensively, sometimes even whole passages, from the *Summa Halensis*, as Oleg Bychkov has shown in his study of aesthetics.[27] The "great affinity" between the Halensian and Albertine *summae* was already highlighted by Victorin Doucet, the editor of the third book of the *Summa Halensis*, who states that "these Summae not infrequently concur" (*illae Summae non raro concordant*) and that Albert "constantly had the Halensian Summa in his hands" (*constanter prae manibus habuerit*).[28] This is not even to mention the *Summa*'s influence on other prominent thirteenth-century authors such as Bonaventure, who likewise

---

24. Ayelet Even-Ezra, "The *Summa Halensis*: A Text in Context," in *The Summa Halensis: Sources and Context*, ed. Lydia Schumacher (Leiden: Brill, 2020), 215–30.

25. Thomas Aquinas, *Quaestiones disputatae De anima*, ed. Bernardo Carlos Bazán (Paris: Les Éditions du Cerf, 1996).

26. See, for example, Beryl Smalley, "William of Auvergne, John of La Rochelle and Saint Thomas on the Old Law," in *Studies in Medieval Thought and Learning from Abelard to Wyclif* (London: Hambledon Press, 1981): 121–211.

27. Oleg Bychkov, "A Propos of Medieval Aesthetics: A Historical Study of Terminology, Sources, and Textual Traditions of Commenting on Beauty in the Thirteenth Century" (PhD thesis, University of Toronto, 1999), 27–29, 211–12.

28. Doucet, "Prolegomena in librum III necnon in libros I et II *Summae fratris Alexandri*," ccxxxv–ccxxxvi.

had this text in his hands (*prae manibus*) when he wrote his commentary on the *Sentences*.²⁹

When these aspects of the *Summa*'s context are taken into account, the text that Roger Bacon sarcastically described as having "the weight of a horse"³⁰ emerges as no mere "Augustinian encyclopedia" but as a pioneering text for early university scholasticism, which likewise represents the first statement of many concepts that would become defining features of the Franciscan intellectual tradition. The translations provided in this volume seek to showcase some of the doctrines where early Franciscans exhibited the greatest creativity and even novelty, including the nature of theology, the knowledge of God, the proof of his existence, the nature of God as infinite, as a transcendental being, as Triune, its Christology, and ideas on free will and moral theology. The doctrines are commented upon below roughly in the order in which the *Summa* treats them, with its first volume devoted to theology proper and the doctrine of God; the two parts of the second volume to creation and sin, respectively; and the third volume to Christology, the law, and grace.

Together with the translations, these comments open doors for exploring the continuity between the Summists' work and that of subsequent Franciscans: not only Bonaventure but also later thinkers like Peter of John Olivi and John Duns Scotus, who have often been regarded as the inaugurators of a new strand in the Franciscan intellectual tradition. At another level, the proximity of the *Summa* to Francis may facilitate efforts to detect the possible correlation between Franciscan ideas and the understanding of the Franciscan ethos that prevailed at the time, as depicted, for instance, in the three biographies of Francis by Thomas of Celano.³¹ In that sense, the *Summa Halensis* has the potential to bring us back to the heart of the Franciscan intellectual

---

29. Ibid., ccxlvi.

30. Roger Bacon, *Opus Minus*, in *Fr. Rogeri Bacon Opera quaedam hactenus inedita*, ed. J. S. Brewer (London: Longman, Green, Longman, and Roberts, 1859), 1:326: *Et adscripserunt ei magnam Summam illam, quae est plusquam pondus unius equi, quam ipse non fecit sed alii. Et tamen propter reverentiam adscripta fuit et vocatur Summa fratris Alexandri etsi ipse eam fecisset vel magnam partem* ("And they ascribed to him [Alexander] that large *Summa*, which weighs more than a horse, which he did not write but others did. And nevertheless, it was ascribed to him out of reverence and called the *Summa fratris Alexandri* as if he himself had written it, or the better part of it").

31. *St. Francis of Assisi: Early Documents, The Founder*, ed. Regis J. Armstrong, J. A. Wayne Hellman, and William J. Short (New York: New City Press, 2000);

tradition and the reasons why certain ideas were formulated in the first place, disclosing the purpose and thus the promise of Franciscan thought, not only in its own time but also for theology and philosophy today.

CHAPTER 1: THE SCIENCE OF THEOLOGY

In the scholastic period, it became common practice in theological treatises to begin with a discussion of the status of theology as a science or field of inquiry. In fact, the *Summa Halensis* was among the first to engage in this kind of inquiry, aside from Roland of Cremona. Both worked largely at the impetus of Aristotle's *Posterior Analytics*, which was increasingly becoming a topic of discussion in the 1240s.[32] The purpose of Aristotle's work in large part was to outline the conditions for determining whether any given field of inquiry satisfies the criteria for a genuine "science."[33]

Is the Discipline of Theology an [Exact] Science?

SH 1, Tr Int, Q1, C1 (n. 1), 1–4

In this regard, the *Summa* argues that the science which concerns God is actually a higher science than other sciences, because it pertains to the cause of all causes, which is self-sufficient, whereas other sciences deal with things that are caused.[34] For this same reason, the science of theology, which is better called wisdom, insofar as it deals with the cause of all things, is more certain than other sciences, namely, because it is the ground of other sciences.

Jacques Dalarun, *La vie retrouvée de François d'Assise* (Paris: Editions Franciscaines, 2015).

32. C. R. Hess, "Roland of Cremona's Place in the History of Thought," *Angelicum* 45 (1968): 429–77, 453. See "Quid sit subiectum theologiae," in *Summae Magistri Rolandi Cremonensis, O. P. Liber Primus* (Bergamo: Umberto Midali, 2015-7), 22–24.

33. B. Niederbacher and G. Leibold, eds., *Theologie als Wissenschaft im Mittelalter: Texte, Übersetzungen, Kommentare* (Münster: Aschendorff, 2006); Christian Trottmann, *Théologie et noétique au XIIIe siècle* (Paris: J. Vrin, 1999); U. Köpf, *Die Anfänge der theologischen Wissenschaftstheorie im 13. Jhr.* (Tübingen: Mohr Siebeck, 1974).

34. Anna-Katharina Strohschneider, "The *Summa Halensis* on Theology and the Sciences: The Influence of Aristotle and Avicenna," in Schumacher, *The Legacy of Early Franciscan Thought*, 49–70.

Although superior to other sciences, wisdom as described here does not yet capture the fullness of the *Summa*'s understanding of theology, the purpose of which is not merely to perfect our understanding of the first cause but rather to perfect our affections by moving them toward goodness, through the principles of love for God and fear of displeasing him. Another name used for theology in the *Summa Halensis* and other contemporary works is Sacred Scripture.[35] The reason theology was effectively conflated with Sacred Scripture at this time is that the latter contains stories about individuals that nonetheless imply universal principles about God and the purpose of human existence—the very subjects proper to theology itself.

About the Difference between Sacred Doctrine [i.e., Theology] and Other Sciences

SH 1, Tr Int, Q1, C2 (n. 2), 4–5

While other sciences have their foundation in creatures, the *Summa* states that theology articulates what is received "from God," thus teaching us what we should believe "about God," thereby leading us "toward God."[36] While the first two functions of theology seem largely speculative in nature, the last one highlights that their ultimate purpose is to inspire piety or devotion to God and related good and moral actions. As this suggests, and as Oleg Bychkov has shown, the *Summa Halensis* already edges in the distinctly Franciscan direction of describing theology as a practical more than a purely theoretical science and thus anticipates the development of this perspective in Bonaventure, Olivi, and Scotus, and others.[37]

---

35. Hess, "Roland of Cremona's Place in the History of Thought," 460. Ulrich Köpf, *Die Anfänge der theologischen Wissenschaftstheorie im 13. Jahrhundert* (Tübingen: Mohr Siebeck, 1974), 24.

36. SH 1, Tr Int, Q1, C2, Ad objecta 1–4 (n. 2), 5. Boyd Taylor Coolman, "On the Subject Matter of Theology in the *Summa Halensis* and St. Thomas Aquinas," *The Thomist* 79 (2015): 439–66.

37. Oleg Bychkov, "The Nature of Theology in Duns Scotus and His Franciscan Predecessors," *Franciscan Studies* 66 (2008): 5–62; Mikolaj Olszewski, "Beginning of the Discussion of Practical or Theoretical Character of Theology: The Positions of Alexander of Hales, Thomas Aquinas, Albert the Great, and Giles of Rome," *Studia Mediewistyczne* 34–35 (1999–2000): 129–46.

What Is the Science of Sacred Scripture About [i.e., What Is Its Subject]?
SH 1, Tr Int, Q1, C3 (n. 3), 5–7

The means by which we acquire the aforementioned knowledge from, about, and toward God, the *Summa* further argues, is Christ, without whom we would not know anything about God or how he intends, and Christ enabled, us to live. On this basis, the *Summa* concludes that "theology is a science about the divine substance that must be cognized through Christ in the course of his work of restoration or salvation."[38] Put differently, theology "instructs the soul in those matters that pertain to salvation."[39]

Is the Way of [Proceeding in] Sacred Scripture That of Discipline or Science?
SH 1, Tr Int, Q1, C4, Ar1 (n. 4), 7–9

While other sciences "operate by way of grasping truth through human reason," the *Summa* elaborates that the wisdom entailed in theology "operates by way of eliciting the affection of piety through what is divinely inspired . . . by way of precepts, examples, admonitions, revelation and prayer, because it is these things that are appropriate for eliciting the affection of piety."[40] The main example of revelation is again that of Christ, and the main precept or admonition is of course to live as he taught us, which may be why moral questions, like Christological ones, consume a great deal of attention in the *Summa Halensis*.

Is the Manner of Sacred Scripture One of Certitude?
SH 1, Tr Int, Q1, C4, Ar2 (n. 5), 9–10

In a subsequent turn of the argument, the *Summa* states that "the way of knowing through inspiration is more certain than the one through human rational thought. Also, what is known from the testimony of the Spirit is more certain than what is known from the evidence gathered from creatures. . . . Therefore, since knowledge in theology is divinely inspired, it is a truer

---

38. SH 1, Tr Int, Q1, C3, Respondeo (n. 3), 6: *Theologia est scientia de substantia divina cognoscenda per Christum in opere reparationis.*
39. SH 1, Tr Int, Q1, C4, Ar1, Respondeo (n. 4), 8.
40. SH 1, Tr Int, Q1, C4, Ar1, Ad objecta 2 (n. 4), 8.

science than other sciences."[41] At first glance, this claim might seem implausible, given that the object of theology is inaccessible to the human mind, whereas the objects of human reason are often empirical and thus manifestly knowable.[42] On the *Summa*'s reasoning, however, it is fully justified, given that knowledge which is delivered by God, the source of all truth, precludes falsity, which commonly plagues human reasoning. Indeed, the pristine source of knowledge is what guarantees its certitude.

The certitude in question is not accessible by any means whatsoever, however. For it comes through the receptivity to revelation that is cultivated through a devotion to God which is not intellectual but volitional. The kind of certitude the *Summa* has in mind here, consequently, is not a certitude of the intellect but of the affections, which comes by way of taste rather than by sight.[43] The emphasis here on taste or the experience of God as a function of the love of God is a distinctly Franciscan one, which becomes the cornerstone of Olivi's theology, as well as a feature of Scotus's, as Oleg Bychkov has shown.[44] For instance, in Olivi's *Questions on Evangelical Perfection* 8 and *Sent*. II, q. 57, experience is the means by which we become conscious of the importance of absolute poverty and free choice, two pillars of the Franciscan practical vision.[45] For Scotus, moreover, experience will become the basis for proving the existence of God.

---

41. SH 1, Tr Int, Q1, C1, Contra a (n. 1), 2: *Quod cognoscitur per divinam inspirationem verius scitur quam quod per humanam ratiocinationem . . . ergo, cum cognitio theologiae sit edita inspiratione divina . . . verius est scientia quam ceterae scientiae.*

42. SH 1, Tr Int, Q2, M3, C5, Respondeo (n. 24), 36.

43. The distinction between taste and sight derives from an anonymous theological text edited by Daniel A. Callus in "The Powers of the Soul: An Early Unpublished Text," *Recherches de Théologie ancienne et médiévale* 19 (1952): 131–70.

44. Oleg Bychkov, "But Everyone Experiences the Opposite: John Duns Scotus's Aesthetic Defense of Anselm's Proof of the Existence of God in Light of Present-Day Thought," *Franciscan Studies* 72 (2014): 259–303.

45. Petrus Ioannis Olivi, *Das Heil der Armen und das Verderben der Reichen*, ed. J. Schlageter, *Franziskanische Forschungen* 34 (Werl: Dietrich-Coelde-Verlag, 1989), 125, 131–32; Petrus Iohannis Olivi, *Quaestiones in secundum librum Sententiarum*, Quaestiones 48–71, ed. B. Jansen (Quaracchi: Typographia Collegii S. Bonaventurae, 1924), 2:316–38.

Is the Manner of Sacred Scripture Uniform, or Does It Have Many Forms?

SH 1, Tr Int, Q1, C4, Ar3 (n. 6), 10–11

According to the *Summa*, the communication of Sacred Scripture can take a great many different forms, including the historical, which conveys facts about the past; the allegorical, whereby we understand one thing through another; the tropological, which concerns morals; and the anagogical, which concerns spiritual and ultimate things. The reason for these and other forms of divine communication is to employ all possible means to instruct us in different ways at different times concerning the way of salvation and to lead us to it.

On the Multitude of Forms That the Manner of Sacred Scripture Exhibits

SH 1, Tr Int, Q1, C4, Ar4 (n. 7), 11–13

In a further discussion of the four standard methods of interpreting scripture, the *Summa* distinguishes between one that is literal, that is, the historical, and three that are spiritual, namely, the anagogical, which leads one upward to the first principle; the allegorical, which announces the hidden things of the first truth; and the tropological or moral, which orders human beings in accordance with the highest goodness.

In different ways, these different forms of interpretation bring us back to the *Summa*'s constant refrain that theology "consists rather in virtue and practical efficiency than in contemplation and [speculative] knowledge."[46] For they are all ultimately oriented toward helping us relate rightly to our first principle and to live accordingly. The key to knowing how to do so, to accessing the principles of right living that theology provides, above all, through Christ, is the affection for God that renders us receptive to his inspiration and his teaching.

CHAPTER 2: THE KNOWLEDGE OF GOD IN THIS LIFE

Is the Human Soul Capable of Knowing God?

SH 1, Tr Int, Q2, M1, C1 (n. 8), 15–16

The *Summa* proceeds from the study of theology as a science to the question whether God is knowable by the human soul. In answering this question,

---

46. SH 1, Tr Int, Q1, C4, Ar2, Ad objecta 2 (n. 5), 9: [*Haec scientia*] *magis enim consistit in virtute et efficacia quam in contemplatione et notitia.*

the Summist quotes Augustine, who says in his book *On Seeing God* [Letter 147, c. 2, n. 7] that, "The difference between seeing and believing is that the things that are present are seen and the things that are absent are believed. By 'things that are present right here,' we understand those things that are instantly accessible to our senses, either mental or corporeal. For example, I see this light by my corporeal sense, and [I see] my will, because it is instantly accessible to my mental sensory awareness, because it is present inside of me."

Thus, every object of knowledge is visible to our mental or corporeal sensory awareness; therefore, if God is invisible, he is thereby also not knowable. The *Summa* qualifies this conclusion with another quotation from the same text of Augustine [Letter 147, c. 15, n. 37]: "If you ask whether God can be seen, I reply: he can. If you ask how I know this, I reply: because we read this in scripture, [Matthew 5:8] which is most true: '*Blessed are the pure in heart, for they shall see God.*' Based on this, the distinction is clear: God is invisible by nature, but visible by his will," in particular, to those whose wills are pure before him and love him absolutely.

While in normal circumstances, or as far as human reason alone is concerned, God is unknowable, the Summist argues here that a love for God, in response to his love for us, opens a door that would not normally be accessible to knowing God. This somewhat voluntarist approach to affirming God's knowability was the way that early Franciscans combined the tendency of newly popular Greek patristic scholars like Pseudo-Dionysius to insist on God's unknowability with the idea of the beatific vision of God.[47] Although the beginnings of a tendency to prioritize love over knowledge are relatively clear in this section, there are signposts to another signature Franciscan doctrine that become obvious only on closer consideration.

These concern the *Summa*'s references to Augustine's distinction between knowledge by direct seeing and knowing remotely, by believing. Whereas the former concerns "things present right here," whether to the senses or the intellect, the latter concerns things that are not thought of as immediately present, although in some cases, they may have been in the past. Those familiar with the later development of the Franciscan intellectual tradition, particularly in Duns Scotus, will be able to detect hints here of the famous distinction between intuitive and abstractive cognition, or between the

---

47. Simon Tugwell, *Albert and Thomas: Selected Writings* (New York: Paulist Press, 1988), 55.

knowledge of things as immediately present and the knowledge of things that have never been or are not now encountered as present.[48]

Can the Divine Substance Be Known in Its Immensity?
SH 1, Tr Int, Q2, M1, C2 (n. 9), 17–18
An approach to knowing God that anticipates this distinction arguably underlies the *Summa*'s whole discussion in this section, including the next question, whether the divine substance can be known in its immensity or infinity. For the *Summa*, the answer to this question is emphatically negative, because the human intellect is finite and can only therefore know the divine substance in a finite way. This, however, is precisely the basis on which the *Summa* argues for the possibility of knowing God in some finite respect, namely, through creatures, and by inferring from their limited qualities the qualities like eternal, infinite, and so on, which Scotus will call "pure perfections," that are proper to the unlimited source of all things, namely, God.

Is the Trinity of Persons Known by Natural Reason?
SH 1, Tr Int, Q2, M1, C3 (n. 10), 18–19
In response to the related question whether the Trinity of persons is known by natural reason, the *Summa* declines to give an affirmative answer, except in regard to circumstances where the mind is subject to grace. After all, things that exceed reason require aid from that which exceeds reason in order to be known by reason itself.

Can God or the Divine Substance Be Known Face to Face in This Life?
SH 1, Tr Int, Q2, M1, C4 (n. 11), 20–21
The same principle applies in the *Summa*'s answer to the question whether God or the divine substance can be known face to face in this life. While

---

48. Stephen Dumont, "Theology as a Science and Duns Scotus's Distinction Between Intuitive and Abstractive Cognition," *Speculum* 64, no. 3 (1989): 579–99. As Oleg Bychkov explains in his article "The Status of the Phenomenal Appearance of the Sensory in Fourteenth-Century Franciscan Thought after Duns Scotus (Peter Aureol to Adam of Wodeham)," *Franciscan Studies* 76 (2018): 267–85, this distinction is further developed by Peter John Olivi, who describes how we become intuitively aware of sensory objects and mental states, which are perceived as "present" to us, in a way that was first mentioned by the *Summa*. The distinction becomes standard in Franciscan thought by the 1300s.

God cannot be known fully or face to face, it is possible to know him "from behind," as it were, through Christ, or through creatures.

Can God's Presence (*Praesentialitas*) Be Naturally Detected Insofar as He Is Present to Creatures?
SH 1, Tr Int, Q2, M1, C6 (n. 13), 22–23

The answer to the next question whether one can naturally know that God is present to all created things is based on the assumption that he is essentially present in a limited sense in things he has made and can be knowable as such.

Is God Known by Reason or by Intelligence?
SH 1, Tr Int, Q2, M2, C4 (n. 17), 27–28

The way in which God is grasped through creatures is by the mind. In affirming this, the *Summa* follows the pseudo-Augustinian work *The Spirit and the Soul* in distinguishing among the operations of reason, intellect, and intelligence.

As noted earlier, the advantage of *The Spirit and the Soul* was that it contained a conglomeration of quasi-Augustinian material which allowed early scholastics to attribute a range of positions to Augustine, particularly on the topic of human knowledge. This facilitated the efforts of early Franciscans to integrate Avicennian psychology into their own Christian tradition. Through the influence of *The Spirit and the Soul*, the *Summa* associated reason with knowledge of things below the soul; intellect with knowledge of things at the level of the self, specifically the human soul and angels; and intelligence with the knowledge of God. Whereas Augustine himself had invoked a distinction between higher and lower reason to explain the relationship between the mind and the senses, the *Summa* transforms it along the lines of the Avicennian distinction between theoretical and practical reason into a distinction within reason itself, which contemplates God in its higher or theoretical part—known as intelligence—and creatures in its lower or practical part—known as reason.[49]

---

49. This has been noted by Theodore Crowley in *Roger Bacon: The Problem of the Soul in His Philosophical Commentaries* (Louvain: Éditions de l'Institut Supérieur de Philosophie, 1950), 188.

Is God Himself (*Se Ipso*) Seen and Known, or Is Something Else Required as a Means of Knowing Him?
SH 1, Tr Int, Q2, M3, C1 (n. 20), 30–31

While we cannot know God in his fullness in this life, the *Summa* reiterates that creatures serve as an adequate means of knowing God partially. Their limited natures give a limited glimpse into who he is and what he is like.

Is God Known by Means of Creatures?
SH 1, Tr Int, Q2, M3, C2 (n. 21), 31–32

The *Summa* recognizes the possible objection that there is no correlation between finite creatures and the infinite God, which seems to undermine the idea that they can mediate knowledge of him. The *Summa* addresses this conundrum by arguing that while creatures are not related to God as he is in himself, they do relate to him as to their formal and final cause. As their formal cause, we will see further below that God provides or contains the model after which every creature is patterned, an idea that would become the cornerstone of Bonaventure's theory of "exemplarity."[50] Through the instantiation of such a divine idea, creatures fulfill their purpose or end in him as their final cause as well and reveal some aspect of his nature.

On the Means of Knowing God through the Grace of Faith
SH 1, Tr Int, Q2, M3, C3 (n. 22), 32–34

This brings us back to the distinction between intuitive and abstractive cognition, which we saw the *Summa* gesturing toward obliquely at the beginning of this section. Here again, the *Summa* reiterates Augustine's distinction in *On Seeing God* (i.e., Letter 147, c. 2, n. 7) between seeing and believing, where the former is concerned with things instantly accessible or present to the mind or to the senses, and the latter with things that are either not presently seen or never have been. On the basis of the foregoing, the *Summa*'s position on knowing God is clear: in this life, God can only be an object of belief or what would later be called abstractive cognition, as he exceeds the scope of human knowledge, sensory or intellectual, in this life.

---

50. On Bonaventure's exemplarity, see Zachary Hayes, "Bonaventure's Trinitarian Theology," in *A Companion to Bonaventure* (Leiden: Brill, 2014), 189–246.

Nevertheless, the *Summa* allows for a kind of limited knowledge of God that can be obtained through the forms of intuitive knowledge that are accessible to human beings in this life, including knowledge of creatures that comes through the senses or knowledge of human ideas and mental states that are achieved through the intellect.

On Rational Proofs of Things to Be Taken on Faith
SH 1, Tr Int, Q2, M3, C4 (n. 23), 34–35

As we will see, these forms of knowledge serve as resources for providing proofs for what is taken on faith. These proofs presuppose faith more than they seek to establish its legitimacy and thus aim primarily to render intelligible whatever is already believed. In this regard, they rely upon the affection for or devotion to God that faith entails, which is in turn the source of their intelligibility and certitude.

Is the Knowledge about God Obtained through the Natural Light of Reason More Certain Than the Knowledge about Creatures?
SH 1, Tr Int, Q2, M3, C5 (n. 24), 35–36

On a related topic, the *Summa* inquires whether the knowledge of God obtained through the natural light of reason is more certain than the knowledge of creatures. In this regard, it distinguishes between knowledge of the existence of a thing, or "that it is," and knowledge of its essence, or "what it is." For the Summist, there is no doubt that the essences of creatures are known with more certainty than the essence of God. However, the existence of God in some way is known with greater certainty than that of creatures. This is because the knowledge of the cause of all things is more certain than that of the effects, as we will see in the section on theistic proof.

To demonstrate this, the *Summa* invokes a distinction—derived from an anonymous text written probably in the late 1220s that proved highly influential for early Franciscans[51]—between an innate or infused habit and a habit acquired through the senses. While creatures are known with more certainty through the habit of knowledge that operates by way of the senses, God is known with more certainty through the innate and infused habits. The former

---

51. Callus, "The Powers of the Soul," 160.

is the means by which he impresses upon human beings the knowledge of himself as the cause of all things, in ways and with effects that will be discussed in the subsequent two sections. The latter is the means by which the innate habit is restored after it is obscured through sin, which renders us ignorant of the knowledge God has imparted to us.

CHAPTER 3: THE NECESSARY EXISTENCE OF GOD

Since the late medieval period, Anselm of Canterbury has been heralded in the West as the first proponent of the so-called ontological argument for God's existence. This kind of argument turns on the assumption that God must possess all perfections, including that of existence. Thus, one need only think about what he is to know that he exists. Although Anselm's proof has garnered considerable attention in the late medieval and modern periods, it was largely neglected in the century or so between his own death and the rise of Alexander of Hales, who was among the first to appropriate and popularize the Benedictine's work, including the famous argument, which appears in chapters 2–3 of Anselm's *Proslogion*.

While we lack the space here to explore the meaning of Anselm's argument in its own right, scholars have increasingly cast doubt on the idea that it was ever intended to offer the sort of ontological proof that has been associated with it to this day.[52] This reading of Anselm more likely derives from the interpretation that was formulated by early Franciscans in a wide range of texts, but above all, the *Summa Halensis*, under the influence of Avicenna's signature proof for the Necessary Existent.[53] In brief, this proof starts from encounters with contingent or "possible beings" that are necessarily brought into existence by another. Such beings trigger an innate sense in the human

---

52. Jean Châtillon, "De Guillaume d'Auxerre à saint Thomas d'Aquin: L'argument de saint Anselme chez les premiers scolastiques du XIIIe siècle," *Spicilegium Beccense* I (Paris, 1959): 209–31, at 226–27; Anton Pegis, "The Bonaventurian Way to God," *Mediaeval Studies* 29 (1967): 206–42, at 211; Lydia Schumacher, "The Lost Legacy of Anselm's Argument: Rethinking the Purpose of Proofs for the Existence of God," *Modern Theology* 27, no. 1 (2011): 87–101; Robert Sokolowski, "Beginning with St. Anselm," in *The God of Faith and Reason* (Washington, DC: The Catholic University of America Press, 1995), 1–11.

53. Scott Matthews, *Reason, Community, and Religious Tradition: Anselm's Argument and the Friars* (Aldershot: Ashgate, 2001), 46–80, esp. 62.

mind that there is a being that is the cause of its own existence and that of all other things. In that sense, Avicenna does not provide a cosmological proof *per se* but sees created realities as catalysts for an ontological proof that moves from the nature of God to his existence.

Does the Divine Substance Necessarily Exist?
SH 1, P1, In1, Tr1, Q1, C1 (n. 25), 40–42

The *Summa* mimics the pattern of this proof by outlining five different ways in which possible or created beings bespeak the reality of a necessary being that makes them possible. First, the very fact that they exist presupposes the existence of something that exists of its own accord. As caused beings, moreover, they gesture toward a first cause; insofar as they are true, they bespeak a source of all truth; as good, they highlight the source of all goods. Finally, the gradation or hierarchy amongst beings calls for a "head" as it were of the hierarchy.

Is the Divine Essence Necessarily Known in Such a Way as to Preclude Thinking of It as Nonexisting?
SH 1, P1, In1, Tr1, Q1, C2, Ar1 (n. 26), 42–44

For the Summists, following Avicenna, these five ways are not cosmological proofs as such but serve instead to activate an innate awareness in the mind that anything that exists, is caused, is true, good, or falls somewhere on the hierarchy of being, must do so through one that is the cause of his own existence, truth, goodness, and so on.[54]

This being is of course God. By thinking of who he is, namely, as the one whose essence is to generate his own existence and that of everything else, consequently, we can know that he exists.

Is It a Property of the Divine Necessity Not to Be Able to Be Thought Not to Exist?
SH 1, P1, In1, Tr1, Q1, C2, Ar2 (n. 27), 44–45

As a matter of fact, the Summists insist, we cannot fail to acknowledge that God exists, unless we willfully refuse to do so. So construed, the kind of

---

54. Pegis, "The Bonaventurian Way to God," 216, quoting Etienne Gilson, *La philosophie de saint Bonaventure*, 2nd ed. (Paris, 1943), 108.

ontological argument that has long been attributed to Anselm is more clearly traceable to the Franciscan reading of Anselm, who as an Augustinian of sorts was not immune to the kind of Avicennian reading of Christian Neoplatonic sources of which early Franciscans were so fond. Although later Franciscans, above all Scotus, did not advance the argument in this exact form, the family resemblance between the different Franciscan renderings of the proof is detectable, for instance, in Scotus's inference from finite or contingent beings to the reality of an infinite being.[55]

CHAPTER 4: THE DIVINE NATURE

The doctrine of God, like the doctrine of the Trinity, represents one of the *Summa*'s areas of sharpest deviation from the tradition of Augustine. While medieval thinkers since Augustine—from Anselm to Peter Lombard and Thomas Aquinas—had largely identified "simplicity" as the most fundamental feature of the divine substance, the *Summa* innovatively emphasized the primacy of God's immensity or infinity, a trend that continued to develop in later Franciscan thought and beyond.[56] At the time, there was relatively little precedent for this new approach to the doctrine of God in the Middle Ages.

Most earlier discussions of infinity—found in Hilary of Poitiers, Isidore of Seville, and Peter Lombard—had described infinity as a feature of God's power, which is evident everywhere in creation and yet surpasses it.[57] The situation changed in the twelfth century with the introduction of the works by Pseudo-Dionysius and other Greek thinkers like John of Damascus, who laid a strong emphasis on the infinity and corresponding unknowability of

---

55. On the innate "sense" for "infinite being" in Scotus's version of the argument, which is anticipated by the *Summa Halensis*, see Bychkov, "But Everyone Experiences the Opposite," 259–303.

56. Tiziana Suarez-Nani, "On Divine Immensity and Infinity in Relation to Space and Time: The Crossroad of the *Summa Halensis*," in Schumacher, *The Legacy of Early Franciscan Thought*, 71–88. Anne Davenport, *The Measure of a Different Greatness: The Intensive Infinite, 1250–1650* (Leiden: Brill, 1999); Meldon C. Wass, *The Infinite God and the 'Summa fratris Alexandri'* (Chicago: Franciscan Herald Press, 1964); Leo Sweeney, *Divine Infinity in Greek and Medieval Thought* (New York: Peter Land, 1996).

57. Schumacher, *Early Franciscan Theology*, 121.

God.[58] In the twelfth century, this emphasis was picked up in the West by Richard of St. Victor, who stressed God's infinity even while counterbalancing it with his simplicity. His work, therefore, laid the foundation for and anticipated the *Summa*'s development of the doctrine of divine infinity.[59]

In this connection, the Summists had to contend with the 1241 Condemnation at Paris, which had brought into disrepute the Greek idea that God is unknowable on account of his infinity.[60] After a period of affirming the two doctrines together, scholastics realized the Greek notion conflicted with their cherished Augustinian idea that God will be known at the end of time.

Is the Divine Essence Finite or Infinite?
SH 1, P1, In1, Tr2, Q1, C1 (n. 34), 54–57

Thus, the Summists had the task of establishing the doctrine of divine infinity as the locus of God's knowability rather than his unknowability.[61] This was something they were arguably motivated to do by their own Franciscan ethos, which found a reflection of God's love in every finite creature. On this basis, therefore, Jacob Wood has rightly observed that they transformed the linchpin of an apophatic or negative theology into a more kataphatic and positive theology.[62]

In this regard, they were aided considerably by Avicenna, who had replaced Aristotle's idea of infinity as something lacking limit and thus order with

---

58. Henri F. Dondaine, *Le corpus Dionysien de l'Université de Paris au XIIIe siècle* (Rome: Edizioni di Storia e Letteratura, 1953).

59. Richard of St. Victor, *De Trinitate: Texte critique avec introduction, notes et tables*, ed. Jean Ribaillier (Paris: J. Vrin, 1958); translation by Ruben Angelici, *Richard of St. Victor: On the Trinity* (Eugene, OR: Cascade Books, 2011).

60. P.-M. De Contenson, "Avicennisme latin et vision de Dieu au début du XIIIe siècle," *Archives d'histoire doctrinale et littéraire du Moyen Age* 34 (1959), 29–97; Henri F. Dondaine, "L'objet et le 'medium' de la vision béatifique chez les théologiens du XIIIe siècle," *Recherches de théologie ancienne et médiévale* 19 (1952): 60–130.

61. On this see Antoine Côté, *L'infinité divine dans la théologie médiévale, 1220–1255* (Paris: Vrin, 2002).

62. Jacob W. Wood, "Kataphasis and Apophasis in Thirteenth Century Theology: The Anthropological Context of the *Triplex Via* in the *Summa fratris Alexandri* and Albert the Great," *The Heythrop Journal* 57 (2016): 293–311.

a positive conception according to which infinity is "a quantity or something possessing a quantity such that anything you take from it you also find something of it different from what you took and you never reach something beyond which there is nothing of it."[63] This definition allowed early Franciscans to describe God as in a sense the "sum total" of all finite beings: the locus of all the exemplars to which they correspond, which are thereby individually known and loved by him.

Does God Know through One or through Many?

SH 1, P1, In1, Tr5, S1, Q un., M2, C3 (n. 166), 248–49

At the same time, the doctrine of infinity made it possible to affirm that God always transcends his creation, and is in no way subject to the multiplicity that characterizes it.

As God knows all things through himself, he always maintains his unity; the diversity of the divine ideas is therefore on the part of the creatures that reflect his nature in different ways. The Dionysian analogy the *Summa* invokes to illustrate this claim is that of a central point in a circle, which encompasses all the many lines that can be drawn out of it without being subject to diversity itself.[64]

Does God Have Knowledge of Singulars?

SH 1, P1, In1, Tr5, S1, Q un., M3, C6 (n. 173), 256–57

While the foregoing might seem to suggest that God only knows in universal terms, the *Summa* insists that he has knowledge of individual or singular things, anticipating already in some way the Scotist idea of *haecceitas* or "thisness." His singular knowledge is even more perfect than human knowledge of individuals, because it does not depend on species abstracted from the senses but is already contained in God's knowledge of himself, which contains a likeness of all things, great and small, of which he is the artificer.

---

63. Jon McGinnis, "Avicennan Infinity: A Select History of the Infinite through Avicenna," *Documenti e Studi sulla Tradizione Filosofica Medievale* 21 (2010): 199–222.

64. SH 1, P1, In1, Tr5, S1, Q un., M3, C6 (n. 173), 256 (Ad obiecta 2).

Is Divine Power Prior to, or Does It Extend Further Than the Divine Will?
SH 1, P1, In1, Tr4, Q1, M2, C2 (n. 135), 206–7

In answering a further question, whether the divine power is prior to or extends further than the divine will, the *Summa* introduces the relatively new distinction, which would become central in the Franciscan tradition, between the absolute and ordained power of God. While God in his absolute power can do far more than he actually wills to do, his ordained power represents what he has actually predetermined to do and does in fact accomplish.[65] For example, God in his ordained power wills to punish the wicked and reward the just.

Is Divine Power Limited by God's Goodness and Justice?
SH 1, P1, In1, Tr4, Q2, M2, C2 (n. 141), 219–21

For the *Summa*, therefore, the answer to the question whether God's power is limited by his goodness or justice is affirmative only with reference to God's ordained power, in which case he always acts according to a certain predetermined will of his own. When God's absolute power is in question, however, he is not limited by his goodness and justice. Thus, he is in principle capable of damning the Apostle Peter and saving Judas, who betrayed Christ. This anticipates the debates in later Franciscan theology, for example, in Scotus, regarding the role of God's power in establishing ethical norms. The debate fundamentally concerns whether the precepts on the "second table of the law," which concern human relations, are arbitrarily mandated by God. Those on the first table, which concern the human relation to God, follow from the natural law, as we will see in the section on moral law.[66]

---

65. William Courtenay, "The Dialectic of Omnipotence in the High and Late Middle Ages," in *Divine Omniscience and Omnipotence in Medieval Philosophy*, ed. T. Rudavsky (Amsterdam: Reidel, 1985), 243–69. Theo Kobush, "The Possible and the Impossible: *Potentia absoluta* and *potentia ordinata* Under Close Scrutiny," in *The Legacy of Early Franciscan Thought*, 207–20.

66. Whereas Allan Wolter has claimed that these laws can be rationalized, Thomas Williams has argued against him that they cannot and thus concludes on this basis that Scotus is a divine command theorist and extreme voluntarist, who does not presume any rational foundation for God's commands. Oleg Bychkov has argued that these ethical norms are neither rational nor arbitrary, but aesthetic. See Bychkov, "In Harmony with Reason: John Duns Scotus's Theo-aesth/ethics," *Open Theology* 1, no. 1 (2014): 45–55.

CHAPTER 5: THE TRANSCENDENTALS

The doctrine of the transcendentals represents one of the most foundational and innovative contributions of the *Summa Halensis*. The inspiration for the doctrine can be traced all the way back to antiquity, when pagan and Christian thinkers alike invoked "being" and its qualities, such as "goodness," "truth," "unity," and so on, to describe the most fundamental metaphysical traits of things, and in the Christian context, their source in God. While figures like Plato, Aristotle, Boethius, and Augustine gestured toward what Jan Aertsen has called a "philosophy of the transcendent," the theory of the transcendentals took an entirely new turn in the philosophy of Avicenna.[67]

Although he did not speak explicitly of "transcendentals"—which were first mentioned by Duns Scotus—he described "first intentions" such as "being" and "thing," which he regarded not only as fundamental qualities of things but also as innate concepts of the mind that serve as the means of knowing things that exhibit such qualities.[68] Avicenna's theory provided the fundamental building blocks for the transcendental vision of the Halensian Summits. However, they were also influenced by their earlier contemporary, Philip the Chancellor, in identifying the common and transcendental properties of being as unity, truth, and goodness, which they followed Philip in correlating or "appropriating" to the three persons of the Trinity: Father, Son, and Spirit.[69] The tradition of outlining these "Trinitarian appropriations," stemming from the Victorines but reaching its height in the Franciscan tradition, quickly became a part of scholastic discussion more generally and is found in the work of Thomas Aquinas.[70]

---

67. Jan Aertsen, *Medieval Philosophy as Transcendental Thought: From Philip the Chancellor to Francisco Suarez* (Leiden: Brill, 2012), 75.

68. Ibid., 84.

69. The first to point out Philip's originality was Henri Pouillon, in "Le premier traité des propriétés transcendentales. La *Summa de bono* du Chancelier Philippe," *Revue Néoscolastique de Philosophie* 42 (1939): 40–77. See also Antonella Fani, "*Communissima*, trascendentali e Trinità: da Filippo il Cancelliere alla prima scuola francescana," *Il Santo: Rivista Francescana di Storia, Dottrina, Arte* 49, no. 1 (2009): 131–54.

70. On Aquinas, see Oleg Bychkov, "Metaphysics as Aesthetics: Aquinas' Metaphysics in Present-day Theological Aesthetics," *Modern Theology* 31, no. 1 (January 2015): 147–78. On the Victorines, see Dominique Poirel, "Scholastic Reasons, Monastic Meditations and Victorine Conciliations: The Question of the

The Essence of "Oneness"

SH 1, P1, In1, Tr3, Q1, M1, C1 (n. 72), 112–13

Where Philip, to say nothing of Aquinas, focused mainly on the metaphysical dimension of transcendental theory, the *Summa* adopted the Avicennian idea that being and its primary determinations are the "first objects of the intellect,"[71] quoting Avicenna as its explicit source for this idea, which subsequently became a fixture in the Franciscan intellectual tradition.[72] Because the transcendentals are known prior to anything else, the *Summa* is quick to point out, they cannot be known except through posterior things, for example, in effects, that is, in beings that exhibit unity, truth, and goodness.

They comprise the means or power of knowing beings rather than the objects of knowledge as such. At the same time, they constitute the image of God, who is being *par excellence*.[73]

How Does "One" Relate to "Being," "True," and "Good"?

SH 1, P1, In1, Tr3, Q1, M1, C2 (n. 73), 113–16

Through the image of God's being and its attendant determinations, therefore, human beings possess the ability to identify any given being as one, or indivisible in itself and distinct from other beings—and thus efficiently caused by the Father; as true, or intelligible in terms of what it is—that is, in terms of a formal cause in the Son; and good, or fit for a certain purpose—insofar as it is ordained by the final cause, the Holy Spirit.[74] So construed, the three determinations of being, namely, unity, truth, and goodness render human beings not only images of God but also more precisely images of the Trinity.

Unity and Plurality of God in the Twelfth Century," in *The Oxford Handbook of the Trinity*, ed. Gilles Emery and Matthew Levering (Oxford: Oxford University Press, 2014), 179–90.

71. SH 1, P1, In1, Tr3, Q1, M1, C1, Respondeo II (n. 72), 113: *Dicendum quod cum sit ens primum intelligibile, eius intentio apud intellectum est nota* (Avicenna, *Meta* 1.6); cf. SH 2.1, In1, S1, Q1, C2 (n. 2), 3.

72. Honnefelder, *Scientia transcendens: Die formale Bestimmung der Seiendheit und Realität in der Metaphysik des Mittelalters und der Neuzeit* (*Duns Scotus, Suárez, Wolff, Kant, Peirce*); Allan B. Wolter, *The Transcendentals and Their Function in the Metaphysics of Duns Scotus* (St. Bonaventure, NY: Franciscan Institute Press, 1946).

73. SH 1, P2, In2, Tr1, Q1, C2, Ar2, Solutio (n. 352), 522: *Deus sicut efficiens, primum eius nomen est ens*.

74. SH 1, P1, In 1, Tr3, Q2, M1, C2, Respondeo (n. 88), 140.

Although these transcendentals enable human beings to know any being in terms of the specific way it is one, true, and good, they also give a glimpse, however limited, into the nature of the God who is their source.

Does the Unity of the Divine Being Allow for a Plurality of Ideas?
SH 1, P1, In1, Tr3, Q1, M2, C4 (n. 80), 130–32

Precisely how they do so becomes clearer when the *Summa* inquires whether divine unity allows for a plurality of ideas. The simple answer is that it does, because every divine idea and being created on the basis of it reflects some aspect of the nature of God and gives a glimpse into his essence in that way. As we have seen, the multiple ideas envisaged here do not compromise the unity of God, because his oneness is the exemplar of all beings that exhibit oneness in diverse and limited ways and thus encompasses and presupposes all finite manifestations of oneness. In that sense, the diversity of the ideas is on the side of creatures rather than of God.

Does Truth Necessarily Have Eternal Existence?
SH 1, P1, In1, Tr3, Q2, M1, C1 (n. 87), 138–39

From the discussion of unity, the *Summa* moves on to inquire about truth, which it claims must be eternal, on the basis of Anselm's argument in *Monologion* 18 that if truth had a beginning or an end, then it would be true that truth did not yet exist before it began, and that it no longer existed after it ended, which means that even when there is supposedly no truth, there is truth.

Does "Truth" Mean Something Different from "Entity," "Unity," and "Goodness"?
SH 1, P1, In1, Tr3, Q2, M1, C2 (n. 88), 139–41

The subsequent question, whether "truth" means something different than "being," "unity," and "goodness," largely reiterates the conclusions already outlined in this regard.

Is the "Good" Fully Identical to "Being" (*Ens*) in Its Meaning?
SH 1, P1, In1, Tr3, Q3, M1, C1, Ar1 (n. 102), 160–61

The next query concerns the good, and specifically, whether it is identical to being. According to the *Summa*, the meanings of "being" and the "good" are not the same, even though things that possess being also always have goodness. This is because a being possesses two ontological levels, first and second, a theme that recurs in various contexts of the *Summa*, for example, in its account of grace. The first kind of goodness is the one that a being has naturally; the second is its orderly existence, or well-being.[75] While the first type of good is inseparable from existence, the second type is separable, because it does not necessarily follow from the fact that a being exists that it exists in accordance with its designated purpose. This is especially true in the case of sin, where a human being turns away from the supreme good and jeopardizes its chances of flourishing.

Are the Beautiful (*Pulchrum*) and the Good Fully Identical as Far as Their Meaning Is Concerned?

SH 1, P1, In1, Tr3, Q3, M1, C1, Ar2 (n. 103), 162–63

Following this inquiry, the *Summa* poses the related question whether the good is identical to the beautiful (*pulchrum*). In answer to this question, the Summist argues that beauty is based more on exemplarity or formal causality—and the idea that this harmonizes different elements in an attractive way—whereas the idea of the good is based on final causality, or the suitability of a given thing for a particular purpose. Though the two notions have commonalities in that both are concerned with excellence (*honestum*), they display excellence in different ways.

More specifically, the term "beautiful" denotes the ability of the good to please our faculty of perception, whereas the term "good" denotes its ability to delight our affective faculty. As the broader of the two concepts, the good encompasses beauty, which is a subset or aspect of it and not a transcendental in its own right like the good.[76] As Aertsen has observed, however, the *Summa*'s discussion of beauty is nonetheless significant in that it instigated a debate about the status of beauty as a transcendental in Albert, Ulrich of

---

75. See Oleg Bychkov, "Decor ex praesentia mali: Aesthetic Explanations of Evil in Thirteenth-Century Franciscan Thought," *Recherches de Théologie et Philosophie Médiévales* 68, no. 2 (2001): 245–69.

76. This has been shown by Aertsen in *Medieval Philosophy as Transcendental Thought* and by Oleg Bychkov in "Suspended Beauty? The Mystery of Aesthetic Experience in the *Summa Halensis*," in Schumacher, *The Legacy of Early Franciscan Thought*, 111–28.

Strasbourg, and the Thomistic tradition, which gained momentum in the twentieth century.[77]

Are the Knowledge and Love of the Highest Good Originally Implanted and Impressed in Our Minds?
SH 1, P1, In1, Tr3, Q3, M2, C1 (n. 108), 169–70

As suggested previously, the knowledge of the highest good is impressed in us naturally through the transcendentals, ensuring that the resource is always available for obtaining well-being, even though appetite for perverse choices sometimes makes one go astray and deviate from the good.

Is Every Created Good So in Its Essence or by Participation?
SH 1, P1, In1, Tr3, Q3, M3, C2, Ar2 (n. 117), 183–86

This natural impression of goodness is the main means through which the human being, like all beings, participates in the goodness of God, namely, by possessing and realizing the capacity to reflect his goodness in a particular way.

Does God Permit Evil to Arise in the Universe?
SH 1, P1, In1, Tr3, Q3, M3, C5, Ar1 (n. 120), 188–89

While on the subject of the highest good, the *Summa* inquires whether God permits evil to arise in the universe. The obvious answer is that God does not cause evil himself; but unlike earlier or near contemporaries such as Peter Lombard, who insisted that God did not want evil to exist or to emerge, and Albert the Great, who only reluctantly allowed for the possibility of redeeming evil, Oleg Bychkov has shown that the *Summa Halensis* advanced the quite remarkable position that evil contributes to the beauty of the universe by throwing the good into greater relief.[78] As the *Summa* states in this section, "when evil is well ordered and occupies its proper place, it presents good things in a more flattering fashion, so that they please us more and become more praiseworthy in comparison with evil ones."

As this suggests, God permitted evil things to exist for the sake of the beauty of good things: "for if evil did not exist, the good would only possess

---

77. On these debates about beauty, see Bychkov, "A Propos of Medieval Aesthetics," 23–27; Bychkov, "Metaphysics as Aesthetics," 147–78.

78. Bychkov, "Decor ex praesentia mali," 250–51 and 265.

absolute beauty, namely, of the good itself; however, when evil exists, the relative beauty of the good grows, so that in comparison with its opposite—evil—the good shines forth more beautifully."[79] Another reason why God allows evil is to derive something good from it, as for example when temptations to do evil, resisted by the holy, enhance and confirm their holiness.

Would the Universe Have Been Better without Evil Things?
SH 1, P1, In1, Tr3, Q3, M3, C5, Ar2 (n. 121), 189-90
In answer to the question whether the universe would have been better without evil things, the *Summa* implies, again quite exceptionally, that the universe is in fact better with evil because this fosters a sort of antithesis in creation that enhances the attractiveness of the created order.

In this regard, as we will see further in the *Summa*'s discussion of free choice, early Franciscans advocated a positive conception of evil as possessing a kind of substantiality that departed quite drastically from earlier theories which saw evil as a privation or absence of the good. The reason for this shift was not to attribute legitimacy to evil as some have supposed, but rather to find a way of depicting it that was consistent with other Franciscan values, in this case, the goal of showing that evil enhances the beauty of God's universe. For the logic behind this sort of perspective, one need look no further than Francis, who thrived on paradoxical principles whereby suffering—God's or ours—represents the optimal means of showing love; strength is made perfect in weakness; and the sinfulness of society poses an opportunity to summon many to genuine repentance.

CHAPTER 6: THE TRINITY

In his magisterial history of Trinitarian doctrine, Théodore de Régnon defended the then novel thesis that the late Middle Ages witnessed the branching off of a new tradition of Trinitarian theological thinking from the previously relatively continuous tradition of Western Trinitarianism founded by Augustine.[80] From this time forward, he contends, there were two main traditions

---

79. SH 1, P1, In1, Tr3, Q3, M3, C5, Ar1 (n. 120), 188–89.
80. Th. de Régnon, *Études de théologie positive sur la Sainte Trinité*, vols. I and II (Paris: V. Retaux, 1892).

of Western Trinitarian thought, including the original tradition of Augustine, which was carried forward by the likes of Anselm, Peter Lombard, and Aquinas, who expressed it in its mature form; and the new tradition, initially formulated by Richard of St. Victor.[81]

Although the Franciscans became responsible for developing and championing the Victorine account in the Middle Ages and beyond, they like Richard did not abandon one of the most fundamental tenets of Western Trinitarian theology, namely, the *filioque*, or the idea that the Spirit proceeds from the Father *and* the Son.[82] They held fast to this cherished position while pioneering a new perspective in the field that seemingly allowed them to articulate more precisely other important aspects of their own ethos and vision, such as an emphasis on the gratuitous love and primacy of God the Father, and the fullness of his self-expression in the Spirit.

Is There Generation in God?
SH 1, P1, In2, Tr un., Q1, Ti1, C1 (n. 295), 414–18

The first question posed in this context is whether there is generation in God. The *Summa* argues for the eternal generation of the Son from the Father on the ground that the highest good does whatever is best, and the greatest and highest thing is to communicate one's whole substance, which is what is involved in the Son's generation. This argument is repeated by Bonaventure in his *Itinerarium* on the basis of his *Sentences Commentary*.[83]

---

81. Russell Friedman distinguishes these two traditions in volume 1 of his *Intellectual Traditions at the Medieval University: The Use of Philosophical Psychology in Trinitarian Theology among the Franciscans and Dominicans, 1250–1350* (Leiden: Brill, 2013), describing them as "relation" and "emanation" accounts of the Trinity, respectively.

82. Maria Calisi, *Trinitarian Perspectives in the Franciscan Theological Tradition* (St. Bonaventure, NY: Franciscan Institute, 2008); Russell L. Friedman, *Medieval Trinitarian Theology from Aquinas to Ockham* (Cambridge: Cambridge University Press, 2010); Nico Den Bok, *Communicating the Most High: A Systematic Study of Person and Trinity in the Theology of Richard of St. Victor (d. 1173)* (Paris: Brepols, 1996); Gervais Dumiege, *Richard de Saint-Victor et l'idée chrétienne de l'amour* (Paris: Presses Universitaires de France, 1952).

83. Bonaventure, *Itinerarium*, in *S. Bonaventurae Opera Omnia*, ed. Collegium a S. Bonaventura, vol. 5 (Quaracchi: Collegium S. Bonaventurae, 1891), ch. 6.2, 310–11.

What Does It Mean to Generate in the Divine Essence?
SH 1, P1, In2, Tr un., Q1, Ti1, C2 (n. 296), 419–21

According to the *Summa*, this act of generation on the part of the Father involves the production of a species of himself, which is itself the product of his act of understanding himself. On this basis, the *Summa* concludes that the generation of the Son follows from God's act of self-understanding.

Is There a Procession of the Holy Spirit?
SH 1, P1, In2, Tr un., Q1, T2, C1 (n. 304), 438–40

In turning to treat the procession of the Holy Spirit, the *Summa* begins with the claim that there are two principles of diffusion in things: nature and will. The most perfect diffusion by nature is generation, whereas the most perfect diffusion of the will is through love. Since it is most praiseworthy to diffuse oneself in both ways rather than in one only, and what is praiseworthy and perfect cannot be lacking in the highest good, namely, God, he is subject to a diffusion of generation, which results in a difference between the one generating and the one generated, namely, Father and Son; and to a diffusion through the mode of love, which we call the procession of the Holy Spirit.

In describing the nature of this love more specifically, the *Summa* departs quite sharply from the longstanding Augustinian tradition that defines the Holy Spirit as the love exchanged between the Father and Son (*dilectio*), in favor of Richard of St. Victor's rendering of the Spirit as their shared love for a third person, or *condilectio*. This kind of love is of the highest order, the *Summa* contends, because it does not merely involve the sort of self-love within God that Augustine envisaged but a more generous and therefore perfect love that wishes that the beloved may be loved by another as much as the lover himself loves the beloved. This presumably is the way in which both the Father and the Son love the Spirit: not only do they love each other, but each one also wishes that the Spirit be loved by the other in the way they themselves receive the other's love. Since this kind of love requires three persons, it is a fitting form of love for the Trinity.

To Whom Does It Belong to Proceed?
SH 1, P1, In2, Tr un., Q1, T2, C2 (n. 305), 441–42

In order further to distinguish the Son's generation from that of the Spirit, the *Summa* differentiates between a principal and a nonprincipal mode of production in God.[84] In the principal mode, the product that is produced has the power to produce another from itself. This is the way in which the Son proceeds from the Father, whose property he retains, insofar as he has the power of producing another from himself, namely, the Holy Spirit. By contrast, the Holy Spirit is produced in the nonprincipal mode, because he does not retain the property of producing another from himself. Put differently, the Father exists in the mode of a first principle or beginning, the Son in the mode of a medium, and the Holy Spirit in the mode of an end.[85]

Although the procession of the Son by way of understanding is principal, and the procession of the Spirit by way of love is nonprincipal, the *Summa* is quick to assert that this does not imply any inequality between the two persons, but only a difference in their respective properties. When we call something "primary" or "nonprimary," that is, we do not designate a priority or posteriority in time but only an order of nature.

Who Proceeds through the Mode of Love or a Gift?
SH 1, P1, In2, Tr. un., Q1, T2, C3, A2 (n. 307), 443–46

As the one from whom both the Son and the Spirit proceed in their respective ways, the *Summa* elaborates, the Father is characterized by a purely gratuitous or giving love, while a love that involves a combination of both receiving and giving pertains to the Son. As the Person of the Trinity who simply receives the love of both the Father and the Son, the Holy Spirit is distinguished by an indebted love, and he stands as the full and final expression of the love that is shared between the other two persons.

While love is common to the whole Trinity when construed along these lines, it is proper to the Holy Spirit when it is considered in its strict sense as the gift or free emanation of shared love (*condilectio*) of the Father and the Son. Although we have seen that the *Summa* departs from Augustine's vision of the *dilectio* or shared love of Father and Son in articulating this position, the foregoing also makes it clear that the *Summa* upholds the

---

84. The use of "production" language is carried forward into the later Franciscan tradition. See J. T. Paasch, *Divine Production in Late Medieval Trinitarian Theology: Henry of Ghent, Duns Scotus and William of Ockham* (Oxford: Oxford University Press, 2012).

85. Zachary Hayes, *The Hidden Centre: Spirituality and Speculative Christology in St. Bonaventure* (St. Bonaventure, NY: Franciscan Institute Press, 1981).

longstanding Augustinian and more broadly Western commitment to the *fililoque* or procession of the Spirit from both the Father and the Son.

CHAPTER 7: CHRISTOLOGY

The Christology of the *Summa Halensis* is another one of its most extensive and influential areas of inquiry, which delves into new topics in the field, doing so at a length that was unprecedented in prior theological treatises. This no doubt reflects the centrality of Christ in Francis of Assisi's own vision.

On the Fittingness of the Incarnation Should Nature Not Have Fallen Due to Sin: Would There Be Any Reason for the Incarnation?
SH 3, In un., Tr1, Q2, T2 (n. 23), 41–42

The first passage translated in this section presents one of the most novel positions of the *Summa*, which would quickly become important for the later Franciscan intellectual tradition, namely, the idea that Christ would become Incarnate regardless of the fall. For all practical purposes, the *Summa* offered the first instance in the West of this position, known as "supralapsarianism," and the reason for doing so seems quite transparent.[86] To render Christ's Incarnation independent of redemption was to link it primarily to the completion or perfection of creation. As the locus of the divine ideas and the one through whom they were initially instantiated, the *Summa* argues, the Son is not only the image of God himself but also the "Archetype" or Exemplar of all created beings.[87]

---

86. In *If Adam Had Not Sinned: The Reason for the Incarnation from Anselm to Scotus* (Washington, D.C.: The Catholic University of America Press, 2020), Justus Hunter observes that Rupert of Deutz (1075–1129) raises the hypothetical question whether Christ would have become incarnate without sin in his commentary on Matthew's Gospel, *De Gloria et honore Filii hominis* (PL 1628, 13.684–86). However, Rupert's account is rather underdeveloped. Robert Grosseteste also entertained the question but probably did so slightly later than and independently of Alexander of Hales in his *Sentences* Commentary.

87. SH 2.1, In1, Tr1, S1, Q1, C3, Ar2, In contrarium a (n. 4), 8: *Mundus sensibilis respondet archetypo, sicut exemplatum exemplari; sed idem est mundus archetypus quod ipse Deus.*

For him to become a created being, and specifically a human being, which has something in common with all beings and is capable in principle of knowing all of them, was therefore in a sense for him to become every creature: to unite himself with all creation and thereby perfect it.[88] In light of Francis's emphasis on the importance of caring for creation, it is hardly surprising that this kind of perspective would take center stage in the *Summa*'s Christology. Although the *Summa* does not go as far as later thinkers like Duns Scotus to argue that Christ would necessarily become Incarnate regardless of the fall—preferring to make a more reserved argument from fittingness—it laid the foundation for that more robust argument by inserting this line of thought into the contours of the tradition.

While foundational for the *Summa*'s Christology, the success of supralapsarianism in this context is very much dependent on the sophisticated metaphysical work the Summists undertake to explain precisely how the divine and the human natures were joined at the Incarnation in what is known as the hypostatic union. The remaining sections translated in this volume deal with the *Summa*'s innovative work in this area. As we will see, the *Summa* offers the first extensive formulation of the so-called substance-accident theory of the hypostatic union, which was more provisionally outlined by William of Auxerre previously, and became a fixture in Franciscan Christology subsequently, including in the work of John Duns Scotus.[89] This theory can be contrasted with the part-whole model of the hypostatic union that was developed later by Thomas Aquinas.

In order to appreciate the *Summa*'s theory, it is important first to understand something of the context in which it was developed.

About Three Opinions (and Doubts That Accompany Them) on the One Who Is Constituted as a Result of the Assumption [of Human Nature]

SH 3, In un., Tr1, Q4, Ti1, D3, M4, C1 (n. 46), 68–70

That context concerns Peter Lombard's articulation in his *Sentences* of three main opinions about the hypostatic union that circulated around his time,

---

88. Lydia Schumacher, "The Centre of Everywhere: Cosmic Christology in Early Franciscan Thought," in *Christ Unabridged: Knowing and Loving the Son of Man*, ed. George Westhaver (London: SCM, 2020), 97–110.

89. Richard Cross, *The Metaphysics of the Incarnation: Thomas Aquinas to Duns Scotus* (Oxford: Oxford University Press, 2005).

and which are reprised in the *Summa* itself. The first of these was the so-called *homo assumptus* theory, most famously advocated by Hugh of St. Victor, not to mention earlier Eastern and Western Fathers.[90] According to this opinion, the Word assumed a human nature and became a particular man who was not already in existence, per adoptionism, or the idea that Christ was a normal man who was somehow co-opted as the messenger of God. As Walter Principe has observed, "this theory carried within itself the seeds of a twofold and in some ways opposed development."[91]

On the one hand, its earliest advocates emphasized the identity of the man assumed with the Word who assumed him to such an extent as to seemingly divinize Christ's human nature. On the other hand, the *homo assumptus* theory affirmed that the Word assumed a certain individual man as opposed to human nature in general and thereby suggested that there are two subjects or supposits in Christ, one of which is man and one of which is God. "Such stress on the duality of Christ coupled with clear statements that there are not two persons in Christ led opponents of the first opinion to describe its supporters as semi-Nestorians."[92] Even though their account differed from that of true Nestorians who went so far as to assign distinct personhood to the distinct subjects, Thomas Aquinas by the 1250s did not hesitate to pronounce this opinion heretical owing to the way it combined two distinct and seemingly tenuously united hypostases in a new *tertium quid*.

The second, subsistence theory stresses that the divine and human natures do not merge in Christ to form a new semidivine, semihuman *tertium quid*. Rather, the Word, who was eternally a simple person, became a composite person at the Incarnation, possessing his divine as well as a human nature, entailing a body and a soul.[93] The Word's assumption of human nature—rather than a particular man—is quite important, insofar as it safeguards the subsistence theory from the suggestion that there are two persons in Christ. On this account, consequently, God became man, or the composite person.[94] However, that person did not *become* God, because the person in question was always God. Thus, the Incarnation did not bring about a change in the

---

90. Marcia Colish, *Peter Lombard* (Leiden: Brill, 1993), 1:400.
91. Walter Principe, *William of Auxerre's Theology of the Hypostatic Union* (Toronto: Pontifical Institute of Medieval Studies, 1963), 65.
92. Ibid., 66; cf. Colish, *Peter Lombard*, 425.
93. Colish, *Peter Lombard*, 401.
94. For more on this concept, see Corey L. Barnes, "Christological Composition in Thirteenth-Century Debates," *The Thomist* 75 (2011): 173–206.

Word—who eternally is the person that he is—but rather in the human nature that now became joined to the Word.

The third opinion, traceable to Augustine, is the so-called *habitus* theory, which speaks of "the humanity of the incarnate Christ as a habit or garment which he puts on."[95] While "it has been general practice to assume that the Lombard's own opinion is only of peripheral importance to an understanding of his text and his presentation of the three theories,"[96] L. O. Nielsen observes in his important study of the doctrine of the Incarnation in the twelfth century that Lombard and members of his school came down clearly on the side of this third theory.[97] By thus affirming that the *habitus*, or human nature, is accidental to the person of the Word, however, such proponents of the *habitus* view made themselves susceptible to two main charges, namely, that the union of the divine and human natures is tenuous at best, and that Christ as man is not "something" (*aliquid*) in his own right.

Because it downplayed or even obliterated the humanity of Christ in this way, opponents contended, the *habitus* theory gave way to what came to be known as "Christological nihilism." In an attempt to suppress such nihilism, Pope Alexander III officially condemned the *habitus* theory in 1177.[98] After this time, the third opinion was universally regarded as heretical, and the first opinion became subject to the growing suspicion that it, too, implied either nihilism or Nestorianism. In practice, consequently, the second opinion won the day. After 1177, it was the favored opinion of scholars as wide-ranging as Simon of Tournai (1130–201), Peter Cantor (d. 1197), Stephen Langton (1150–228), and Godfrey of Poitiers.[99] While the first opinion was still debated in the university context until at least the 1230s—and even in the *Summa Halensis*—it seems to have garnered very little active support from the late twelfth century.[100]

---

95. Colish, *Peter Lombard*, 402; cf. 417–38, on Lombard's own Christology.

96. Lauge Olaf Nielsen, *Theology and Philosophy in the Twelfth Century: A Study of Gilbert Porreta's Thinking and the Theological Expositions of the Doctrine of the Incarnation During the Period 1130–180* (Leiden: Brill, 1982), 244.

97. Ibid., 359.

98. Ibid., 329.

99. Ibid., 68.

100. Walter Principe, *Hugh of St. Cher's Theology of the Hypostatic Union* (Toronto: Pontifical Institute of Mediaeval Studies, 1970), 59; cf. *William of Auxerre*, 202.

Be that as it may, there was still considerable work to do on the part of the post-1177 generation to show more clearly how Christ is *aliquid*, or something and not merely an accident, while at the same time demonstrating his unity-in-duality, and scholars had very different ways of going about this, whether through a substance-accident, part-whole model, or some other means. Remarkably, the task was one the Halensian Summists above all accomplished not by forswearing all talk of accidentals but rather by giving a much more robust account of the sense in which the human nature of Christ can be understood as an accident in relation to the subject or substance of the Word.

Doubts about the Third Opinion
SH 3, In un., Tr1, Q4, Ti1, D3, M4, C4 (n. 56), 80–82

Drawing on the Avicennian metaphysics that was popular at the time, early Franciscans adopted the pluralist theory of forms, which entailed that accidents have a sort of existence in their own right even though they cannot exist independently of the subject in which they inhere. So construed, accidents do not represent mere modes of being of the form in which they inhere, but forms over above this, which taken together as a "bundle" constitute the identity of the being. This way of putting things allowed early Franciscans to affirm that Christ's human nature is truly "something" even though it comes after and is therefore parasitic upon his divine nature.

In addition to affirming the substantiality of Christ's human nature, post-1177 theologians faced the challenge of demonstrating that Christ's two natures do not threaten the unity of his being.

Is a Person Assumed?
SH 3, In un., Tr1, Q4, Ti1, D2, C4 (n. 35), 54–56

This matter came to a head in the question whether Christ assumed a human person. The problem with him assuming a human person is that this would rival his divine personhood and create a sort of split personality. To circumnavigate the problem, the Summists distinguished between three features of human personhood, namely, singularity, incommunicability, and dignity, a distinction that was in fact found earlier in William of Auxerre.[101] What makes

---

101. This threefold distinction itself had a prehistory that Magdalena Bieniak describes in *The Body-Soul Problem at Paris 1200–50* (Leuven: Leuven University

a person a singular being is the body-soul composite; as all human beings have this feature, the quality of singularity is communicable. By contrast, incommunicability is represented by the unique bundle of properties or accidental forms that is specific to one person and no other.

Although the first two distinctions of singularity and incommunicability fully establish a person's individuality, the final distinction is the ultimate arbiter of personhood, according to the *Summa*. For it is derived from what is most dignified or excellent in all persons, namely, their unique rational capacities. On the ground that the very Mind and Word of God is found in Christ, the *Summa* insists that his personhood was that of the Son of God rather than that of the man Jesus.[102] That again is not to undermine the fullness of Christ's humanity, however.

Is Christ an Individual Insofar as He Is a Man?
SH 3, Tr1, Q4, T1, M4, C3, Ar3 (n. 52), 75–77

To reaffirm this, the *Summa* invokes Richard of St. Victor's definition of an individual—or hypostasis—as an "incommunicable substance which has certain distinguishing features" and of a person as an "incommunicable substance of a rational nature which is distinguished through the property of dignity."

According to these definitions, the *Summa* argues, every person is a hypostasis, even though not every hypostasis is a person, that is, rational. Whereas most nonpersonal hypostases would be nonrational beings, the *Summa* claims that Richard's definitions allow for the possibility of a hypostasis that both happens to be distinguished by all the properties that make someone human, namely, singularity and incommunicability, and still derives actual personhood from the Son of God. Since the term "hypostasis" can refer both to an "individual" and a "person," moreover, it encompasses both Christ's human and divine natures in their full integrity without positing a dual personality.

Press, 2010), chapter 1.2. According to Walter Principe, *William of Auxerre*, 85, the distinction of dignity has its origins in Faustus of Riez, and possibly Boethius before him; it was invoked by Stephen Langton, Godfrey of Poitiers, and others. However, William's schematization of singularity, incommunicability, and dignity was followed almost universally by the next generation of theologians.

102. SH 3, In un., Tr1, Q4, Tii, D2, C4, Solutio (n. 35), 55.

Is Christ One or Two [Things]?

SH 3, In un., Tr1, Q4, Ti1, D3, M4, C3, Ar1 (n. 50), 73-74

As further support for this position, the *Summa* distinguishes between "being a nature" and "being *of* a nature." According to the *Summa*, Christ is divine and not human in his essential nature. However, he is able to be of human nature through divine causality. For the *Summa*, in summary, Christ is *of* multiple things even though he is not himself multiple things—just as a human being is not multiplied in virtue of being a body-soul compound.

Does the Union Take Place in the Person?

SH 3, In un., Tr1, Q4, Ti2, C1 (n. 57), 82-84

In an effort to explain this kind of union further, the *Summa* invokes an analogy to the way a branch from a pear tree is united to an apple or some other base tree into which it is grafted.

In this case, both natures, namely, pear and apple, remain intact: apples never become pears, nor vice versa—and yet no third entity results from this union—such as a tree that is neither a pear tree nor an apple tree. Rather, one comes to be "of the other," namely, a pear tree becomes part of an apple tree, because through the grafting, the dominant entity, that is, the apple tree, draws the other one into unity with itself, so that it grows out of it but is not the same thing as it. Here, there is ultimately only one hypostasis or one tree, which entails two distinct natures, of pear and apple.

According to the *Summa*, this is the way the Son of God is united to the human nature, because he draws human nature into a unity with his own hypostasis.

Does This Union Produce Any Change in What Is So United?

SH 3, In un., Tr1, Q4, Ti2, C7, Ar1 (n. 63), 92-93

This union does not result in any change in the Word itself but only on the side of the humanity that is now grafted on to the divine person. In other words, the Son of God does not move from not-being human to being human through the union, but that which he joins to himself, namely, human nature, moves from not-being divine to being divine, through union with the Second Person of the Trinity.[103]

---

103. SH 3, In. un., Tr1, Q4, Ti2, C7, Ar1, Ad tertium 3 (n. 63), 93.

Is Christ God Insofar as He Is a Man?

SH 3, Tr1, Q4, T1, D3, M4, C3, Ar2 (n. 51), 74–75

Following Alexander of Hales, who was among the first to start thinking, if not explicitly, in terms of the "communication of attributes" between the divine and human natures, the *Summa* finally considers the sense in which things said of God can also be said of Christ as man. Here, the author applies the rule that anything that can be predicated of the human can be predicated of the divine nature, and vice versa, so long as the appropriate nature is mentioned as a qualifier. For instance, Christ remits sins insofar as he is God.

CHAPTER 8: FREE CHOICE

Does Free Choice Exist?

SH 2.1, In4, Tr1, S2, Q3, Ti3, M1 (n. 389), 466–67

The Middle Ages inherited a relatively continuous tradition of thinking about free choice from Augustine, Anselm, and Bernard of Clairvaux.[104] Albeit in different ways, these thinkers advocated the position that free choice involves willing only the good and not evil. For them, an evil choice or sin represents a form of slavery. This position was upheld in one form or another by many of the *Summa*'s immediate predecessors and contemporaries, from Peter Lombard to the secular master William of Auxerre, whose *Summa aurea* offers one of the first in-depth treatises on free choice in the post-Lombard period;[105] a similar view is also found in Philip the Chancellor and the Dominicans Roland of Cremona and Hugh of St. Cher.

Is Free Choice Called "Free" for the Reason That It Is Indifferent to [Choosing] Good or Evil?

SH 2.1, In4, Tr1, S2, Q3, Ti3, M2, C3, Ar1 (n. 397), 475–76

In a radical departure from this tradition, articulated first and foremost by Alexander of Hales, the *Summa Halensis* advances the idea that free choice

---

104. See Lydia Schumacher, "Free Will in the *Summa Halensis*," in Schumacher, *The Legacy of Early Franciscan Thought*, 129–50.

105. William of Auxerre, *Summa aurea*, book 2, vol. 1, Spicilegium Bonaventurianum 17, ed. Jean Ribaillier (Paris: Grottaferrata, 1982), 274–309; see also book 2, vol. 2, Spicilegium Bonaventurianum 18 (1982), 470–510. See a fuller account of William's doctrine of free choice in Riccardo Saccenti, *Conservare la retta volontà: L'atto morale nelle dottrine di Filippo il Cancelliere e Ugo di Saint-Cher (1225-1235)* (Bologna: Società Editrice il Mulino, 2013), 116–21.

is indifferent to good and evil and can choose between either one of them. The Summist acknowledges that the human being is made in the image of God, but denies that we are unchangeably good as he is on the ground that we are created. In elaborating this case, the *Summa* invokes a more recently recovered authority, John of Damascus, who of course had been known to Peter Lombard and was popularized by Philip the Chancellor, though he was not drawn on in this particular respect previously.

According to *The Orthodox Faith* 2.27, everything that is created or generated from nothing is subject to change. By affirming this, the Damascene himself intended only to suggest that human beings are capable of doing or not doing, or of desiring or not desiring, any given thing.[106] The point of his argument, in other words, was to highlight that human beings are not determined to any specific good choice. Nevertheless, the *Summa* interprets his words to mean that free choice may vacillate between good and evil options.[107] Although there was a time, prior to the fall, when human beings chose only the good, as they do by grace postlapse, free choice under these circumstances consists nonetheless in the power to do good or evil, precisely because this in the *Summa*'s view is the logical corollary of being created.[108]

About Anselm's Definition of Free Will
SH 2.1, In4, Tr1, S2, Q3, Ti3, M2, C2, Ar1, Pr1 (n. 393), 472

This radical position was not so easy to reconcile with the leading authorities on free choice, Anselm, Augustine, and Bernard. Thus, the *Summa* proceeds to dedicate an entire section to the exposition of their opinions, and to seek essentially to explain away the thrust of their perspectives in order to justify its own. The first definition of free choice the *Summa* considers is that of Anselm in *Free Choice of the Will* 13, which states that "free choice is the power of preserving rectitude for its own sake."[109] This view poses a problem for the Summists' definition of free choice, which involves the options of preserving or deserting rectitude.[110] To get around the problem and co-opt

---

106. SH 2.1, In4, Tr1, S2, Q3, Ti3, M3, C2, Ad 1 (n. 403), 480, citing *The Orthodox Faith* 2.26.
107. SH 2.1, In4, Tr1, S2, Q3, Ti3, M2, C3, Ar1, obiectum a (n. 397), 475.
108. SH 2.1, In4, Tr1, S2, Q3, Ti3, M3, C4, Respondeo (n. 405), 482.
109. SH 2.1, In4, Tr1, S2, Q3, Ti3, M2, C2, Ar1, Pr1, 1 (n. 393), 472.
110. Ibid.

Anselm's definition for its own purposes, the *Summa* observes that the power of preserving rectitude can be understood in several ways, namely, on the part of the one who preserves rectitude, on the part of what is preserved, that is, "the right thing to do," and in terms of the means through which it is preserved. When all three of these factors are taken into account, no power of preserving rectitude can exist without rectitude actually being implemented. However, when we consider the power to preserve rectitude exclusively in terms of the nature of the one who preserves rectitude, the power of preserving rectitude can be said to exist even if no rectitude is actually upheld. On this basis, the Summist concludes that the power to preserve rectitude that Anselm describes does not necessarily entail acting rightly. In this way, the Summist justifies the view that free choice can result in evil.

About Augustine's Definition of Free Will
SH 2.1, In4, Tr1, S2, Q3, Ti3, M2, C2, Ar1, Pr2 (n. 394), 472–3
The next definition the Summist considers is that of Augustine, or at least Lombard's rendition of Augustine, which states: "free choice is the operation of will and reason by which the good is chosen through the assistance of grace and evil resisted also by grace."[111] In grappling with this definition, the Summist distinguishes between the liberty of nature, which entails freedom from force or compulsion; the liberty of grace, which involves freedom from sin; and the liberty of glory, which concerns freedom from misery. According to the *Summa*, the idea that free choice is incompatible with sin does not refer to the liberty of nature, which entails both good and evil, but to the liberties of grace and glory only. This is the *Summa*'s way of justifying its opinion in the face of Augustinian sentiments to the contrary.

About Bernard's Definition of Free Will
SH 2.1, In4, Tr1, S2, Q3, Ti3, M2, C2, Ar1, Pr3 (n. 395), 473–4
Finally, the *Summa* addresses the definition of Bernard of Clairvaux in his *De libero arbitrio* 2.4: "free choice is consent on the basis of the freedom of the will that cannot be lost and the judgment of reason that cannot be

---

111. SH 2.1, In4, Tr1, S2, Q3, Ti3, M2, C2, Ar1, Pr2, 1 (n. 394), 472. See also Augustine, *On Reprimand and Grace* 11. 32 (PL 44, 935); Peter Lombard, *II Sent.*, d. 24, c. 3, 421.

changed."¹¹² According to Bernard, this consent is a medium between the sense of the mind and the sense of the flesh. While the sense of the mind cannot pertain to evil, the sense of the flesh cannot pertain to anything good. When understood in terms the mind, consequently, Bernard says that "no one would try to say that free choice is a power or faculty that can alternate between good and evil."¹¹³ As the medium between the mind and the senses, however, consensus is indifferent to good and evil. For it is capable of preferring what is good and ultimately God or of declining it.¹¹⁴

How Do These Three Definitions Differ among Themselves?
SH 2.1, In4, Tr1, S2, Q3, Ti3, M2, C2, Ar2 (n. 396), 474–75
In comparing the three definitions outlined above, the Summist associates them with three of the four Aristotelian causes: efficient, final, material, and formal. Bernard's definition of free choice as consent concerns the efficient or moving cause, insofar as it has to do with whether we choose to follow God or not. Anselm's definition pertains to the final cause of free choice, namely, righteousness for its own sake, and Augustine's deals with the powers of reason and will which serve as the material cause of free choice.

Do Humans Possess the Same Kind of Free Choice in the States of Innocence, Sin, and Grace?
SH 2.1, In4, Tr1, S2, Q3, Ti3, M3, C4 (n. 405), 482
According to the *Summa*, the nature of free will as indifferent to good and evil remains the same in the states of innocence, or before sin, and after it, as well as in the glory of heaven. Although human beings who existed prior to sin were initially made good, this did not change the fact that their fundamental nature involved the capacity to do otherwise.

Do Those to Whom Free Choice Is Appropriate Have It in Equal Degree?
SH 2.1, In4, Tr1, S2, Q3, Ti3, M4, C1 (n. 407), 484–85
Furthermore, the Summists argue that humans have that capacity in equal measure and only their choices as to what to do with it vary.

---

112. SH 2.1, In4, Tr1, S2, Q3, Ti3, M2, C2, Ar1, Pr3, 1 (n. 395), 473, citing Bernard of Clairvaux, *On Grace and Free Choice* 3.7 (PL 182, 1005).
113. Ibid., citing Bernard of Clairvaux, *On Grace and Free Choice* 10.35.
114. SH 2.1, In4, Tr1, S2, Q3, Ti3, M2, C2, Ar2, Solutio (n. 396), 474.

Is Free Choice Reason or Will, or Some Power That Is Neither Reason Nor Will?

SH 2.1, In4, Tr1, S2, Q3, Ti3, M2, C1, Ar3 (n. 392), 470–71

Following its discussion of free choice, the *Summa Halensis* takes decisive steps in a debate stemming from Lombard as to whether free choice consists primarily in reason and will or in something beyond them. While Lombard himself advocated the view that free choice consists in reason and will together, many following him, including Praepositinus of Cremona, Stephen Langton, William of Auxerre, Hugh of St. Cher, and Roland of Cremona all take the more intellectualist line affirming that free choice consists primarily in right reason.[115] As Saccenti observes, however, Philip the Chancellor represents a new phase in work on free choice. He breaks from his predecessors to argue that free choice is identical with the will rather than reason. In his opinion, the will rather than reason possesses the power to act or not to act and thus to acquire or lose merit.[116]

This definition proved influential for Alexander of Hales, who is to credit for developing the Franciscan position on the question of whether free choice consists in reason or the will.[117] Following Alexander, the Summist holds that free choice is a faculty which contains both reason and will, which entails a preliminary cognitive act that is needed to weigh what one should do. For the *Summa*, however, free choice is ultimately a matter of willing to do what one should do and so in essence pertains more to the will than reason.[118]

Is Merit or Demerit Estimated Based on the Power of Free Choice?

SH 2.1, In4, Tr1, S2, Q3, Ti3, M7 (n. 416), 490

Following Philip the Chancellor, the *Summa* concludes that this is precisely the reason why we are able to acquire merit, namely, on the basis of what we choose to do with our knowledge of what is right or wrong.

---

115. D. Odon Lottin, *Psychologie et morale aux XIIe et XIIIe siècles*. Vol. 1, *Problèmes de psychologie* (Gembloux: J. Duculot, 1942), 50, 67, 96–103.

116. Ibid., 73–74; *Philippi Cancellarii Parisiensis Summa de bono*, ed. Nicolas Wicki (Bern: Francke, 1985), 173; cf. Saccenti, *Conservare la retta volontà*, 124.

117. *Magistri Alexandri de Hales Quaestiones disputatae 'Antequam esset frater,'* vol. 1 (Quaracchi: Collegii S. Bonaventurae, 1960), Q. XXXIII, disp. 2, memb. 2, no. 50, 583.

118. SH 2.1, In4, Tr1, S2, Q3, Ti3, M2, C1, Ar3 (n. 392), 470–71; Lottin, *Psychologie et morale*, 1:140–49.

As this suggests, the Summist's view of free choice as flexible between good and evil is instrumental to a larger Franciscan perspective on how salvation is forfeited or achieved. While it is always the case that God gives us the ability to know and do what is right, it is our decision what to do with it. This is a more moderate version of the voluntarism that would become a key feature of Franciscan thought from Duns Scotus onward.[119] Yet it is a form of voluntarism nonetheless which is not so much designed to validate evil as a legitimate and substantial option as it places the onus on human beings for the consequences of their decisions.

CHAPTER 9: MORAL THEOLOGY

The field of moral theology, and specifically moral law, plays a prominent role in the *Summa Halensis*, whose third volume contains a treatise on law of more than five hundred pages that was the first of its kind in the period of early university scholasticism. This treatise is itself based on the *Tractatus de legibus* of John of La Rochelle, who we have seen was largely responsible for the *Summa*'s third volume.[120] Earlier thinkers and contemporaries, such as Peter of Poitiers, Prepositinus, Philip the Chancellor, William of Auxerre, and Roland of Cremona, had focused the treatises on moral theology within

---

119. Olivier Boulnois, *Duns Scot: La rigeur de la charité* (Paris: Le Cerf, 1998); Allan B. Wolter, *Duns Scotus on the Will and Morality* (Washington, DC: The Catholic University of America Press, 1997); Bonnie Kent, *Virtues of the Will: The Transformation of Ethics in the Late Thirteenth Century* (Washington, DC: The Catholic University of America Press, 1995); Bychkov, "In Harmony with Reason," 45–55.

120. This work has recently been edited by Riccardo Saccenti, *Iohannes de Rupella: Quaestiones disputatae de legibus* (Rome: Quarrachi, 2021); and translated by Michael Basse, *Summa theologica Halensis: De legibus et praeceptis: Lateinischer Text mit Übersetzung und Kommentar* (Berlin: De Gruyter, 2018). See also the important studies of this text by Aloysius Obiwulu, *Tractatus de Legibus in Thirteenth-Century Scholasticism: A Critical Study and Interpretation of Law in Summa Fratris Alexandri, Albertus Magnus and Thomas Aquinas* (Münster: LIT, 2003); Beryl Smalley, "William of Auvergne, John of La Rochelle and Saint Thomas on the Old Law"; and M. V. Dougherty, "Twenty Moral Dilemmas from Two Early Thirteenth-Century Summaries of Theology: William of Auxerre's *Summa aurea* and the Franciscan *Summa Halensiana*," in idem., ed., *Moral Dilemmas in Medieval Thought from Gratian to Aquinas* (Cambridge: Cambridge University Press, 2011), 41–84.

their major theological works on the theme of moral virtues and vices.[121] The same is true later for Thomas Aquinas, who famously filled volumes 2.1 and 2.2 of his *Summa Theologiae* with material proper to what has often been called "virtue ethics." Devoting extensive space to law, where others focused on virtues, bespeaks a budding Franciscan interest in divine commands, which arguably mimics Francis's concern for the literal adherence to Christ's example, and which would quickly become popular with later Franciscans, such as William of Ockham.[122]

While Ockham has been accused—rightly or wrongly—of advocating a moral theology which hinges on obedience to completely arbitrary divine rulings, which in his view may even command persons to perform evil acts, the *Summa Halensis* ensures that its rendering of divine commands is firmly rooted in what human beings can verify as right and good.[123] This effect is achieved through the articulation of a "tiered" theory of law that moves from the eternal to the natural law, then to the Mosaic Law or Ten Commandments, and finally, to the law of the gospel.

What Is Eternal Law?
SH 3, P2, In1, Q un., C3 (n. 226), 316–19

Whereas William of Auxerre was the first to incorporate a discussion of natural law, usually treated in exclusively legal treatises, into a theological

---

121. *Petri Pictaviensis Sententiarum libri quinque*, ed. Dom Hugh Mathoud (Paris, 1655), repr. PL 211, 789–1280; P. Moore, *The Works of Peter of Poitiers: Master in Theology and Chancellor of Paris (1193–1205)* (South Bend, IN: University of Notre Dame Press, 1936); G. Lacombe, *Prepositini Cancellarii Parisiensis (1206–1210) opera omnia I—La vie et les oeuvres de Prevostin* (Caen: Le Soulchoir, 1927). William of Auxerre was the first to incorporate a discussion of natural law, usually treated in exclusively legal treatises, into a theological account of the virtues, which nonetheless took priority, as O. Lottin observes in *Psychologie et morale aux XIIe et XIIIe siècles* (Louvain: Abbaye du Mont César, 1948), 2.1:75. For an example of the focus on virtues and vices, see Roland of Cremona, *Summae Magistri Rolandi Cremonensis, O. P. Liber Tercius* (Bergamo: Umberto Midali, 2017).

122. See Marilyn McCord Adams's response to this position in "The Structure of Ockham's Moral Theory," *Franciscan Studies* 46 (1986), 1–35; Thomas M. Osborne Jr., "Ockham as a Divine-Command Theorist," *Religious Studies* 41, no. 1 (March 2005): 1–22. See also Riccardo Saccenti's survey of the doctrine of natural law in the Middle Ages and the Franciscan tradition in *Debating Medieval Natural Law: A Survey* (South Bend, IN: University of Notre Dame Press, 2016).

123. This is also true of Scotus, as Bychkov shows in "In Harmony with Reason."

account of the virtues, John of La Rochelle was the first theologian systematically to develop an account of the eternal law that exists above our minds, in the mind of God, for which he drew inspiration from Augustine.[124]

According to John, this law is impressed upon our souls,[125] and is that by which all things are ultimately ordained towards what is good.[126] Although God himself does not do evil, John allows that he orders evil to the good and thus incorporates it under the auspices of his eternal law.

Is the Natural Law Universally Derived from the Eternal Law?
SH 3, P2, In1, Q un., C7, Ar4 (n. 233), 328–29

As the means by which all things are ordered by God to the good, the eternal law is the basis for the natural law, which ordains both irrational and rational creatures to perform their proper functions, which in the case of rational beings are not determined but subject to free choice.

Is the Natural Law a Cognitive or Motive Habit?
SH 3, P2, In2, Q2, C2 (n. 244), 343–44

Much like free choice itself, the natural law involves both reason and will and their operation, that is, knowing the law, wanting to fulfill it, and actually doing so. Since the fulfillment of the law is enacted by the will, however, the *Summa* here as previously preserves a kind of primacy for this faculty over reason in what will quickly evolve into a distinctly Franciscan form of voluntarism.

Can the Natural Law Be Erased?
SH 3, P2, In2, Q3, C1 (n. 246), 346–47

When it comes to the question whether the natural law can be erased from the soul, the *Summa* distinguishes between two ways in which this could happen: in essence or in effect. The natural law cannot be erased in essence

---

124. Lottin, *Psychologie et morale aux XIIe et XIIIe siècles*, 2.1:52–53, 75. See also Brady, "Law in the *Summa Fratris Alexandri*," 138–39, where the author credits John with systematizing Augustine's thought on the eternal law and providing the first concerted discussion on this score. Lesley Smith discusses John's innovations regarding the eternal law in *The Ten Commandments: Interpreting the Bible in the Medieval World* (Leiden: Brill, 2014), 18–25. Aquinas follows John in Summa Theologiae 2.1.93.

125. SH 3, P2, In1, Q un., C1 (n. 224), 314. SH 3, P2, In1, Q un., C2 (n. 225), 316.

126. SH 3, P2, In1, Q un., C1 (n. 224), 314.

because it is constitutive of the impressed image of God. This can never disappear in the human being, because that would imply a failure on God's part to make himself knowable to us. Nevertheless, John admits that the law can sometimes be erased in its effect, when the soul turns away from God and becomes so darkened by sin as to become ignorant of the law which always potentially illumines its moral deliberations.

Does the Natural Law Ordain Us to God?
SH 3, P2, In2, Q4, M2, C1 (n. 250), 353
Because the natural law is impressed on all human beings as images of God, they possess in it not only knowledge of what is right to do but also of God himself.

Does the Natural Law Instruct Us to Love God above All Things?
SH 3, P2, In2, Q4, M2, C3 (n. 252), 357–58
In loving the self, consequently, John argues that we necessarily love above all else the origin of our being and its conservation, albeit not in itself and absolutely but precisely insofar as it is our origin. After all, the soul cannot naturally love God more than itself because nature does not extend beyond itself. By the same token, we love those similar to ourselves in species, because we love other things like ourselves by nature, which means the love of the self also entails the love of the neighbor.

Is the Law of Moses Necessary for Salvation?
SH 3, P2, In3, Tr1, Q1, C2 (n. 260), 369–70
Following the inquiry concerning natural law, John turns to consider the law of Moses or the Ten Commandments and the law of the gospel, arguing that the former is necessary for salvation because it elucidates the meaning of the gospel law.

Is the Law of the Gospel the Same as the Natural Law?
SH 3, P2, In4, Tr1, Q4 (n. 546), 843–45
The Law of Moses, on his account, gives a privileged and complete expression of the natural law, which humanity needed after the fall into sin led to ignorance of the natural law.[127] It is necessary for salvation insofar as it renders explicit the requirements God has imposed upon us through the natural law

---

127. SH 3, P2, In1, Q. un., C7, Ar4 (n. 233), 328–29.

and outlines a number of ceremonial and judicial precepts which effected salvation until the coming of Christ, whose redeeming work they prefigured.[128] As this suggests, there is no real difference between the content of the law of Moses and that of Christ.[129] The main difference concerns the means by which salvation is carried out under the two orders.[130]

Is the Law of the Gospel the Same as the Law of Moses?
SH 3, P2, In4, Tr1, Q5 (n. 547), 845–46

As John insists, the law of Moses and the gospel are one law in terms of their universal import but differ as to the way they were given—through a mere man, or through Christ. They also differ regarding the ends they can achieve. While the end of Mosaic law is to deflect evil through fear, the end of the gospel is principally to do good through love. This brings us to the question regarding the relationship of the natural law to the law of the gospel.[131] These laws are likewise intricately related and differ mainly in terms of the more or less precise concept of the God who is their arbitrator.

While the natural law says that God must be loved, because he is our benefactor and creator, the law of the gospel, for instance, says that he is to be loved, because he is good and the redeemer. Likewise, the natural law says that we must love our neighbors because they are human and conform to us in species and because we are made by the same creator. The law of grace, however, dictates that the neighbor must be loved because they are a child of God, or at least can be, and because they are made in the image of God, by whom all who are redeemed are redeemed. This confirms that the obligation to love God and neighbor in the natural law and the law of the gospel stem from different causes, but the former is ordained to and perfected through the latter.

What we find in the *Summa*, consequently, is an understanding of how we do what is good that closely mirrors its understanding of how we know the truth. In the latter case, we are impressed with an innate knowledge of the first truth, that is God, which gives us access to the means of knowing all truth and ultimately God himself. In the former, we are impressed with

---

128. SH 3, P2, In3, Tr1, Q1, C2 (n. 260), 369–70.
129. SH 3, P2, In4, Tr1, Q8, Respondeo (n. 560), 866.
130. SH 3, P2, In3, Tr1, Q1, C1 (n. 259), 366–69.
131. SH3, P2, In4, Tr1, Q4 (n. 546), 843–45.

an innate knowledge of the good, through natural law, which gives us access to the means of doing what is right and ultimately loving God as well as neighbor. The failure to do this is certainly possible, but not for want of the capacity to do good and love God, which God perpetually makes available to us in the form of his image. As ever in the Franciscan account, the failure is down to an ignorance and neglect of the capacity that stems from an excessive love for goods other than God.

NOTE ON THE TEXT AND TRANSLATION

The current translation is intended for a variety of audiences, ranging from the academic audience, which includes undergraduate or graduate students with no reading knowledge of Latin, as well as scholars who would like to familiarize themselves with this source quickly, to the Franciscan community at large, or anyone interested in the Western medieval or more specifically Franciscan intellectual tradition.

To create the current translation, the 1924–1948 Quaracchi edition of the *Summa Halensis* was used. While the translation is a joint product of both translators/editors, Lydia Schumacher was primarily responsible for Chapters 3, 4, 6, and 9, and Oleg Bychkov for Chapters 1, 2, 5, 7, and 8.

Although the translation styles of the two translators of this volume differ, the general strategy can be described as follows. The best way of translating a Latin text for a present-day reader is not by making a calque of the Latin in English, that is, by rendering all Latin roots that are also used in English by cognate English words. The exact replication of the Latin syntax is also not advisable. Those who can read Latin do not need such a calque translation, and those who cannot will not benefit from it in any way. Calque translations create unnecessary awkwardness and tediousness even in the cases of the best Latin prose, while scholastic texts such as the *Summa* often exhibit broken and awkward syntax even in Latin, and it makes no sense to replicate it in English. Thus the translators attempted to render both Latin terms and Latin grammar in ways that would be most intelligible and transparent to a present-day English-speaking reader. At the same time, as this translation is intended as a research tool, an attempt has been made not to stray too far from the text and make the rendition so free and loose that it cannot be matched more or less exactly to the Latin. Thus the Latin syntax has been followed in all cases where it is possible to do so without disrupting the English syntax, and freer renditions have been made where the Latin is too awkward or too broken to be followed exactly.

REFERENCES IN THE *SUMMA HALENSIS*

The *Summa Halensis* often quotes authoritative sources without giving the complete reference for its quotations, which was not customary at the time. The editors of the Latin text have therefore attempted to supply full references in the apparatus. In order to assist the reader in locating the *Summa*'s sources, we have included in square brackets or footnotes references to the *Summa*'s sources in cases where the author was explicitly mentioned in the text but have not included references to implicit citations, many of which can be found listed in the edition of the Latin text..

References to the *Summa Halensis* give the book (liber) rather than the volume (tome) number. Thus, we cite books 1, 2.1, 2.2, 3 instead of volumes 1, 2, 3, 4, in order to avoid any confusion with the unedited fourth book of the *Summa*. The subject of volume 1 is primarily the nature of God; volume 2, creation and human nature; volume 3, sin and vice; and volume 4, the Incarnation and law.

CHAPTER 1

THE SCIENCE OF THEOLOGY

IS THE DISCIPLINE OF THEOLOGY AN [EXACT] SCIENCE?

SH 1, Tr Int, Q1, C1 (n. 1), 1–4
Objections:

1. Augustine, *83 Questions*, q. 48: "Some things are taken on faith and are never a matter of understanding, for example, every history that deals with singular events and human deeds." Therefore, since the discipline of theology is for the most part historical, as is clear from the law and the gospel, it is about the things that are never a matter of understanding. But there cannot be a science about things that are not a matter of understanding, for science deals with intelligible things; it remains, therefore, that the discipline of theology is not a science.

2. As Aristotle says at the beginning of his *Metaphysics* [1.1], "Experience is of singular individual things, while art deals with universals: for art comes into existence when, after having had multiple experiences of similar things, one starts to group them under one and the same class"; but the discipline of theology for the most part does not deal with universals, but with singular and individual things, as is clear from historical narratives in it. Therefore, it is not an art or science.

3. Truth is received in three ways in disciplines: by way of opinion, belief, or science; opinion is formed on the basis of things subject to opinion; belief is formed on the basis of credible things; science is formed on the basis of intelligible things. However, science never derives from things pertaining to opinion or belief as such. Now since theology as such deals with matters of belief, according to John 20:31, *"But these are written that you might believe,"* therefore it does not operate as a science.

4. Augustine, *On the Trinity*, Bk. 14 [1.3]: "I do not attribute to 'science' whatever humans are capable of knowing as regards human affairs, where there is much empty vanity and harmful curiosity, but [I] only [attribute to science] that by which a most salutary faith, which leads one to true blessedness, is born, nourished, and strengthened." Therefore, all that this "science" generates is faith; therefore, it is not science in the true sense of the word,

especially since faith is a way of grasping that is "situated above opinion but below science."

To the contrary:

a. That which is known through divine inspiration is known more truly than that which is known through human reasoning, because divine inspiration allows for no falsity, while the latter occurs frequently in reasoning. Therefore, since knowledge in theology is divinely inspired (2 Timothy 3:16: "*All scripture is given by inspiration of God*"; and 2 Peter 1:21: "*The holy men of God spoke as they were inspired by the Holy Spirit*"), it is a science in a truer sense than other sciences.

b. Augustine says in Bk. 14[1.2] of *On the Trinity*: theology is a science dealing with things that pertain to our salvation. Therefore, it is a science.

Solution:

First of all, one must note that there could be a science of the cause and a science of the caused. Now, the science of the cause of [all] causes is certainly self-sufficient. At the same time, a science of the caused, be they [lower] causes or merely effects, is not self-sufficient, because those things relate to, and depend on, the cause of [all] causes. Hence, we conclude that theology, which is a science about God, who is the cause of all causes, is self-sufficient. But the name of "science" [technically speaking] is applied to the sciences of the caused, while the science of the cause of all causes is [actually] called "wisdom." For this reason even Aristotle says that First Philosophy, which is self-sufficient and deals with the cause of all causes, should be called "wisdom." By the same token, the discipline of theology, which surpasses all other sciences, must be called "wisdom." Hence Deuteronomy 4:6: "*This is our wisdom and understanding in the sight of the nations.*"

In addition, it must be noted that there is [the sort of] science that perfects our cognition by way of truth, and also there is [the sort of] science that moves our affection toward goodness. The first kind is like cognition through [the faculty of] sight, and therefore should be called science in an absolute sense. The second kind is like cognition by way of taste, and for this reason should be called wisdom, from the taste of affection, according to what is said in Ecclesiasticus 6:22: "*Wisdom is like her name.*"[1]

---

1. A pun lost in the English: "wisdom" (*sapientia*) has the same root in Latin as "flavor" (*sapor*).

Therefore, theology, which perfects the soul by way of affection, moving it toward the good through the principles of fear and love, is more appropriately and mainly wisdom. First Philosophy, which is the philosophers' theology[2] and deals with the cause of all causes but perfects our cognition by way of skill and reasoning, is less appropriately called wisdom. As for the rest of the sciences, which are about subsequent [levels of] causes and about the effects, they should not be called "wisdoms" but sciences [strictly speaking].

For these reasons one must say that the discipline of theology is wisdom in the strict sense of the term wisdom. As for First Philosophy, which is the knowledge of first causes, which are goodness, wisdom, and power, it is wisdom in the sense of science. As for other sciences, which study accidents of a subject through their respective causes, they are sciences in the sense of science.

Replies to the objections:

1. To the first it must be said that history functions differently in sacred scripture compared to other disciplines. Indeed, in other disciplines the purpose of historical narratives is to relay "singular and individual deeds" of the people, and no inner meaning is intended. For this reason, because these historical narratives are about individual and temporal acts, they do indeed deal with those things that are "never a matter of understanding." However, in sacred scripture historical narratives are not intended to signify the individual acts of humans, but they are supposed to signify universal principles of action and conditions that pertain to instructing the audience and shaping the contemplation of the divine mysteries. For example, Abel's suffering is introduced to signify the passion of Christ and the just, Cain's malice in order to signify the perversity of the unjust, and so forth. Thus, in [the sort of] history that is found in sacred scripture an individual fact is introduced in order to signify a universal [principle,] and this is where one can speak of understanding and science [in it].

2. To the second it must be said that "universal" can be used in four senses: in predication (an example: "man"); in exemplifying (an example: the shape of an [individual] shoe standing for a number of shoes, or the life of Job

---

2. That is, part of philosophy that deals with transcendence, or the divine; in Arabic texts (known to thirteenth-century schoolmen in translation) metaphysics is aptly called الإلاهيات, i.e., "divine matters," "divinity."

standing for the lives of a number of people); in signifying (an example: Jacob signifying a just man who was associated with both Rachel and Leah, for he exerted himself in both the contemplative and active lives); in reference to causality (an example: God as the universal cause of the creation of things, or Christ as the universal cause of the restoration of humans). Now in view of this one must say that sacred scripture does contain universals. For sacred scripture does have general pronouncements, such as "*The fear of the Lord is the beginning of wisdom*" (Proverbs 1:7); "*The end of the commandment is charity*" (1 Timothy 1:5), and the like. In such universal pronouncements we have "universal" understood in the first sense, that of predication. It also has particular or individual pronouncements, which appear in historical, prophetic, and other contexts. In these, if one takes their surface meaning, one can find "universal" in the second sense, that is, in the sense of exemplifying [something]. For example, literally the stories of Abraham and Job are about individual events, but they are told in scripture to provide an example of good conduct. On this account Romans 15:4: "*Whatsoever things were written, were written for our learning*"; and James 5:10: "*Take the prophets for an example of patience and suffering affliction.*" As for the inner and spiritual meaning, there are "universals" in pronouncements about individual things in the third sense, namely, universals of signification, for from one universal principle they point to many [individual] things. If one takes both senses of scripture, inner and outer, expressed either in general or in individual pronouncements, insofar as they provide some way to God, who is the universal cause of the creation of things, or to Christ, who is the universal cause of the restoration of humans—there are "universals" in it in the fourth sense, the sense of causation. Therefore, having made these distinctions, in this sense one can say that sacred doctrine [i.e., theology] is about universal principles.

3. To the third it must be said that, according to Augustine's distinction in *83 Questions* [q. 48], "there are three kinds of things pertaining to belief. Some are those that are always taken on faith and are never a matter of understanding, as any historical narrative. Others are believed in the course of understanding them, as all rational arguments, either about numbers or about some disciplines. Others are first believed and then understood: such are things pertaining to the divine that can only be understood by those of pure heart, which is attained if one sticks to the precepts designed to promote a good life." From this it appears that there is a category of "things pertaining to belief" that is never associated with science, such as historical [narratives

of] deeds. Then there are some [such things] that do go together with science, for example, the credibility of the arguments made in the [scholarly] disciplines. Finally, there are some that dispose one toward understanding and science, as is the case with matters pertaining to the divine. Whence, according to an alternative reading[3] of Isaiah 7:9, "*Unless you believe, you will not understand.*" Therefore, it is not mutually repugnant for theology to be both about matters of belief and a science at the same time.

4. The reply to the fourth is already clear, because this science first generates belief or faith, and later, after the heart has been cleansed by faith that operates through love, it generates understanding. Hence, this is the difference between this discipline, which is wisdom, from others, which are sciences: in this discipline, "belief" leads to "understanding," while in those other disciplines "understanding" leads to "belief"—for one assents [to something] by the very fact of understanding [it].

As for what is added, namely, that "belief is below science and above opinion," one must make a distinction: there is belief that derives from probable reasons, and of such belief it is true that it is below science; there is also belief or faith that is inspired to assent to primary truth for its own sake, and this type is above any science. It is precisely to this sort of belief that the grasp of the sacred teaching disposes one, and it is at this sort of belief that it is aimed.

Also, one could object as follows: "every [singular] science is of some [single] kind of subject, whose parts and accidents it considers in themselves," as the Philosopher says [in *Posterior Analytics* 1.28]; however, Boethius says in his book *On the Trinity* [4] that "God is not a subject"; therefore, one cannot examine God in the same way one examines an accident of a subject; therefore, theology, which is knowledge about God, will not be a science.

To this, one must say that the way of "knowing forms that are embedded in matter is different from the way of knowing forms that are separate from matter," as Boethius shows in his book *On the Trinity* [2]. In the first case, form inheres in its subject by means of some cause. In such cases "[singular] science" is indeed understood to be "of a [singular] kind of subject" and it "considers accidents of the subject." However, the way of knowing forms and things that are separate from matter, such as the divinity and trinity of

---

3. That is, according to the *Itala* version, which was, unlike the Vulgate, a Latin translation from the Septuagint.

persons, is different. In such cases, through operation we become aware of the power, and through the power, of the very substance of divinity,[4] as in Romans 1:20: *"The invisible things of God . . . are seen, being understood by the things that are made, even his eternal power and godhead."*

In addition to that, the way of knowing simple things is different from the way of knowing composites. Indeed, composites are known by way of resolving them into their parts, and therefore a "[singular] science," which is of composites, indeed, "is of a single kind of subject, whose parts it considers." However, one cannot assume this way of knowing as regards simple things, which do not admit of parts—for divinity, as a simple thing, cannot be known by this way of knowing, but by the one described earlier.

ABOUT THE DIFFERENCE BETWEEN SACRED DOCTRINE [I.E., THEOLOGY] AND OTHER SCIENCES

SH 1, Tr Int, Q1, C2 (n. 2), 4–5

It is asked, then: is the discipline of theology simply one of the sciences, or does it contain them, or is contained under them, for example, under some part of philosophy?

One raises the following objections:

1. Ecclesiasticus 1:1: *"All wisdom is from the Lord God."* Therefore, every wisdom or science is theological or divine, because the science of theology is nothing but divine science.

2. Theological or divine science is called "divine" either because it is from God (and then every other science would be "divine"), or because it is about God: but according to this First Philosophy is [also] divine and theological, because it is [also] about God. And then the [science of] sacred scripture will simply be a science like all others, or [at least] like First Philosophy [i.e., in the same sense of the word].

3. If it is called "divine" because it is brought forth by the divine Spirit, then one can object as follows. Indeed, it is true that "all truth, no matter who might utter it, is from the Holy Spirit," as the Gloss[5] on 1 Corinthians 12:3 says: *"No one can say that Jesus is the Lord, [but by the Holy Spirit]"*;

---

4. See a similar context in pseudo-Dionysius, *Celestial Hierarchy* 11.2: εἰς οὐσίαν καὶ δύναμιν καὶ ἐνέργειαν (see a direct quote from this text in what follows).

5. Peter Lombard's gloss on 1 Corinthians 12:3 (PL 191, 1651).

therefore, every truth of any science whatsoever is brought forth by the Holy Spirit; but then, just as theology is a science by virtue of being brought forth by the divine Spirit, so every other science will be theological.

4. If [a science] is called "theological" or "divine" because it is obtained through divine revelation, one can object as follows, according to Romans 1:19, which speaks about the philosophers' knowledge about God: "*Whatever is known of God is manifest in them: for God has revealed it to them* [that is, the philosophers]." Therefore, philosophical knowledge about God was obtained through revelation; therefore, it is theological.

From these arguments, then, it seems that theology is like one of the other sciences.

To the contrary:

a. Every human science is acquired through either discovery or teaching. However, theology is an inspired, not acquired discipline, as far as its origin is concerned, as 2 Timothy 3:16 says; therefore, it is not like the other sciences.

b. All human sciences are founded upon evidence coming from creatures, which is the basis for all experience, as Aristotle says in his *Metaphysics* [1.1]: "All science and art happen through experience: for it is experience that produces art." But theological teaching is based upon evidence coming from faith, according to the alternative reading of Isaiah 7:9: "*Unless you believe, you will not understand.*" Therefore, it is not like other sciences.

c. 1 Corinthians 2:7 says: "*We speak the wisdom of God in a mystery, even the hidden wisdom.*" The Gloss [comments]: "So that the pseudo-apostles may not be privy to it," "because it is not in the words, but in virtue, and it is not graspable by human reason, but can be believed through the works of the Spirit"; therefore, theology is not like other sciences.

d. According to Hugh of St. Victor [*On the Sacraments* I, Prol. 2], other sciences are "about the works of creation, which are apparent from the natural state of things, while theology is about the works of restoration," which become apparent in [the light of] faith, and not from the very nature of things or as a result of human reasoning, as the commentary on Romans 1:19 says: "*That which may be known of God*"; "that is, which is known of God by natural reason, because there are many things about God that cannot be known naturally." Therefore, it is not the same as the other sciences.

e. Other sciences operate only with significations of words, while this discipline operates not only with significations of words, but also of things, as in Galatians 4:22: "*For it is written that Abraham had two sons*"; and it follows [4:24]: "*which was said allegorically*"; and in 1 Corinthians 2:7: "*We speak the wisdom of God in a mystery*," which is glossed as follows: "by explaining the mysteries of the Old Testament, which signify Christ, as in the sacrifices of Abel or Abraham."

f. All other sciences proceed, according to the order of rational thought, from [rational] principles to conclusions, which teach the intellect rather than move our affection. However, sacred scripture proceeds, according to the order of practical instruction, from [practical] principles to actions, so that our affection could be moved, by fear and love, on the basis of faith in God's justice and mercy. Hence, it is said in Deuteronomy 6:5: "*You will love the Lord your God*," etc. And later [6:13] it says: "*You will fear the Lord your God*," etc. And in Exodus 20:5: "*For I the Lord your God am a jealous God, avenging*," etc., and "*showing mercy*," etc.

Solution:

From the preceding it follows that theology is not like any other science, nor should it be listed among them. Nor is it under any part of philosophy. This is what must be conceded.

Answer to objections 1–4:

One must reply to the objections in the following manner: sacred doctrine [i.e., theology] is called "divine" or "theological" because it is (1) *from* God, (2) *about* God, and (3) *it leads to* God.

"From God." This is also applicable to other sciences, but not in the same way as it is to sacred scripture. Indeed, there is the true as true, and the true as good: both variations are from the Holy Spirit. Now when the true is taken as good, this "good" is either "moral good" or "good given by grace." If we consider "good given by grace," then there is a connection to the Holy Spirit, who is goodness. In this sense it is from the Holy Spirit according to his own ways: this is why this doctrine is described as being brought forth by the Holy Spirit. However, in other sciences, the speculative ones, the true is taken as true, and even the good as true. And even if the true is taken as good, as for example in practical moral disciplines, "good" is understood not as given by grace, but as moral: therefore, they are not called "brought forth by the Holy Spirit."

"About God." Theology is "about God" not in the same sense as other sciences, for example, First Philosophy, because they do not treat of God in the context of the mystery of the Trinity or the sacrament of the restoration of humanity.

"Leads to God." It is such through the principles of fear and love based on faith in God's mercy and justice: which is not characteristic of any other science. This argument makes the answer to objections clear.

WHAT IS THE SCIENCE OF SACRED SCRIPTURE ABOUT [I.E., WHAT IS ITS SUBJECT]?

SH 1, Tr Int, Q1, C3 (n. 3), 5-7

Arguments pro and contra:

Various things are said on this matter.

I. Hugh of St. Victor in the book of the *Sentences* [i.e., *On the Sacraments* I, Prol. 2] says: "The subject of sacred scripture is the works of restoration, while that of the other sciences—the works of creation."

To the contrary:

1. Genesis 1 deals with the works of creation.

2. Theology is a science about God; therefore, it is a science about the cause of the works of both creation and restoration. Therefore, the subject of sacred scripture is not the works of restoration, but rather the cause itself, which is God.

II. 3. Peter Lombard in the *Sentences* [1.1.1], following Augustine's *On Christian Doctrine* [1.2.2], says: "the contents of both the New and the Old Testaments include things and signs"; therefore, the subject of sacred scripture is things and signs.

To the contrary:

4. The science about things and the science about signs is not the same science, but sciences are divided into ones that deal with real things and ones that deal with speech, that is, with signification or signs of things; therefore, the sciences about things and about signs are different.

5. The kinds of things that theology deals with, according to Augustine [*On Christian Teaching* 1.3], are the things "that are to be enjoyed and used, which are enjoyed and used"; but this includes every kind of thing; therefore, theology is about all things.

III. 6. Others say that the subject of sacred scripture is "the whole Christ, both the head and the body, Christ and the Church, the groom and the bride," according to the Gloss on the beginning of the Psalter, because "divine scripture does not contain anything that does not pertain to Christ or to the Church."

To the contrary:

7. "*Christ is the end of the law*" (Romans 10:4) and "*He is the consummation of words/sermons*"[6] (Ecclesiasticus 43:29); therefore, he is not the subject.

Reply:

The subject of sciences is taken in two senses: [the subject] "about which" and "[the subject] that is included." The "subject about which" can be taken in three senses, according to the words of Dionysius in his *Celestial Hierarchy* [11.2]: "All understanding of the divine is divided by the heavenly intelligence into three areas: essence, power, and operation." According to this, if we take the subject of sacred scripture in the sense of "operation," we can say that it is the work of restoration of humankind. If, however, we take the subject of sacred scripture in the sense of "power," we shall say that it is Christ, who is "*the power of God and the wisdom of God*" (1 Corinthians 1:24). If, finally, we take the subject of sacred scripture in the sense of "essence," we shall say that it is God, or the divine substance. For this reason, according to this, theology is a science about the divine substance that must become known through Christ in [the course of] the work of restoration.

Replies to the objections:

1. To the first objection against the way Hugh assigns [the subject,] namely, that "Genesis 1 deals with the works of creation," one must reply that a science can consider something for two reasons: either because it belongs to the kind of things that this science is about, or because it clarifies what this science treats. In the first sense, sacred scripture deals with the works of restoration, but in the second sense it deals with the works of creation. For this reason Hugh of St. Victor says in the *Sentences* [i.e., *On the Sacraments* I, Prol. 3]: "In order to approach the works of restoration in a more substantial way, first, at the very beginning of the narration (Genesis 1), it narrates how the works of creation came about. For it could not appropriately show how humans were

---

6. The SH uses a truncated phrase from the Vulgate *consummatio sermonum ipse est*, which, if translated out of context, suggests that Christ is somehow the end of words or sermons. The full text of the passage reads *consummatio autem sermonum: "ipse est in omnibus"* and can be translated as "'*he is in all*' is the pinnacle of verbal expression."

restored without first showing how they fell—nor can it appropriately show their fall without first explaining how they were created by God. However, in order to show how humans were first created, one had to lay out the creation of the entire world, for the world was made to benefit humans."

2. To the second objection, when one objects against the same [Hugh] that "theology is a science about the cause of the works of both creation and restoration," this must be conceded. However, it does not follow from this that the subject matter of divine scripture is not the works of restoration, because the highest cause, which is God, is revealed through the work of restoration, through the power—Christ—as has been said, so that through operation we might become aware of the power, and through the power, of divinity, as in Romans 1:20: *The invisible things of God*—namely, *power and godhead—are seen, being understood by the things that are made.*

Therefore, note that according to Hugh [ibid., 2], "the work of constitution is the creation of the world with all its elements, while the work of restoration is the incarnation of the Word with all its sacraments. Now the subject matter of worldly or secular sciences is the work of creation, and the subject matter of divine scripture is the work of restoration."

3. To the other objection, the one against assigning the subject matter of sacred scripture in [Peter Lombard's] *Sentences* as "including things and signs," one must say that "things and signs" are the subject matter "*that is included*" in sacred scripture, not the subject matter *about* which it is. Therefore, Hugh, following Augustine, appropriately said that the subject matter of sacred scripture "includes things and signs." However, the subject matter *about* which sacred scripture is, is the divine substance that becomes known through Christ in the work of restoration. The same can be said of First Philosophy, namely, that the subject matter *that it includes* is all things. Hence, it is said to be about all, because it includes being according to its every specific difference, according to the different divisions of being, namely, potential being, actual being, single and multiple being, substantial and accidental being, and so forth. However, the subject matter *about* which it is—the primary thrust—is being that is one in its actuality, which is first substance, on which all things depend. Thus, in some sense the subject matter which sacred scripture includes is things and signs, while the subject matter *about* which its principal thrust is, is what we have said.[7]

7. That is, divine substance, etc.

4. As for the objection that a science about things and a science about signs is not one science, one must reply that this is the case when the rationale for considering things is separate from the rationale for considering signs. In the present case, however, they are not separate, for both are related to one thing, which is the restoration of humans to the likeness of God, or the conformity of humans to God through the work of restoration performed by Christ.

5. As for the objection that theology is about all things, because it deals with things under every angle, one must reply that even if it does deal with all things, it does not deal with them under different angles, but under one angle, which is to enable the human being, who is restored through the sacraments of the incarnation (which are constituted in between things to be enjoyed and things to be used), to arrive at things to be enjoyed (which are the Father, the Son, and the Holy Spirit, the unchangeable good) through things to be used. Therefore, even if it deals with all things generically, it does not deal with all things under all angles and according to all aspects, but under one proper angle and aspect, which has been specified.

6. To the objection against assigning [a specific subject matter] for the reason that the subject matter of sacred scripture is proposed as the whole Christ, both the head and the body, one must concede in the way that was described above.

7. And when one objects that "Christ is the end; therefore, he is not the subject matter," one must reply that the consequence is false. In the same way, the subject matter of a virtue that is for the sake of some end (such as faith, hope, and charity) is the same as that end. For example, the highest truth is both the subject matter and the end of faith, which believes in the highest truth for the sake of the highest truth. Similarly, charity loves the highest good for the sake of the highest good. However, it is not the same way as regards virtues that pertain to those which are for the sake of some end, for example, as regards justice and fortitude, but the subject matter of such a virtue is different from its end. Indeed, it is the arduous and most difficult things that constitute the subject matter of fortitude, but its end is the highest good—for it tolerates and approaches difficult things for the sake of the highest good. One could speak similarly about a science that is for the sake of some end, which is sacred scripture, because its subject matter and its end are the same. Hence, it does not follow: "Christ is the end; therefore, he is not the subject matter."

IS THE WAY OF [PROCEEDING IN] SACRED SCRIPTURE THAT OF DISCIPLINE OR SCIENCE?

SH 1, Tr Int, Q1, C4, Ar1 (n. 4), 7–9

Objections to the first article:

1. Any poetic manner is nonscientific and alien to any discipline, because this manner is historical and metaphorical, neither of which is characteristic of a [scientific] discipline. But the theological manner is poetic, historical, or parabolic;[8] therefore, it is not scientific.

2. Every scientific manner proceeds by way of defining, taking things apart [conceptual analysis], and putting them back together [conceptual synthesis]. However, the way of sacred scripture is not like this; therefore, it is not scientific.

3. Every scientific manner uses a manifest or direct way of speaking. At the same time, the manner of sacred scripture uses mystical speech; therefore, it is not scientific.

Reply:

It must be said that the way of sacred scripture is not that of science in the sense in which human reason understands it. It operates by organizing divine wisdom in order to instruct the soul in those matters that pertain to salvation. Therefore, Augustine says in *On the Trinity*, Bk. 14 [1.3]: "I do not attribute to this science whatever humans are capable of knowing as regards human affairs, where there is much vanity or harmful curiosity, but only that by which most salutary faith, which leads one to true blessedness, is born, nourished, and strengthened." And this sort of science deals with things that pertain to one's salvation.

Answer to objections:

1. To the first one must reply using the words of Dionysius, who says in the *Celestial Hierarchy* [2.1]: "Taking into consideration [the nature of] our intellect, theology unskillfully[9] used poetic sacred forms [to speak] of intel-

---

8. That is, uses parable, which is a kind of metaphor.

9. I translate according to pseudo-Dionysius's original text, which says "unskillfully" or "artlessly" (ἀτεχνῶς). Medieval translators starting with Eriugena for some reason (perhaps, their corrupt manuscript had οὐκ ἀτεχνῶς?) rendered the phrase as *valde artificialiter* ("very skillfully"), which is the text the SH uses. It seems that his argument would make much more sense if one assumed the original meaning: theology uses "unskillful" (i.e., nonscientific or imprecise) poetic

lectual matters that have no form." "For the divine ray can only illumine us if it is wrapped anagogically in a variety of sacred veils, and not in any other way," "because it is not possible for our mind to ascend to the immaterial contemplation of the celestial hierarchies except with the help of the material guidance which befits its own nature." For this reason, "forms of formless things and figures of figureless things spring forth beautifully in sacred scripture." For this reason also, "it is most appropriate to conceal divine enigmas by elaborate speech and make the sacred and secret truth of supraworldly intellects unapproachable by the multitude: for not everyone is sacred, and not everybody is entitled to knowledge or science, as sacred texts say." From these words of Dionysius it is clear that the reason why sacred scripture "unskillfully"[10] operates in a poetic manner is, perhaps, the need of our own intellect, which lacks comprehension of divine things. The second reason is the dignity of this [sort of] truth, which must be concealed from evil men.

2. To the second one must reply that there are different [scientific] styles: one operates by way of grasping truth through human reason; the other operates by way of [eliciting] the affection of piety through what is divinely inspired.

Now, it is the first manner that should operate through defining, taking things apart [analysis], and putting them back together [synthesis]. And this manner is appropriate for human sciences, because it is precisely the grasping of truth by the human reason that is reflected in dividing [concepts,] definitions, and rational arguments.

The second manner must operate by way of precepts, examples, admonitions, revelations, and prayer, because it is these things that are appropriate for [eliciting] the affection of piety. And it is this manner that is characteristic of sacred scripture.

Hence, Titus 1:1 refers to [scripture as] knowledge or science "*according to piety.*" Besides, the manner that operates by way of precepts is present in the law and in the gospel; the one that operates by way of examples is present in history texts; the one that operates by way of admonitions is present in the books of Solomon and in the Epistles; the one that operates by way of

---

language and therefore is not a discipline; however, theology uses such language to cater to the weakness of the human intellect.

10. See previous note; the SH actually has "very skillfully."

revelations is present in the Prophets; and the one that operates by way of prayer is present in the Psalter.

Also note that the manners of two types of sciences—one that is concerned with shaping our affection along the lines of piety, and the other that is concerned with shaping the intellect alone for the cognition of truth—are different. And the one that is concerned with shaping our affection proceeds in ways that have just been described, because precepts, examples, admonitions, revelations, and prayers incite affections of piety. For piety is "worship of God," as Augustine says in *On the Trinity* 12[14.22], introducing the alternative version[11] of Job 28:28: "*Behold, piety is wisdom.*" For it is a worship of God "through which we presently desire to see him and believe and hope to see him in the future": we desire by charity, we believe by faith, and we hope by hope, and the discipline of piety is formed according to these three virtues.

3. To the third one must say that, just as it is appropriate for human science to use clear speech, so it is appropriate for the divine wisdom to use cryptic speech. For there is wisdom in mystery, according to 1 Corinthians 2:7: "*We speak wisdom, which is hidden in a mystery.*" As for the reason for the cryptic nature [of this sort of speech], it is triple. The first is the merit of faith: for the merit consists [precisely] in believing what you do not see. On this account, Revelation 5:1 says: "*And I saw on the right hand of him who sat . . . a book written within and without, sealed with seven seals.*"

The second reason is the exercise of perseverance and patience. On this account, Daniel 12:4 says: "*Shut up the words, and seal the book, even to the established time: many will come and go, and knowledge will multiply.*"

The third reason is the dignity of truth, which must be hidden from evil men, as in Matthew 7:6: "*Give not that which is holy to the dogs, neither cast you your pearls before swine.*"

IS THE MANNER OF SACRED SCRIPTURE ONE OF CERTITUDE?

SH 1, Tr Int, Q1, C4, Ar2 (n. 5), 9–10

Namely, is the approach of sacred scripture more certain than in other sciences?

---

11. That is, the one based on the text of the *Itala*, which is based on the Septuagint.

Objections:

1. Other sciences rely on the intellect, while theology relies on faith. Since [cognition through] the intellect is more certain than faith, the approach of other sciences is more certain than that of theology.

2. The science that proceeds from the principles that are of themselves clear to the intellect is more certain than the one that proceeds from the principles that are hidden from the intellect. But while other sciences proceed from the principles that are of themselves clear to the intellect, theology is based on the principles that are hidden from the intellect, for they are the principles of faith. Therefore, other sciences have a more certain way of proceeding.

3. The science that is based on literal speech is more certain than the one that uses metaphorical speech.

4. The one that uses univocal and simple speech is more certain than the one that uses equivocation and statements with multiple senses, for such result in dubious meaning. So it seems that the approach of other sciences is more certain than in theology.

To the contrary:

The way of knowing through inspiration is more certain than the one through human rational thought. Also, what is known from the testimony of the Spirit is more certain than what is known from the evidence gathered from creatures. Also, what is known by way of taste is more certain than what is known by way of sight. Therefore, since the way of sacred scripture is the way of knowing through inspiration, from the testimony of the Spirit, and by way of taste, while in other sciences the way of knowing is through rational thinking, from the evidence gathered from creatures, and by way of sight, it is clear that the way of knowing in theology is more certain than in other sciences.

Reply:

There is a certitude of speculation and that of experience. In addition to those, there is a certitude of intellect and a certitude of affection. Also, there is a certitude as far as the spiritual [part of the] soul is concerned and a certitude as far as the animal [part of the] soul is concerned. I say, then, that the theological approach is more certain by the certitude of experience, by the certitude of affection, which is by way of taste (as in Psalms [118:103]: "*How sweet are your words to my taste!*"), but not more certain as far as intellectual speculation goes, which operates by way of seeing. Also, it is more certain to the spiritual self but less certain to the animal self, as in 1 Corinthians 2:14: "*But the animal man does not perceive the things of the Spirit of God . . . but the spiritual man discerns all.*"

Reply to the objections:

1. A reply to the first objection is clear now: faith is more certain than the intellect in other sciences by the certitude of affection, not by the certitude of speculation.

2. To the second one must say that there are principles of truth as truth, and there are principles of truth as goodness. Now, other sciences proceed from the principles of truth as truth, which are self-evident. Theology, however, proceeds from the principles of truth as goodness, which are self-evident insofar as goodness is concerned, but concealed and hidden insofar as truth is concerned. Hence, this discipline is based on virtue rather than on science, and it is wisdom rather than science, for it consists in virtue and practical efficiency rather than in contemplation and [speculative] knowledge, as in 1 Corinthians 2:4: "*And my speech is not in enticing words of human wisdom, but in the demonstration of the Spirit and of power.*"

3. To the third one must say that there is a [kind of] certitude [that is sufficient] for the animal soul, which only has knowledge from sense experience, and there is a [kind of] certitude [that is sufficient] for the spiritual soul, which has the spirit[ual capacity] to contemplate the divine. Now for the animal soul an approach through mystical pronouncements does not possess certitude, although it does for the spiritual soul, as in 1 Corinthians, 2:9–10: "*what eye has not seen, nor ear heard, what has not entered into the heart of man . . . [God] has revealed to us by his Spirit: for the spirit searches all things.*"

Besides, as has been said, it is characteristic of this science to proceed by way of mystery, and therefore by using obscure speech; therefore, because the way of obscure and mystical speech is characteristic of this science, this way will be more certain for the soul that is disposed to [receive] this science, namely, to the spiritual, not the animal soul.

4. To the final point, one must say that the standards of "certitude" in the sciences of the human and divine spirit are different. The first kind is constricted by the limits of a single human intellect, which can only understand one thing at a time. The second kind, however, knows no such restriction, for the divine Spirit, who is responsible for this science, is "*one but multiple*" (Wisdom 7:22). Hence the approach in sacred doctrine: there is one literal meaning, but there are multiple hidden meanings. And this does not

diminish certitude for the soul that is disposed to [receive] this [kind of certitude,] that is, the spiritual soul, as was said.

IS THE MANNER OF SACRED SCRIPTURE UNIFORM, OR DOES IT HAVE MANY FORMS?

SH 1, Tr Int, Q1, C4, Ar3 (n. 6), 10–11

That it has many forms:

a. Hebrews 1:1: "*God, long ago speaking to our fathers in many and various ways by the prophets,*" etc. One takes from this that the manner was not uniform in the Old Testament.

b. Ephesians 3:8, 10: "*Unto me, who am less than any of the saints, is this grace given, that I should preach among the gentiles the unsearchable riches of Christ.*" And it follows: "*in order that the wisdom of God that has many forms might be known to the principalities and powers through the church.*" One takes from this that the manner is not uniform in the New Testament.

c. As Bede says in *On the Beginning of Genesis*, the sense in the words of sacred scripture is fourfold: "Four are the senses of sacred scripture: historical, which tells of the deeds past; allegorical, where something is understood through something else; tropological, i.e., moral talk, which treats of ordering one's mores; and anagogical, which directs us to higher matters when we intend to treat the highest and heavenly subjects. For example, 'Jerusalem' in a historical sense is a city; allegorically speaking it stands for the church; tropologically, i.e., ethically, speaking, it signifies the soul of every faithful person; anagogically speaking, it signifies the heavenly life of all, who will see God *with open face* (2 Corinthians 3:18)." Therefore, one understands sacred scripture in many ways.

d. The law exhibits a commanding manner; the historical books exhibit a historical manner that works by example; the books of Solomon exhibit a manner of exhortation; the Psalms exhibit a prayerful manner; the Prophets exhibit a revelatory manner. One takes from this, then, that the Old Testament exhibits no uniform manner.

e. The gospel exhibits a historical manner insofar as it narrates Christ's life and deeds; a demanding and counseling manner as far as Christ's teaching is concerned; Paul's and the Canonical Letters exhibit an admonishing manner; the Acts exhibit a historical manner; the Revelation exhibits a revelatory manner. Therefore, there is no uniform manner in the New Testament.

f. Dionysius says in the *Celestial Hierarchy* [2.2–3]: "The holy mysteries are manifested in two manners: one of consonance, by means of similar representations, and the other of complete discordance and unfittingness, through unlike forms." [The example of the manner of proceeding] through similar representations: "when they celebrate the Lord's pronouncements as Reason, and Intellect, and Essence, proclaiming the Intellect and Wisdom of God, as well as his truly existing subsistence." [The example of the manner of proceeding] through dissimilar representations: "when It is named Invisible, Infinite and Incomprehensible, in such terms as indicate not what It is, but what It is not." One takes from this, therefore, that the manner of manifestation of sacred scripture is not uniform.

To the contrary:

1. Romans 15:4: *Whatsoever things were written, were written for our learning.* Therefore, if a uniform manner is more suitable *for our learning* than a multiform, because our intellects are confused by multiple forms, it remains that the manner of sacred scripture should be uniform.

2. Our intellect is easier instructed by fewer things than by more numerous things, because "the fewer the better"; therefore, the manner must be uniform.

3. The manner that is uniform is more clear and easier than the one that has many forms; but the manner of scripture must be more clear and manifest, for it is said in Habakkuk 2:2: *Write the vision, and make it plain . . . that he may run who reads it.* It remains, therefore, that the manner must be uniform.

Reply:

One must reply that the manner of sacred scripture must have many forms. There are three reasons for that. First, by reason of the efficient [cause], that is, the Holy Spirit, who is, as Wisdom 7:22 says, "*a spirit that is intelligent, holy, unique, manifold*." For this reason, in order to accommodate its efficient [cause], sacred knowledge must be manifold or have many forms. Second, by reason of the material [cause], which is the "*wisdom of God that has many forms*." For this reason, its manner must have many forms in order to fit its material [cause]. Third, by reason of the final [cause], which is instruction in the matters that pertain to our salvation. Now, one's status can have many different forms: at the time of the law; after the time of the law; at the time of prophecy; at the time of grace. Moreover, one's status even within one of these statuses can have many forms: indeed, some are weak in matters pertaining to faith; some are recalcitrant—in various ways!—in matters that pertain to good behavior; some are fortunate in their lives, and some are misfortunate; some are good, and some are sinners. It remains that instruction provided by sacred scripture, whose aim is our salvation, must come in many forms, so that its manner may correspond to its end.

Reply to the objections:

1. To the objection that a manner that has many forms confuses the intellect one must reply that this is not true. In fact, such a manner [more efficiently] instructs the intellect. Indeed, one's intellect can be dull, acute, or mediocre. Respectively, the demonstration of truth to a dull, acute, or mediocre intellect must proceed differently and by using different methods, in order that a dull intellect might grasp something in some form if it is not grasping it in another. In addition to that, simple babes should be instructed differently than perfect adults, just as the Apostle says in 1 Corinthians 3:1–2: "*As unto babes in Christ, I have fed you with milk, and not with meat: for hitherto you were not able* [to digest it], *neither yet now you are able.*" For this reason a manner that has many forms is necessary.

2. One must deny the second objection by using the same argument. Indeed, "our intellect is easier instructed by fewer things"—but only when one speaks of one singular person with a certain status. However, if one considers the differences in intellectual capacity of different persons, as well as their different statuses, this thesis is not true.

3. One can reply in a similar fashion to the third objection, that "the manner that is uniform is more clear and easier than the one that has many forms." One must reply that this thesis is not true when one speaks of a manner that has many forms that is applied to clarify one thing, but according to different forms.

ON THE MULTITUDE OF FORMS THAT THE MANNER OF SACRED SCRIPTURE EXHIBITS

SH 1, Tr Int, Q1, C4, Ar4 (n. 7), 11–13

I. First, it is asked about the multitude of senses of sacred scripture.

a. And it seems, based on the aforesaid authoritative statement by Bede, that the multitude of senses of sacred scripture consists of four senses: historical, allegorical, tropological, and anagogical.

However, there are objections against this:

1. Indeed, Hugh of St. Victor proposes merely three senses: historical, allegorical, and tropological. Hence, he says in Bk. III of his *Sentences* [i.e., *On the Sacraments* I, Prol. 4]: "History is the narration of what happened, which is the primary sense of the text; allegory is when by way of the narration of an event some other event is signified, either in the past or in the future; tropology is when by way of the narration of an event what ought to be done is signified." This account leaves Bede's fourth sense, anagogical, superfluous.

2. Sacred scripture contains proverbs and parables designed for literal interpretation; and it is clear that the parabolic manner is not the same as historical, allegorical, tropological, or anagogical; therefore, there are more senses than those four, and the aforesaid list is insufficient.

3. Augustine, in the book *On the Usefulness of Believing* [3.5], says: "All scriptural texts under the name of 'Old Testament' are traditionally interpreted in four ways: historically, when what is written is what is taught; etiologically, when why it is written is what is taught; analogically, when the correspondence between the two Testaments is taught; or allegorically, when it is taught that it is not to be taken literally but to be understood spiritually." One takes from these statements that there is one mystical sense and three literal senses, while Bede's aforesaid list has one literal and three mystical senses.

Reply:

One must reply that, since the first truth is one and triple, the manner of knowing the first truth is also triple in one: one literal manner and three spiritual: anagogical, which leads one upwards to the first principle; allegorical, which announces the hidden things of the first truth; and tropological or moral, which orders one in accordance with the highest goodness. Therefore, the anagogical sense refers to the Father, the allegorical to the Son, and the moral to the Holy Spirit.

For the number of senses can be accounted for in the following way: either the sense is literal and external, or spiritual and internal. There is only one sense of the first kind. The second kind has several variations. Thus, it refers either to morals or to faith. And if it refers to faith, it is faith in the divine or at the human level. The first variation is moral [sense]; the second, anagogical; the third, allegorical.

Another way of accounting for [their number] is by saying that the sense of sacred scripture either concerns the cause or the effect. If it concerns the eternal cause—God—then the sense is anagogical. If it concerns the effect, there can be two scenarios: the effect that has been achieved or the effect that is to be achieved. If it concerns the effect to be achieved, then the sense is moral or tropological. If it concerns the effect that has been achieved, then there are two scenarios. The first is when [sacred scripture] is understood "in the primary sense of the text," that is, taking into consideration what the words mean, and this is the literal or historical sense, for "history is narration of what happened, which is the primary sense of the text," according to Hugh. The second is when one takes into consideration what the events mean, and this is the allegorical sense, according to what Hugh says: "allegory is when by way of a narration of an event some other event—past, present, or future—is signified."

Reply to the objections:

1. Note, then, that Hugh of St. Victor, who stated that the subject matter of divine scriptures is the works of restoration, posited only three senses of sacred scripture, which are founded in the work, namely, historical, allegorical, and tropological. Bede, however, who thought that the subject matter of divine scriptures is not only the work of restoration, but also the [first] cause, added the anagogical sense, which refers to the cause, just as the other three refer to the effect.

2. As for the objection about the parabolic sense, one must reply that it is reduced to the historical. However, the historical sense has two meanings: either it deals with things or with likenesses of things. An account of what happened deals with things; parables deal with likenesses of things. For a parable is a likeness of things, when one arrives at what it means by way of a likeness that is different from the thing itself. For this reason, Augustine [in *Against Lying* 10.24] says about gospel parables that one must take them not as if they really happened, but as if they could happen.

3. To the third objection one must reply that Augustine in the book *On the Usefulness of Believing* distinguishes between different senses not based on the understanding [itself] or on that which is understood, but on the manner of understanding. For this reason the first three senses are understood as literal, for those three senses coincide with the literal sense as far as the manner of speaking is concerned. However, the fourth sense contains all the three spiritual senses, so there is no conflict.

II. Next, it is asked about the literal sense: is it founded upon truth?

1. For sometimes it seems that it is founded on lies: Judges 9:8, "*The trees went forth to anoint a king over them*"; but this does not seem to belong to the knowledge of truth: Job 13:7, "*God does not need our lies.*"

Reply:

I reply that there are two types of truth in speech: either that which is told can be true, or that for the sake of which it is told can be true. Therefore, one must say that parables of this sort are true as far as that for the sake of which they are told is true, for their aim is to designate some event or thing in a truthful manner. In this way, one pays attention not to what their primary meaning is, but what their secondary meaning is. For this reason one must note that historical accounts are true in terms of what the words mean, and parabolic statements are true in terms of the things that are signified [secondarily through primary meanings].

III. Also, one wonders about the spiritual or mystical [sense], which mostly uses likenesses of bodily and transitory things.

1. Indeed, since similar likenesses[12] are more suitable for the demonstration of divine things than dissimilar likenesses, the mystical sense would have to operate with the most similar likenesses; therefore, since likenesses of spiritual things are more similar to the divine than likenesses of bodily things, the mystical sense must only use spiritual likenesses.

2. It is unfitting to use ugly images of the highest beauty; however, ugly images are those drawn from crude material things, as well as disorderly things such as anger, fury, and lust; therefore, such images should be excluded while explaining something about God; therefore, the mystical senses of scripture proceed in an unfitting manner when they call God fire, a cornerstone, a wild beast, a lion, a worm, and such, as well as [present him as] furious, angry, and lustful.

To the contrary:

a. Dionysius [in *Celestial Hierarchies* 2.3–4]: "Negations are true of the divine, while affirmations are loose," because these affirmations "do not show what God is, but rather what he is not." Therefore, if dissimilar images are more suitable for negation than for affirmation, a demonstration by means of dissimilar images is more suitable for a demonstration of the divine than one by means of similar images.

b. More sumptuous forms seduce the intellect of the simple-minded, who believe that the divine or heavenly essences are things of the same sort as these sumptuous images; at the same time, dissimilar forms reduce the intellect; therefore, dissimilar forms are more suitable for the mystical sense than similar forms. For this reason Dionysius writes [ibid.]: "The nobler images

---

12. The language of pseudo-Dionysius in the *Celestial Hierarchy*.

tend to seduce us into supposing that the heavenly essences are some kind of golden forms, or men shining like lightning ... or such other similar forms as are assigned by theology to the celestial intelligences. But lest this befall those whose mind has conceived nothing higher than visible beauties, the wisdom of the holy theologians ... descends to the level of the ugly, not allowing our material," that is, intellect, "to remain attached to those unseemly images."

c. Dionysius says [ibid.]: "No single existing thing is entirely deprived of participation in the beautiful, for, as the true Word says in Genesis 1:31, '*all things are very beautiful*.' Holy contemplations can therefore be drawn[13] from all things and form dissimilar likenesses with invisible and immaterial things based on material things."

Solution:

This must be conceded. The reply must be in line with what Dionysius says, because the manifestation of the divine happens in two ways: (1) through similar things, as when the divine is venerated based on the attributes of spiritual creatures, which are like the divine, such as reason, intellect, and wisdom; (2) through dissimilar things, as when it is venerated based on attributes of bodily things. And this [according to Dionysius] happens in three ways [ibid., 2.5]: "For sometimes [deity] is celebrated by means of lofty [images], as when it is called the Sun of justice, or the Morning Star ... sometimes by means of intermediate [images], as when we call him fire flashing forth ... sometimes by means of the lowest images, as when we call him a cornerstone, or a wild beast ... or even a worm."

And according to Dionysius, there are many reasons why these are [more] suitable. The first is that they rather negate than affirm, and therefore they are more true, because "negations are truer when speaking of the divine." The second is that "our intellect is rather reduced" by them. For this reason, when our intellect, desiring to know God, perceives these forms, it is never satisfied by them, as it never believes God to be of this sort, as it would through the sort of speech [about God] that would use the likenesses of spiritual things. The third reason is that "holy contemplations can be drawn from all things and form suitable likenesses of heavenly [things] out of base parts of matter," because, drawing their existence out of true goodness, the latter contain images of intelligible beauty. The fourth reason is to conceal

---

13. Reading *elicere* for *intelligere*.

the divine from the unworthy and evil ones. For this reason Dionysius writes: "In this way all the prophets prefer unlike symbols for holy things, so that divine things may not be accessible to the unworthy." The fifth reason is that the intellect is guided by these [images]. For this reason Dionysius says: "The forms of deformed things are beautifully procured [for us] in order to assure our ascent to contemplations of invisible things which we cannot immediately achieve."

Reply to the objections:

1–2. The reply to the objections is clear from what has been said.

This is the way to end this question, which is, as it were, an overture to the following investigation. It is clear from what has been said that the teaching of theology is about the substance of God that effects the work of restoration of humans through Christ. For this reason, theological investigation starts with the excellence of divine sublimity and continues by treating Christ and those things that pertain to the work of restoration.

CHAPTER 2

THE KNOWLEDGE OF GOD IN THIS LIFE

IS THE HUMAN SOUL CAPABLE OF KNOWING GOD?

SH 1, Tr Int, Q2, M1, C1 (n. 8), 15–16
Arguments in favor:

1. Augustine in the book *On Seeing God* [Letter 147.8.20] says: "God by his nature is invisible: not only the Father but the entire triune God"; but for God to be visible is the same as to be knowable. For, as the same book says [ibid., 2.7], "The difference between seeing and believing is that the things that are present are seen and the things that are absent are believed. By 'things that are present right here' we understand those things that are instantly accessible to our senses, either corporeal or mental. For example, I see this light by my corporeal sense, and [I see] my will, because it is instantly accessible to my mental sensory awareness, for it is present inside of me." However, every object of knowledge is visible to our mental or corporeal sensory awareness; therefore, if God is invisible, he is thereby also not knowable.

2. Augustine says in the same book [ibid., 15.37]: "'*No one has ever seen nor could see God, for he dwells in inaccessible light*' [1 Timothy 6:16], and by nature God is invisible as he is incorruptible. And just as he will remain incorruptible in the future, not just now, in the same way he will always remain invisible, and not just now."

3. John Damascene says [in *On the Orthodox Faith* 1.4]: "God is infinite and incomprehensible"; however, all that is known by the mind is comprehended by the intellect; therefore, God is not knowable.

4. All knowledge of the infinite, insofar as it is infinite, is infinite—because if it were finite, it could not extend over something that is infinite. Therefore, since God's substance is infinite, it could only be known by infinite knowledge; but no finite power can generate infinite knowledge, because no finite power produces an infinite act; therefore, since every power of the rational soul is finite, the soul cannot generate an action that is the knowledge of God's infinite substance.

5. A less advanced capacity of the human being by its nature is not capable of knowing the most advanced capacity of the human being: for example,

our imagination or sensory power cannot know our mind or rational faculty. Therefore, [even] the most advanced capacity of the human being is incapable of knowing something that is incomparably better and superior to this capacity; therefore, God [could not be known even] by our mind, which is our most advanced capacity.

Arguments to the contrary:

a. Augustine says in Book I of the *Soliloquies* [8.15]: "Both God and the demonstrations of the sciences are intelligible, but in very different ways. For both light and the earth are visible—however, the earth cannot be seen unless it is illuminated by light. In a similar way, the demonstrations of the sciences cannot be seen unless they are illuminated, as it were, by a sun of their own," namely, by God.

b. The Gloss on Romans 1:19, "*That which may be known of God is manifest in them*," says: "That is, that which can be known my means of reason, as if it said: they have in themselves the capacity to know that which can be known about God." And the same text [Romans 1:20] says: "*From the creation of the world, the invisible things of God are clearly seen through the things that are made, even his eternal power and divine nature.*" And Wisdom 13:5 says: "*From the greatness and beauty of created things their Creator could be seen and known.*"

c. Just as the purpose of affective rationality is to love the good, in the same way the purpose of cognitive rationality is to know the truth. Therefore, if the highest good is the object of desire for affective rationality, then the highest truth is knowable by cognitive rationality.

Reply:

Augustine says in *To Pauline on Seeing God* [Letter 147.15.37]: "If you ask whether God can be seen, I reply: he can. If you ask how I know this, I reply: because we read this in scripture [Matthew 5:8], which is most true: '*Blessed are the pure in heart, for they shall see God.*'"

Replies to objections:

1. Therefore, to the first objection one must reply in keeping with the words of Augustine: "If you ask how God can be called 'invisible' if he can be seen, I reply: he is invisible by nature; however, he can be seen when he wills it and in the manner in which he wills." Based on this, the distinction is clear: God is invisible by nature, but visible by his will. On this basis, one must distinguish between something that is visible by necessity and something that is visible according to the will. Things that are necessarily visible include

bodies and beings that are perceptible by the senses. Things that are visible voluntarily include spiritual beings, such as angels and God himself. And this is what Augustine says in the same book [6.18], summing up Ambrose's authoritative statement [in his Commentary on Luke's Gospel 1.24] where he comments on Luke 1:11, "*And an angel appeared*," etc.: "Things perceptible by the senses are not visible in the same way as he who is not visible by nature but by will, for if he does not wish it, he is not seen, and if he wishes it, he is seen. For God appeared to Abraham when he willed, but he did not appear to others because he did not will to do so."

2. To the second objection, that "by nature [God] is invisible as he is incorruptible," one must reply by following Augustine in *On Seeing God* [Letter 147.20.48]: "Bodies are generally called 'visible things'; for this reason God is called 'invisible' lest one believe he is a body—not because he has deprived pure hearts of a vision of his substance, for this highest reward is promised to those who love God when the Lord himself says in John 14:21: '*He who loves me shall be loved by my Father, and I will love him, and will manifest myself to him.*'"

3. To the third objection, one must reply in a similar manner by following Augustine's distinction in *On Seeing God* [ibid., 9.2]: "'To see' something is not the same as 'to grasp something visually in its entirety.' For 'to be seen' amounts to being present and perceived in any way whatever by the senses. However, 'to be grasped visually in its entirety' means to be seen in such a way that nothing of this thing is hidden from the observer, or that its boundaries are within one's range of observation. For example, nothing of the present [activity of your] will is hidden from you, and the boundaries of your finger ring are within your range of observation. I gave two examples: one pertains to our mental gaze, and the other to our corporeal eyes." Augustine's words make it clear that it is not logical to state that "God cannot be [wholly] understood; therefore, he cannot be known."

4. To the fourth objection, one must reply with Boethius in *Consolation of Philosophy* [V, pr. 4], that "those things that are known, are known not according to their nature, but to the extent of the capacity of the one who knows." Therefore, knowledge is not called finite or infinite based on whether the object of knowledge is finite or infinite, but based on whether the [cognitive] faculty of the one who knows is finite or infinite. Indeed, "that which is known, is known in the mode of the one who knows, not in

the mode of the object of knowledge."[1] This is clear as regards every manner of knowing, whether it be sensory, imaginative, or intellective cognition. Therefore, it does not follow that if the divine substance is infinite, then the knowledge of it that the human intellect has is [also] infinite. Quite the opposite: because the human intellect is finite, it will also know the divine substance in a finite way.

5. To the fifth objection, one must reply that materiality prohibits the senses, which are capacities of a lower rank, from knowing superior capacities, such as the intellect. Indeed, no faculty whose being and operation depend on matter can grasp the form or thing that is abstracted from matter.[2] For this reason, because the sensory faculty depends on matter in its being and operation, it cannot know the mind, or the intellect, which is a thing and form that is abstracted from matter.[3] On the other hand, the very immateriality and simplicity of spiritual powers ensures that the mind or the intellect can know[4] something that is better and superior to itself, namely, the divine substance, which is [equally] simple and immaterial. And in this respect [the mind] is God's image, according to Augustine, *On the Trinity* [14.8.11]: [the mind is] "the image of God insofar as it can grasp God and participate in him: it can grasp him by means of cognition and participate in him through love." This makes it clear that the objection is incoherent.

CAN THE DIVINE SUBSTANCE BE KNOWN IN ITS IMMENSITY?

SH 1, Tr Int, Q2, M1, C2 (n. 9), 17–18
Arguments in favor:
1. Romans 1:20: "*The invisible things of God,*" etc. The Gloss [on this passage says:] "He created stars of such beauty that it is possible to know, by looking at them, how great and how awesome their Creator is." Therefore, one can have the knowledge of "how great God is"; however, he possesses

---

1. A common statement found in Averroes, Avicenna, *Book of Causes*, and *Book of Intelligences*, among others.
2. That is, immaterial forms or things.
3. That is, an immaterial thing.
4. Reading *cognoscitiva* for *cognoscibilis*, which must be a scribal or transcription error.

greatness by virtue of his infinite and immense power: indeed, for God, to possess greatness is the same as to possess magnitude; but as Augustine says [in *On the Trinity* 6.7.8], [God] "possesses magnitude not in terms of bulk, but in terms of power"; therefore, God can be known in his immensity or infinity [because his power is such].

2. Ephesians 3:19 says: "*that you might be filled with all the fullness of God*"; but "*all the fullness of God*" is his immensity; as for this "filling," it happens through knowledge and love; therefore, God's immensity will be able to be known.

3. John 15:15 says: "*For all the things that I have heard from my Father, I have made known to you*"; however, "all" in this statement stands for power, truth, goodness, eternity, and even immensity, for all these things are known to the Son; therefore, he made known to the apostles God's very eternity and immensity.

4. All things that exist in God, such as eternity, truth, and immensity, are one; therefore, if his truth can be known, so can his immensity.

To the contrary:

a. Ambrose at the beginning of his *Commentary on Luke* 1 [.25] says: "'*No one has ever seen God*' [John 1:18], because no one has seen or grasped, either by their mind or by their eyes, that fullness of divinity that abides in God."

b. Boethius [in *Consolation of Philosophy* V, pr. 4] says: "All that is known or cognized is cognized not according to its nature but according to the capacity of the knower." Therefore, since the ability of the [human] soul that receives knowledge is finite, and the divine substance due to its immensity is infinite, [the divine substance] will not be able to be known in its immensity by a rational soul.

Solution:

One must reply that knowledge about God can be either positive or privative. When we acquire privative knowledge, we learn about what God is not; when we gain positive knowledge, we learn what God is. Now the divine substance cannot be known by a rational soul by way of positive knowledge, but it can be known by way of privative knowledge.

Replies to objections:

1. To the first objection, that "it is possible to know the greatness of the Creator by looking at creatures," one must reply that it is possible to know how great God is by way of privation, but not in a positive way. For example, we learn by way of privation how great he is in duration by calling him

"eternal," that is, without beginning and end. Similarly, we learn how great he is in terms of fullness by calling him "uncircumscribed," that is, by denying [that God has] place and location. Similarly, [we learn] how great he is in terms of power by calling him "immense," that is, by denying that his power can be measured. However, it is not possible to determine how great his magnitude, power, or duration are by using a positive way of knowing.

2. Augustine [Letter 147.23.53] replies to the second objection by saying that the statement from Ephesians 3:19, *"that you might be filled with all the fullness of God,"* is not to be taken in the sense that we will have the fullness that he has: "For they will be filled with all of God's fullness not in the sense that they will have become fully divine themselves, but in the sense that they will have become completely filled with God."

3. To the third objection, one must reply that the phrase *"I have made all things known to you"* [John 15:15] must be understood in the sense that "I preordained to make all things known to you," where "all things" stands for creatures, and not universally for all the conditions of God's immense and infinite capacity for being. Nevertheless, even if we did say that it stands for divine immensity, eternity, and such things, then one must make a distinction: the statement that has the form "the divine essence, in its immensity (namely, being immense, such as it is), can be known" is true. Or [one can put it this way:] "it can be known according to its immensity," and in this form, it is false, because [in this second case] the characteristic of "immensity" defines the cognition that the knower[5] can have (for if it defined the cognition that could be had about this object of knowledge, it would be true, in the same sense as before).

4. To the last objection, one must reply that the following way of arguing is not logical when one speaks of the divine: "in the divine, wisdom, goodness, and immensity are one and the same thing; therefore, what is predicated of one of them is also predicated of another." Indeed, even though these names refer to one and the same thing as far as their principal signified is concerned, nevertheless, they differ by reason of their connotation and mode of signification. For example, although knowledge and will are one and the same thing in God, nevertheless, the argument "he knows bad things; therefore, he wills bad things" is illogical. So is the last objection.

---

5. That is, the human knower.

IS THE TRINITY OF PERSONS KNOWN BY NATURAL REASON?

SH 1, Tr Int, Q2, M1, C3 (n. 10), 18–19

And it seems that it is:

a. Romans 1:20: "*The invisible things of God, even his eternal power and divine nature . . . are seen, being understood through the things that are made.*" The Gloss on this text says that these three things—*the invisible things*, *eternal power*, and *divine nature*—stand for the Trinity of persons; therefore, the philosophers were able to know the Trinity of persons by the natural light of reason.

b. The Philosopher at the beginning of the book *On the Heavens* [1.1–2] shows that the number three belongs to all things, including physical entities, mathematics, and the divine. In physical things, for instance, there is motion away from the center, motion toward the center, and motion around the center; in mathematics, there is a line, surface, and [three-dimensional] body; it is similar as regards the divine. Therefore, he says: "we ourselves attribute to this number, based on the properties of created things, [the capacity] to glorify one God, the eminent creator." Therefore, the Philosopher himself also had a knowledge of the Trinity by the natural light of reason.

c. [Hermes] Trismegistus says: "The monad generated the monad and turns its yearning back upon itself." Therefore, Trismegistus had a notion of the Trinity, because the generating monad is the Father, the generated monad is the Son, and the yearning is the Holy Spirit.

d. Augustine in *On the Trinity*[6] says: the philosophers said that "wisdom is tripartite," which signifies the Trinity. "For with whom else would [the three parts of philosophy] be associated except with the originator of all creatures, the giver of intelligence, and the one who inspires love?" Here Augustine wants to say that natural philosophy is about those things that pertain to [physical] nature; rational philosophy is about those things that pertain to reason and intelligence; and moral philosophy is about those things that pertain to love. Therefore, natural philosophy is associated with the originator, the Father; rational philosophy is associated with wisdom, the Son; and moral philosophy is associated with love or goodness, the Holy Spirit.

---

6. Or, rather, *City of God* 11.25.

To the contrary:

1. Romans 1:20: "*The invisible things of God*," etc. The Gloss says: "Augustine says that the knowledge of the philosophers did not extend to the third person, namely, the Holy Spirit, based on Exodus 8:18 where the Pharaoh's magicians fell short at the third sign. Indeed, the best pagan philosophers have philosophized about τὸ ἀγαθόν, that is, the highest Father, and about the νοῦς, that is, his intellect. However, the magicians fell short at the third sign because the philosophers were not able to reach as far as the third person." I reply, according to the Gloss, that "they did not have the knowledge of the Trinity itself as far as the personal properties [of persons] are concerned, and the only way they could have it would be either through instruction or through inspiration. However, they did have and could have the knowledge of the Trinity as far as what is appropriated to the persons is concerned, namely, power, wisdom, and goodness." However, there is an objection: to the extent that they knew what was appropriated to the Father and the Son, they also knew what was appropriated to the Holy Spirit. But to the extent that they did not know the Holy Spirit's personal properties, they also did not know the personal properties of the Father and the Son. Therefore, to the extent that they had no knowledge of the person of the Holy Spirit, they also had no knowledge of the persons of the Father and the Son, and to the extent that they did know the persons of the Father and the Son, they also knew the person of the Holy Spirit.

2. Did Trismegistus not know the persons through their personal properties when he said: "The monad generated the monad and a yearning that proceeds [from it]"?

3. Richard of St. Victor [*On the Trinity* 1.4] says: "I believe without a doubt that there is no shortage not only of probable but also of compelling arguments in order to explain the things whose existence is necessary"; but nothing exists with such necessity as the Trinity of the persons; therefore, there could be compelling arguments and natural reasons that elucidate it; therefore, the Trinity can be known through the natural light of reason.

Reply:

By means of the natural light of reason alone one cannot have a knowledge of the Trinity as far as the personal properties [of the persons] are concerned. However, one can have [such a knowledge] by means of the natural light of reason that is aided by some grace, either the one that is given as God pleases or the one that makes one pleasing [to God]. And the reason for this is that our intellect, which is clouded by the original corruption, falls short of [the understanding of] those things that exist in the truest sense—and therefore falls short of [the understanding of] the things that are at the highest threshold of intelligibility—and also [falls short] of [the understanding of] those things that exist in the most tenuous sense (and therefore are at the lowest threshold of intelligibility, such as [the successive process of physical] motion and [the passing of] time)—just as our sensory capacity falls short of [perceiving] the extremes, that is, the things that exceed [our sensory capacity] or fall below its threshold. The consequence is as follows: because the divine persons in the unity of the divine essence exist in the highest and truest sense, our clouded intellect falls short [of understanding them]. Nor is this something remarkable, because, as Aristotle says in the *First Philosophy* [i.e., *Metaphysics* 2.1], "in respect to the natural things that are most manifest, our intellect behaves in the same way as the eye of the owl in respect to the sun."

Replies to the objections:

1. The reply to the first objection is that [the philosophers] are said to have fallen short on multiple accounts as far as the knowledge of the third person is concerned because they have fallen short as far as the knowledge of goodness is concerned. First, because they were not aware of the most powerful effect of goodness, namely, the Incarnation and redemption. Second, because although they were aware of goodness, they did not worship it as highest and first nevertheless, because they attributed to it their own [ideas of what is] good. Third, because although they were aware of what is appropriated to the two persons, namely, power and wisdom, they were not aware of what is appropriated to the third person, namely, goodness.

2. To the second objection, one must reply that even though Trismegistus did have in mind the personal properties [of the persons] when he said, "The monad generated the monad," etc., he did not have that knowledge through the natural light of reason, but either through instruction or through inspiration.

3. To the third objection, one must reply that there is no lack of an argument that proves [the existence of] the Trinity: that is, a middle term exists, on the basis of which one can necessarily infer the existence of the Trinity; on our part, however, there is a lack of ability to draw this conclusion. Therefore, there is no lack on the part of the thing itself, but there is such a lack on the part of our intellect that draws conclusions, which is not able to find

the middle term and, once found, apply it to conclude to the truth. For this reason, Richard says in the same place [*On the Trinity* 1.4]: "There is no shortage of arguments about those things whose existence is necessary, even though they happen to elude our efforts."

CAN GOD OR THE DIVINE SUBSTANCE BE KNOWN FACE TO FACE IN THIS LIFE?

SH 1, Tr Int, Q2, M1, C4 (n. 11), 20–21
It is proved that it can:

1. Genesis 32:30: "*I saw the Lord face to face,*" etc. Augustine, in *On the Trinity* [2.17.28]: "The 'face' is that form, assuming which the Son '*thought it not robbery to be equal*' [Philippians 2:6] with the Father"; therefore, Jacob personally saw God's very form and face.

2. Numbers 12:8: "*With him,*" that is, Moses, "*I speak face to face,*" and "*he sees God openly, that is, not in an obscure manner (per aenigmata)*"; therefore, also Moses personally saw God's form and shape without any [intervening] image, that is [he saw him face] to face.

3. Isaiah 6:1–3: "*I saw the Lord sitting upon a throne, high and lifted up, and the whole earth was full,*" etc. Therefore, Isaiah saw God in his majesty; therefore, [he saw God's] form and shape.

4. 2 Corinthians 3:18: "*But we, with open face beholding the glory of the Lord, are changed into the same image with increasing clarity*"; therefore, we see God's glory without any obstruction; therefore, without any [intervening] image, or clearly.

5. Exodus 33:11: "*And the Lord spoke to Moses face to face, as a man speaks to his friend.*"

To the contrary:

a. 1 Corinthians 13:12: "*For now we see through a glass, darkly (in aenigmate), but then face to face.*" The Gloss on this passage says that "glass and darkness (*aenigma*) stand for the images or likenesses (*similitudines*) that help us understand God" at present; therefore, at present he cannot be seen in his [true] form or [face] to face.

b. Exodus 33:20: "*You will not be able to see my face, for no man shall see me and live*"; and it follows [Exodus 33:23]: "*You will see my back parts, but you will not be able to see my face.*" It remains, then, that he will not be able to be seen in his form or [face] to face.

Also, it is asked how seeing the *back parts* of God is different from seeing his face.

Reply:

[The expression] "God's face" is used in many senses. One sense is when "God's face" stands for his presence through grace; this sense is used in Psalms [113:7]: "*The earth shook at the face* [i.e., presence] *of the Lord,*" etc. Another sense is when "face" stands for his bodily presence, as in Psalms [79:4]: "*Show us your face,*" etc., or in the case of Moses in Exodus 33:14: "*My face* [i.e., presence] *will go before you.*" The third sense is when "face" stands for his presence through glory in his own form, as in Job 33:26: "*You will see his face with joy,*" and in 1 Corinthians 13:12: "*But then face to face.*"

Using the same type of reasoning, the expression "back parts" of God, or knowledge by means of back parts, has three meanings: one sense is natural reasons; the other sense is figurative speech; the third sense is creatures.

If one understands "face" as God's presence through grace, in this sense knowledge by means of "face" will be knowledge through the presence or contemplation of grace. It is in this sense that one must take Genesis 32:30: "*I saw the Lord face to face.*" And [some] knowledge by means of the natural light of reason, as it were, rides on the "back" of this knowledge: although this [natural] knowledge does not receive God's presence [face to face] in an affective way, as it happens in knowledge through grace, nevertheless, it does accept intellectually some truth about God, as it were, "from the back."

Also, if one takes "face" as God's bodily presence, in this sense the "back parts" of the Lord refer to the figurative passages in the Law that foreshadow the Incarnation. Therefore, those who lived under the Old Law also were able to see, as it were, "from the back" through some images of things to come. We, however, see him, as it were, face to face, because we believe in him and accept him as having become present in the flesh, which is the way the Apostle's statement from 2 Corinthians 3:18 interprets "face": "*But we, with open face,*" etc., where the Apostle adds this after having spoken about the veil of figurative speech.

Also, if one takes "face," in the third sense, as the presence of glory, in this sense the "back parts" of God can be understood as creatures. For there is a knowledge of God in his [proper] form, and there is a knowledge of God through his effects. However, to know God through his effects amounts to knowing him "from the back," while to know him as he is in himself is to know him face to face. And it is in this sense that it is said to Moses [in Exodus

33:23]: "*You will see my back parts, but you will not be able to see my face*," because at present we know God through his effects, which is the sense that Romans 1:20 uses [when it speaks of] "*the invisible things of God,*" etc. However, in the future we will know him as he is in himself.

Also, note that according to Augustine [in *On the Trinity* 2.17.28], [the expression] "face" of God refers to his divine form, and, following this logic, God's "back parts" can refer to his human form. And in this sense one can interpret the statement to Moses, "*you will see my back parts,*" in the sense that you will see [me] in the flesh, "*but you will not be able to see my face.*"[7]

Note that the expression "face" of God also can refer to intellectual vision, whether it may happen by means of some [material] thing or by means of an intelligible species, namely, abstracted from matter. And in this sense [God's] "back parts" refer to corporeal vision or to imaginary vision. And this is the sense in which [Exodus 33:11], "*And the Lord spoke to Moses face to face,*" should be taken, because God appeared to him under the guise of an intelligible species. Also the phrase from Numbers 12:8, "*he sees God openly, and not in an obscure manner*" (*per aenigmata aut figuras*), [should be understood in this sense], so that *aenigma* might stand for imaginary vision, and *figura* for corporeal vision. For God did appear to corporeal vision in some external shape, as for example he appeared to Moses in Exodus [3:2] in a bush, and he also appeared to imaginary vision, as for example in Jacob's dreams in Genesis 28:12. And the statement in Numbers 12:6 should be understood as referring to these two types of vision: "*If there be a prophet among you, I will appear to him in a vision*" (namely, in a corporeal vision) or "*in a dream,*" namely, in an imaginary vision. God also appears under the guise of an intelligible species to intellectual vision, as [he appeared] to Moses in Numbers 12. . . .

CAN GOD'S PRESENCE (*PRAESENTIALITAS*) BE NATURALLY DETECTED INSOFAR AS HE IS PRESENT TO CREATURES?

SH 1, Tr Int, Q2, M1, C6 (n. 13), 22–23

In other words, can one naturally know that God is present to all [created] things?

---

7. That is, his true divine form.

And it seems that one can:

a. Romans 1:20: "*The invisible things of God*," etc. The Gloss [on this passage reads]: "The fact that [the universe] is governed shows us that he is present to every thing."

To the contrary:

1. Knowledge through grace is greater than natural knowledge; however, [even] knowledge through grace does not necessarily show us that he is present [to everyone] through grace; therefore, natural knowledge is much less capable of making us certain of his essential presence to things, for the threshold of certainty there[8] is even higher.

2. Ambrose [says in his *Commentary on Luke* 1.27]: "When he is considered absent, he is seen, and when he is present, he is not seen."

Reply:

One must reply that God can be naturally known to be essentially present to things; however, he cannot be known to be present [to someone] through grace. This is because in natural cognition the middle term is the created effect, which can be understood. At the same time, "grace" refers to acceptance [of someone] in God [himself], and for this reason it is not in our power to grasp the presence of grace [in someone], and therefore nor [can we grasp] that God is present [in someone] through grace.

Replies to the objections:

To Ambrose's authoritative statement one can reply as follows, following the interpretation of many commentators: the phrase "when he is considered absent" means "when one does not believe, in his humility, that God is present [to him]"; God "is seen" because then he is present through grace; also, "when he is present" (through grace), "he is not seen," because [then] one does not think, in his humility, that God is present [to him]. However, one must note, following Augustine's position in his book *On Seeing God* [Letter 147.12.29], that Ambrose's intention was to comment on the passage from John 14:9: "*I have been so long with you*," etc., "*Philip, he who has seen me*," etc. According to this interpretation, then, what Ambrose is saying is that,

---

8. The translation of *illa* is left deliberately ambiguous. Because Medieval Latin is inconsistent in its use of indicative pronouns *hic* and *ille* to indicate "the former" or "the latter," one cannot rely on grammar here. As for the sense, either interpretation would result in faulty logic: "cognition through grace" certainly cannot be more certain for humans than natural knowledge, but if natural knowledge is more certain, then how can cognition through grace be "greater"?

although God is present everywhere through his immensity, nevertheless, he is considered to be absent due to his incomprehensibility. And in this light his authoritative statement is explained as follows: "when he is considered absent," that is, incomprehensible, then "he is seen," that is, known; also, "when he is present, he is not seen," because his presence is not believed to be incomprehensible. This is why Christ was present to Philip and the other apostles, but they failed to see him, because they did not think[9] of him as absent, that is, incomprehensible. For this reason Augustine in his book *On Seeing God*, commenting on Ambrose's statement, says: "'When he is considered absent, he is seen'; he does not say 'when he is absent' but 'when he is considered absent': for he who *'fills heaven and earth'* is never absent, nor is there a space too tight for him to fit in, nor so large that it would thin him out, for he is everywhere in his entirety, and he is contained by no place. And he who understands these things, stretching his mind to its capacity, sees God even when he is considered to be absent." ...

IS GOD KNOWN BY REASON OR BY INTELLIGENCE?

SH 1, Tr Int, Q2, M2, C4 (n. 17), 27–28

Now, since knowledge about God comes not through the senses but through the intellect, and if one considers the intellect, according to Augustine,[10] one finds more than one grasping faculty, including reason and intelligence, the next question is: Is God known by reason or by intelligence alone?

Arguments in favor:

a. Psalms [4:7 says]: "*The light of your countenance is imprinted on us.*" The Gloss [comments]: "The 'light of your countenance' is reason, which serves the purpose of knowing God."

b. We know God by that faculty in our soul which is higher; however, [Augustine] says in *On Free Choice of the Will* [2.6.13] that "nothing is higher than reason"; therefore, God is known by reason.

To the contrary:

1. [Pseudo-]Augustine, ascribing five grasping faculties to the soul in the book *On the Soul and Spirit* [c. 11]—the senses, imagination, reason, intellect, and intelligence—says: "The sensory capacity is the faculty that perceives

---

9. An alternative reading of three MSS is "did not know him as absent."
10. Pseudo-Augustine, *The Spirit and the Soul* 11.

corporeal forms when [bodies] are present. The imagination is the faculty that perceives corporeal forms when [bodies] are absent. Reason is the faculty that perceives the universal and abstract natures of bodies, such as genera, species, [specific] differences, properties, and accidents—for it abstracts from bodies their universal natures, to which bodies serve as substrates, and it does this not by acting [physically] but by considering [them mentally]. The intellect is the faculty that recognizes created spirits. However, intelligence is the faculty that recognizes the uncreated spirit," namely, God. It remains, then, that God is known by intelligence, not by reason.

2. Boethius, distinguishing between grasping faculties in *Consolation of Philosophy* [5, pr. 4], says: "The sensory capacity intuits the form (*species*) that is lodged in its underlying matter; the imagination, however, conjures up forms by themselves, without matter; reason, in its turn, transcends even that capacity and ponders in its universality the [universal] form itself that is present in singular things. Intelligence, going beyond the reach of universality, by its pure mental gaze contemplates the simple form itself." Therefore, since the divine essence is a simple form—moreover, such a form that is not present in singular things in the manner of a universal form—it remains that it is known by intelligence, and not by reason.

3. Boethius says in the same place: "A superior power includes inferior powers, but no inferior power rises to the level of the superior power in any way; nor are the senses able to know anything beyond material things, nor can the imagination observe universal forms, nor can reason grasp simple forms."

Reply to the objections:

1. There is a general and a strict sense of the word "reason" (*ratio*). In its broad sense, "reason" includes intelligence, intellect, and "reason" in its strict meaning. Indeed, if one considers the rational power insofar as it relates to something that is above it, namely, God, it is called intelligence. [If one considers the rational power] insofar as it relates to something that is at the same level as itself, namely, spiritual nature, it is called intellect. [Finally, if one considers the rational power] insofar as it relates to something that is below it, namely, bodily natures, it is called "reason" in a strict sense. And this is how Augustine understands this in his book *On the Soul and Spirit* [12].

Or, to put this differently: employing a twofold distinction, Augustine says [ibid., 11 and 34] that reason is subdivided into two [parts], namely, into a higher and a lower, or a male and a female [part]. The higher part serves the purpose of contemplating God and eternal things, and the lower part serves the purpose of contemplating creatures and temporal things. Wisdom pertains to the higher part, and science pertains to the lower part.

Taking this into consideration, one must reply that God is grasped by reason insofar as the term "reason" is extended to include the higher part, which is called mind or intelligence, and not insofar as the term "reason" is restricted to designate the lower part, which serves the purpose of contemplating creatures and lower natures.

2–3. As for the statements of Boethius, one must reply that "reason" can be understood in its role as "reason" and in its role as "intelligence." Similarly, "intelligence" can be understood in its role as "intelligence" and in its role as "reason." However, reason's proper role is to perceive how things are arranged as one among many: for example, [to perceive] a universal form in singular things, or how one thing follows from another or is after another, for example, a conclusion from the principles. However, the role of intelligence is to grasp the simple form itself: not [how] one [is] through another or after another, but [to grasp] simultaneously the entire totality. Now in our present state reason in us functions in its role as reason, and even intelligence functions in its role as reason: because our intelligence grasps the simple form, which is God, not as simple and simultaneous, but as a universal cause in its many effects; also [it grasps it] by means of something else, that is, through its effects, or creatures. As for reason functioning as intelligence and intelligence functioning as intelligence, this [only] happens in the divine intellect. Therefore, Boethius says in his book *Consolation of Philosophy* [V, pr. 5] that reason belongs only to the human being, and intelligence to God. This is precisely what he says: "Mere sensation, which is deprived of all cognitive activity, stoops down even to immobile marine animals, such as shell mollusks; as for the imagination, it is present in mobile beasts, which also possess some instinct of fleeing or pursuing; however, reason is only present in humankind, just as intelligence is only present in God." . . .

IS GOD HIMSELF (SE IPSO) SEEN AND KNOWN, OR IS SOMETHING ELSE REQUIRED AS A MEANS OF KNOWING HIM?

SH 1, Tr Int, Q2, M3, C1 (n. 20), 30–31
Objections:

1. The relationship between the divine light on the one hand, and the intellect and objects of knowledge on the other is the same as the relationship

between corporeal light on the one hand, and the sensory faculty and objects of sense on the other. As Augustine says in his book *Soliloquies* [1.8.15], "both the earth and light are visible. However, the earth cannot be seen unless it is illuminated by light. Similarly, what the sciences show us can only be understood if they are illumined, as it were, by a sun of their own"—and this [sun] is God. Therefore, if corporeal light can be seen on its own, and not by means of something else, then the light that is God [also] can be seen on its own, and not by means of something else.

2. According to Augustine [*Literal Commentary on Genesis* 12.7], there are three kinds of vision: corporeal, imaginary, and intellectual. The third kind perceives the "things that are not like anything else except themselves," as Augustine's gloss[11] on 1 Corinthians 12:2 says; therefore, [God] cannot be seen by means of an image or likeness. As for [the confirmation] that God is seen by the third kind of vision, it is contained in a gloss on Romans 1:20, "*The invisible things of God*," etc., [which says] that the philosophers saw God by the third kind of vision.

3. Augustine [in *On True Religion* 55.113] says that "the mind is shaped by the first truth itself, with no nature coming between them." Therefore, no other nature that would serve as a means of knowing God comes between first truth and the mind.

To the contrary:

a. 1 Corinthians 13:12: "*Now we see through a mirror, by way of mystery.*" The Gloss says: "*through a mirror, by way of mystery,* that is, by means of an obscure image: for we see some creatures in which some likeness of God shines through." And it follows: "Just as the word 'mirror' stands for 'image,' in the same way the word 'mystery' stands for 'likeness,' albeit an obscure one. Therefore, both words stand for 'likenesses' that can assist us in knowing God, albeit in an obscure manner." It remains, then, that at present God is only known by means of likenesses [from the world] of creatures.

b. Dionysius says at the beginning of the *Celestial Hierarchy* [c. 1, n. 3]: "It is not possible for our mind to ascend to the immaterial contemplation of the celestial hierarchy, unless it uses material things to lead to that end, understanding the beauties that appear to the senses as likenesses or images of invisible beauty."[12] It remains, then, that spiritual creatures can only be

---

11. That is, *Literal Commentary on Genesis* 12.6.
12. I used the Greek text to amend the translation, since the Latin version has an unclear passage in the middle that is not in the Greek: ἐπεὶ μηδὲ δυνατόν ἐστι

perceived by means of [material] likenesses; therefore, all the more so the uncreated spiritual substance itself.

Reply:

In our present condition, we cannot know God without an intermediary. As to whether God can be known without an intermediary in our future condition, this is a matter for inquiry elsewhere.

Reply to the objections:

1. To the first, one must reply that "to be seen by himself (*se ipso*)"[13] can have two meanings: to be the efficient or the material cause [of his own visibility, i.e., "to be himself seen"]. Therefore, one must reply that even [material] light is seen 'by itself' in the sense of being the efficient cause [of its own visibility], because there is no other cause apart from light itself that makes it visible.[14] But there is also some material cause of light's visibility, for example air or color. Therefore, light becomes visible "by itself" as the efficient cause [of its own visibility], but not as the material cause. That is, [it is not visible] in itself, namely, in its spiritual and absolute nature, but in another nature, for example in air or color. In the same way, the eternal light at present is seen "by itself," but not "in itself," but in creatures, which are, as it were, a material medium that channels that light to the intellect.

2. To the second, one must reply that "intellectual vision" has two senses: in one sense, "intellectual vision" signifies cognition by the intellect, whether it happens by means of a likeness of the thing that we understand or through [an immediate contact with] the thing itself. And this is how "intellectual vision" is taken in Romans 1:20 and in the Gloss. In another sense, "intellectual vision" is equivalent to "heavenly vision," and in this sense not every cognition by the intellect is called "intellectual vision," but only such a cognition by which a thing is seen not by means of its likeness that is different

---

τῷ καθ' ἡμᾶς νοῖ πρὸς τὴν ἄϋλον ἐκείνην ἀνατάθηναι τῶν οὐρανίων ἱεραρχιῶν μίμησίν τε καὶ θεωρίαν, εἰ μὴ τῇ κατ' αὐτὸν ὑλαίᾳ χειραγωγίᾳ χρήσαιτο τὰ μὲν φαινόμενα κάλλη τῆς ἀφανοῦς εὐπρεπείας ἀπεικονίσματα λογιζόμενος.

13. Although what the text attempts to say is clear in both Latin and English, the phrasing is awkward in both languages. The Latin ablative construction *se ipso* communicates that God himself (or "of himself," "by himself") is seen, rather than an intervening image, but it can also be interpreted in terms of agency: "by himself" as being the agent or efficient cause of creating the possibility of being seen by us. The translation attempts to maintain clarity in English by shifting between two possible translations, and some of the ambiguity that is obvious in the Latin is lost as a result.

14. Reading *videri* for *videre*, which is either an editorial or a scribal error.

from the thing itself. And this is how it is taken in the Gloss on 2 Corinthians 12:2, "*caught up to the third heaven*," which says: "The third kind of vision is the one by which love is intellectually seen; [this type of vision] contains things of which there are no images that are like them." And it continues: "For there are no two different ways of seeing love: one when it is present in [its own] form by virtue of which it exists, and another when it is absent, by means of some image that is similar to it." Therefore, one must say that if "intellectual vision" is taken in the former sense, then God is seen [in this way] at present, but if it is taken in the latter sense, then God will be seen [in this way] in heaven.

3. To the third, one must reply that the word "nature" can mean two things: (1) either a certain substance, or (2) a condition or state of that substance. If we take "nature" to mean "a certain substance," using the term in this sense Augustine [in *On True Religion*] says that "no nature, such as an intellectual substance, comes between the mind and God," such as an angel, which would shape and perfect the mind in the way that the philosophers have falsely claimed, saying that the human intellect is perfected and actuated by an angelic intellect. However, if we take "nature" to mean "a condition or state of a substance," in this sense it is not inappropriate for there to be some state or condition of the mind that would allow it to see God. The mind, then, would use this state or condition—or even other intelligible species—as an image that would enable it to see God.

IS GOD KNOWN BY MEANS OF CREATURES?

SH 1, Tr Int, Q2, M3, C2 (n. 21), 31–32
And it seems that he is not:

1. All knowledge is through agreement; but there is no agreement between God and creatures: neither in genus, nor in species, nor in number; therefore, one cannot know him through creatures.

2. All knowledge that is founded on the discursive movement of reason is founded on some relation (*habitudo*); however, there is no relation between creatures and God; therefore, one cannot know him through creatures. Proof of the minor:[15] there is no proportion between the finite and the infinite; but

---

15. The Latin edition gives *mediae* ("middle [proposition]"), which is the term that the SH sometimes uses in the sense of "minor premise."

God is infinite, while creatures are finite; therefore, there is no common proportion or relation [between the two].

3. Augustine says in *On Free Choice of the Will* [2.13.36]: "The powerful mental gaze, after it has observed many immutable things, will focus itself on the highest truth, by means of which all other things become clear, and remaining fixed on it will forget everything else"; thus, when [our mind] understands the first truth, it arrives at this truth and it forgets everything else; therefore, it does not understand this truth by means of those other things.

4. Since the soul is naturally capable of understanding the first truth, there is no lack on the part of the soul; however, the divine light is always present to it; therefore, the soul sees it always and with no intermediaries.

5. The Gloss on Matthew 11:27, *"No one knows the Father except the Son,"* says: "The Father is revealed through the Son." Therefore, we see God through the Son, not through creatures. A passage from [Lombard's] *Sentences* [I, d. 5, c. 1] on the same topic says: "God the Father, who both wanted and was able to reveal himself most truly to all souls with cognitive powers, in order to reveal himself, generated him who is identical to the one who had generated." Therefore, it is the Son who more appropriately serves the purpose of revealing God.

To the contrary:

a. The Gloss on Romans 1:20, *"The invisible things of God,"* says: "God, who was invisible by nature, has made his masterpiece in order to reveal the artist by its conspicuous nature." Therefore, we see God through creatures.

b. 1 Corinthians 13:12: *"Now we see through a mirror, by way of mystery."*

Reply to the objections:

1. To the first objection, one must reply that there are two types of agreement: univocal and analogical. Things can agree univocally in genus, in species, or in number. An example of analogical agreement would be substance and accident: they agree in that they are both [a type of] being, which is predicated of them in terms of priority: substance as [a type of] being serves as a substrate to its accidents, and therefore "being" is predicated in a primary sense of substance, which is "being" essentially, and in a secondary sense of accidents, which are "beings" [by virtue of being] in something else. Therefore, one must reply that there is no univocal agreement between God and creatures, but there is an analogical one. For example, if "good" is predicated of God and of creatures, it is predicated of God essentially, and of

creatures in terms of participation. This suggests that the predication "good" of God and of creatures is analogical.

2. To the second objection, one must reply that the divine substance can be considered in itself or as a cause. Considered in itself, it is "like some sea of infinite substance."[16] However, if it is considered as a cause, it can be viewed either as the efficient cause or the final cause, because God is the "*alpha and the omega*" [Revelation 1:28]. In this second way, God is considered insofar as he encloses created reality within boundaries: the "before" boundary insofar as he is its efficient cause, and the "after" boundary as its final cause. And in this sense a relation between the finite and the infinite can be admitted: not [to God] as he is in himself, but [to God] as he is the final cause [of creation].

3. To the third objection, one must reply that there are two ways of directing our mental gaze at the truth itself: insofar as it exists in itself and insofar as it exists in creatures. One cannot fix one's mental gaze on truth under the first scenario, but one can under the second. Therefore, one must reply that cognition can be in its formative stage (*in fieri*) or in its complete stage (*in facto esse*). Our cognition of God is always in its formative stage in this life, but in our future life it will be in its complete stage. It is in this sense that one must understand Augustine's statement to the effect that our mind "forgets everything else." This is clear [from the following example]: when someone is in the process of manufacturing an artifact, they have their tools with them; but once the artifact is finished, they throw down the tools. As Augustine says, "in this present state we need likenesses."[17]

4. To the fourth objection, one must reply that the lack is on the part of our nature: [as Aristotle says in *Metaphysics* 2.1], "in respect to the natural things that are most manifest our intellect behaves in the same way as the eye of the owl in respect to the sun." Just as our sight fails to see the brightest and the dimmest objects, in the same way our intellect fails to comprehend the brightest objects, for example, the Trinity, on account of the intensity of light. Similarly, it fails to grasp the dimmest objects, such as the passage of time and motion. Therefore, our intellect is deficient in knowing the eternal as the brightest object, and in grasping the passage of time and motion as

---

16. John Damascene, *On the Orthodox Faith* 1.9.
17. This is not an exact quote, but Augustine uses similar language in *On the Trinity* 15.9.16.

the dimmest objects. Therefore, just as our weak eye is unable to gaze [directly] at the disk of the sun, but is able to detect it by [seeing how it illumines] the air, in the same way we can see God through creatures.

5. To the fifth, one must reply that there are two ways of seeing God—through the Word and through creatures—just as there are two ways of seeing a [material] thing—directly in the light and through its reflection in a mirror—except that light is the formal cause of seeing, and the mirror is the material cause. Similarly, God is seen through the Word as in the light and through creatures as through a mirror.

ON THE MEANS OF KNOWING GOD THROUGH THE GRACE OF FAITH

SH 1, Tr Int, Q2, M3, C3 (n. 22), 32–34
Since cognition through grace [can vary and consists of cognition through the grace] of faith, the gifts of the intellect and wisdom, prophecy, and rapture, at this point we only inquire about the means of knowing [God] through the grace of faith, because no adult can be saved without this type of knowledge. We will discuss other types in appropriate sections.

I. a. Regarding this matter, the first opinion to be introduced is that of Augustine in his book *On Seeing God* [i.e., Letter 147.2.7]: "We say that the difference between seeing and believing is that the things that are present are seen and the things that are absent are believed. By 'things that are present right here' we understand all those things that are instantly accessible (*praesto*) to our sensory awareness, either mental or bodily. Therefore, borrowing the term [*praesto*] they are called 'present' (*praesentia*)."[18] It remains, based on this statement, that cognition through faith is not the same as vision, but is the cognition of things that are absent.

To the contrary:

1. 1 Corinthians 13:12: "*Now we see through a mirror, by way of mystery, but then face to face.*" This suggests that there are two senses of "seeing": (1) seeing "*through a mirror, by way of mystery,*" and (2) seeing the appearance (*species*)[19]

---

18. This, of course, is a false etymology, since the participle *praesens* comes from a different verb.

19. It is possible that the summists meant to say *per faciem* instead of *per speciem* and the text was corrupted (e.g., Borgh. lat. 359 and Vat. lat. 701 have *per speciem*, so it is not a transcription error); however, *facies* and *species* can both

[of something directly]. Therefore, since believing amounts to *"seeing through a mirror, by way of mystery,"* believing is seeing; therefore, the difference between believing and seeing that Augustine suggests amounts to nothing.

2. If belief amounts to knowledge of things absent, then, since both the imagination and memory are of things that are absent, imaginative and commemorative knowledge will also be [types of] belief; but then imagining and recalling would amount to believing, which is clearly false. It remains, therefore, that it is incorrect to distinguish between seeing and believing based on whether their objects are present or absent.

II. The next question is: Is knowledge based on faith scientific knowledge (*scientia*)?[20]

That it is:

a. Based on 1 John 3:2, *"but we know (scimus) that when he will appear, we will be like him,"* Augustine says in On Seeing God [i.e., Letter 147.5.12]: "He applies the terminology of 'knowing' (*scire*) to himself regarding things that have not yet happened, [which implies] that he has learned them not by seeing but by believing"; therefore, believing amounts to knowing scientifically (*scire*); therefore, faith is scientific knowledge.

b. Augustine says in the same work [3.8]: "Our scientific knowledge consists of things that have been seen and things that have been taken on faith"; however, when the soul accepts something based on things taken on faith it is [called] faith; therefore, faith is scientific knowledge.

To the contrary:

1. The intellect has three types of acceptance: opinion, belief (or faith), and scientific knowledge; therefore, if opinion never amounts to scientific knowledge, nor does belief (or faith).

---

mean "appearance" and be used synonymously (cf. the Arabic وجه, which also means both "face" and "appearance").

20. It is rather difficult to translate adequately into English the terminological difference that exists between the two Latin roots that mean "knowledge": on the one hand, *notitia* and *cognitio* (related to the ancient Indo-European root *jnâ-*, cognate of the Greek γνῶσις and the English "know"), and on the other hand *scientia* (with the original meaning of "distinguishing"), which usually renders the Greek ἐπιστήμη. Yet the distinction is of crucial importance to medieval discussions of theology, and it will be maintained by rendering *scientia* as "scientific knowledge."

Reply to the objections:

I. 1. To the first objection one must reply that there are two senses of "seeing something": seeing in itself and seeing in something else. We refer to seeing something in the proper sense when it is seen in itself, and in an improper sense when it is seen in something else. Based on this [distinction], one must reply that believing is seeing something in something else, and not in itself, and therefore [it is seeing] in an improper sense. And Augustine says the same thing in *On Seeing God* [i.e., Letter 147.3.8]: "If we—not inappropriately—apply the terminology of 'knowing' (*scire*) to the cases when we believe something to be most certain, it happens that we also refer to ourselves as mentally seeing the things that properly belong to the realm of belief, despite the fact that they are not part of our sensory awareness." However, as he says himself [ibid., 2.7], properly speaking it is the "things that are absent from our sensory awareness that are believed, if we see appropriate evidence that is adduced to prove them. The things that are seen, however, are those that are instantly accessible (*praesto*) to our sensory awareness, either mental or bodily. Therefore, they are called 'present' (*praesentia*)."[21] The situation is thus clarified: that which is believed is not seen in itself in the proper sense, but in the evidence [presented to prove it]. As for the things that are seen in the proper sense, they become known when they are present by themselves. Therefore, note Augustine's example [ibid.]: "I see this light by my corporeal sight, and I see my wishes by my mental gaze. However, if someone were to reveal to me his wishes, I would believe him, and not see [his wishes]. This is because I would only hear his words that would indicate his wishes, but the wishes themselves that he is telling me about would not be perceived either by my corporeal sight or by my mental gaze. [Also, I would believe him only] as long as I treated his words as trustworthy evidence, because if I thought he were lying, his words would not amount to credible evidence, and therefore I would not believe them."

I. 2. Augustine replies to the second objection in his book *On Seeing God* [ibid.]: "However, my statement 'those things are believed of which our sensory system is not immediately aware' should not be taken in the sense that those things that we did see at a certain point in time" (for example, those that we imagine), or [those things] that "we recall having seen" (such as objects of our memories), and "of which we are certain that they are

---

21. See note to argument I.a.

currently, when we are recalling them, not here," "should be included among those things that are believed, but among those things that are seen." For "seeing" amounts to grasping a thing by one's corporeal senses or by one's mental gaze, while "believing" is applied to things which we do not recall ever to have seen, either by our corporeal sight or by our mental gaze.

Reply:

II. To the last question, whether faith can be called scientific knowledge, one must distinguish between the following senses of "scientific knowledge": strict, common, and the most common. In its strict sense, scientific knowledge means knowing things through their causes, as the Philosopher says [in *Metaphysics* 1.3.1]: "Knowing scientifically amounts to knowing the cause of the thing." In its common sense, scientific knowledge means seeing things through one's intellect, which is the sense that Augustine uses in *On Seeing God* [16.38]: "As for the things that can be seen corporeally, they cannot be part of any knowledge (*scientia*) unless a mind is present that can receive such things after they have been announced" [by the senses]. The most common sense of scientific knowledge is illustrated in the following statement from Augustine's *On Seeing God* [3.8]: "Our knowledge (*scientia*) consists of things that have been seen and things that have been believed. The difference is that we ourselves serve as witnesses to things that we see or have seen, while we are moved to believe in things that we believe in by others who serve as witnesses [to those things]. This is because the signs of the things which we neither see nor recall ourselves to have seen are given in the form of speech, written testimony, or other evidence, and upon seeing [this evidence,] things that have not been seen are believed. Therefore, it is not inappropriate to say that we know (*scire*) not only those things that we see or have seen, but also those things in which we believe based on trustworthy witnesses or accounts."

ON RATIONAL PROOFS OF THINGS TO BE TAKEN ON FAITH

SH 1, Tr Int, Q2, M3, C4 (n. 23), 34–35

The next question proceeds by way of comparing cognition through the natural light of reason with cognition through the grace of faith.

1. St. Gregory says [in *Sermons on the Gospels* 2.26.1]: "The faith for which human reason furnishes a proof has no merit"; therefore, to prove [what is taken on] faith amounts to taking away the merit of faith.

2. Hebrews 11:1: "*Faith is the substance of things hoped for, the evidence (argumentum) of things not seen.*" Therefore, since faith is the *evidence (argumentum)*, it is something that proves, not something that is proved.

3. Since an authoritative statement says that "nothing is more certain to a person than their faith," and all proofs are accomplished through something more certain [than what needs to be proved], therefore, faith cannot be proved; therefore, reasons that are adduced to prove what is to be believed are futile and useless.

4. The things that are to be believed are beyond the scope of every intellect and reason; however, all things that are proved by the natural light of reason are within the scope of the intellect and reason; therefore, things to be believed cannot be proved by the natural light of reason.

To the contrary:

a. Richard [of St. Victor] in *On the Trinity* [1.4] says: "I believe without a doubt that there is no shortage not only of probable but also of compelling arguments in order to explain things whose existence is necessary." Therefore, since the existence of things to be believed is most necessary, most compelling arguments to prove them exist.

Reply:

As some have well said, there are three reasons for attempting to prove objects of belief by natural reasons. First, [one can attempt proofs] for our own sake: [namely, for the sake of our own] understanding of the truth that we believe in, which we must always keep investigating, according to what Psalms [104:4] says: "*Seek his face evermore.*" Therefore, in order to secure this understanding of the truth that we believe in, we can think of some proofs, and the grace of faith itself illumines us to find them. Second, [one can attempt proofs] in order to advance the simple ones to a perfect faith. For just as the simple ones are moved to the love of God by material goods, in the same way they advance to a perfect or greater faith by means of proofs of this sort. For this reason it is said to prelates in 1 Peter 3:15: "*be ready always to give a reason to every person that asks you a reason of the hope and faith that is in you.*" Third, [one can attempt proofs] in order to call back the unfaithful ones to faith. For just as John Damascene says in [*On the Orthodox Faith*] 1[.3], "although the knowledge of God's existence is naturally present to us, nevertheless, the pernicious malice of human nature has taken such a powerful hold of humans that they dare deny God's existence, as in David's words [in Psalms 52:1]: '*A fool said in his heart: there is no God*'"; therefore, in order to call back such persons [to faith], one needs proofs.

Reply to the objections:

1. To the first objection, one must reply that although objects of faith are known both by the natural light of reason and through faith, knowing through reason is different from knowing through faith. Indeed, when we know objects of belief by the natural light of reason, we assent to truth on account of our own evidence that we have in ourselves, namely, that rational argument that convinces our intellect. However, when we know through faith, we assent to truth not on account of our own evidence but on account of some other type of evidence, namely, divine or the one that comes from the first truth. This is what Augustine spoke about in aforesaid references.

As for the objection that "the faith [for which human reason furnishes a proof] has no merit," one must reply that "human reason furnishes a proof" to the one who relies on reason alone and believes that something is true [only] on account of rational arguments; it is true that this [sort of reliance on reason alone] takes away the merit of faith. However, human reason does not furnish a proof to the one who does not rely on reason, but rather assents to truth on account of the evidence provided by the first truth, because although such a person may entertain rational arguments that prove objects of faith, nevertheless, they do not rely on them: this is how it is with the faithful. This is symbolized by the scene with the Samaritans who said to the woman in John 4:42: "*Now we believe, not because of your saying.*"

2. To the second objection, that faith is the evidence (*argumentum*), etc., some gave an elegant reply that the relationship between reason and faith is different in matters logical and theological. Indeed, in logic, reasons generate belief; this is why we speak of a [logical] argument when belief is generated by means of offering reasons about a dubious thing. In theology, however, the situation is reversed, because [here] it is belief that generates reasons; this is why a [theological] argument is when belief leads to the formation of reasons. Indeed, faith by means of which one believes is the light of the soul, and the more one is illumined by this light, the more one is attuned to finding reasons that could prove what one believes.

3. Replying to the third objection, that "nothing is more certain to a person than their faith," one must make a distinction: there is the intellectual certitude of contemplation, which operates in the same way as vision, and there is affective certitude, which operates in the same way as the will or love that

fixate on [their object]. It is in this second sense that the statement about "faith being more certain" must be taken, not in the first sense.

4. To the fourth objection, one must reply that some things are proved by means of something that is prior, and some things are proved by means of something that is posterior. An example of the former is when effects are proved through their cause. An example of the latter is when a cause is proved through its effects. Now, when the [human] intellect or reason uses the former method, both that which is proved and the middle term by which it is proved are within the scope of the human intellect. For this reason, objects of belief are not proved that way. However, when [the human intellect] uses the latter method, and when[22] the middle term [of the proof] is within the scope of the human intellect, or near there, nothing prevents it from proving a truth that lies beyond the scope of the human intellect or reason, for the "*invisible things of God . . .* [and] *even his eternal power and Godhead,* [are understood] *by the things that are made*" (Romans 1:20). And this is the way objects of belief are proved.

IS THE KNOWLEDGE ABOUT GOD OBTAINED THROUGH THE NATURAL LIGHT OF REASON MORE CERTAIN THAN THE KNOWLEDGE ABOUT CREATURES?

SH 1, Tr Int, Q2, M3, C5 (n. 24), 35–36
Objections to this are as follows:

1. Things that are seen in the light are seen more clearly than those seen in the dark; but creatures are seen, as it were, in the light, while the divine substance is seen, as it were, in the dark, as in Psalms 17:13: "*He made darkness his secret place.*" The Gloss [on this passage says]: "He is hidden in that darkness of mortal life, where we are guided by faith, not by sight." Therefore, creatures are known with more certainty.

2. The knowledge by which it is known about a thing "that it is" and "what it is" is more certain than the knowledge [about a thing] by which it is known "that it is" and "what it is not," [especially] when it is not [even] possible to know about this thing "what it is"; however, knowledge about creatures is of the former kind, while knowledge about God is of the latter kind, as Dionysius and Damascene say; therefore, knowledge about creatures is more certain.

---

22. Reading "et si" for the "etsi" of the edition.

3. The middle term is known with more certainty than the conclusion; however, creatures are the middle term of knowledge in our present state, as Romans 1:20 says; therefore, creatures are known with more certainty.

To the contrary:

a. Light is seen more clearly than what is seen in this light; but the relation between God and intelligible things is the same as the relation between light and visible things, as Augustine says in *Soliloquies* 1[8.15]: "Just as we notice three things about the sun—that it exists, that it shines, and that it illuminates [other things]—in the same way we must notice three things about God, who is most hidden: that he exists, that he is capable of understanding, and that he makes other things intelligible."

Reply:

As was said previously, one can know about a thing "that it is" [or of its existence] and "what it is" [or its essence]. The essences of creatures are known with more certainty than the essence of God. However, the existence of God in some way is known with more certainty. Indeed, certainty is of many kinds, for there is sensory certainty and intellectual certainty. Also, intellectual certainty can be of two kinds: habitual or actual. Also, habitual certainty can be of many kinds, depending on whether it is an innate habit, infused habit, or a habit that is acquired by way of the senses. Therefore, one must reply that creatures are known with more certainty than God in two ways, namely, by the certainty of the senses and of the habit that is acquired by way of the objects of sense. However, God is known with more certainty [also] in two ways, namely, by the certainty of the innate and infused habits: in the first way by everybody, and in the second way by the faithful.

Reply to the objections:

1. To the first objection, one must reply that knowing a thing "in the light" amounts to knowing its essence (or "what it is"), its size, and its quality—and we know creatures by this sort of knowledge with more certainty than we know God. However, nothing prevents us from becoming aware of God's existence (or "that he is") with more certainty, in the way described previously.

2. This clarifies the solution to the second objection.

3. To the third objection, one must reply that created things do serve as a middle term for knowing God, insofar as our knowledge of God comes by way of a habit acquired from sensory experience. And in this sense, as was said previously, [our knowledge] of creatures is more certain than that

of God. However, it does not follow therefore that our knowledge of God by way of innate and infused habits is not more certain [than that of creatures].

Thus ends this inquiry about knowing God by the natural light of reason, [which was undertaken] in order to draw up the limits of inquiries about the Unity and Trinity of the divine substance.

CHAPTER 3

THE NECESSARY EXISTENCE OF GOD

Two things must be shown concerning the essential nature of the divine substance. First, that the divine substance exists by necessity; second, that it is necessarily known to exist in such a way that it cannot be thought not to exist.

DOES THE DIVINE SUBSTANCE NECESSARILY EXIST?

SH 1, P1, In1, Tr1, Q1, C1 (n. 25), 40–42

To demonstrate the first point [that the divine substance necessarily exists], many arguments are brought forward in accordance with different ways of thinking about the divine essence.

I. In the book *On the Trinity* [1.6], Richard of St. Victor proves that God exists through the notion of being or existence, by proposing this distinction: "everything that exists or is able to exist either has its being from eternity or began to be in time. Similarly, all that exists or is able to exist either has being from itself, or from something other than itself. Therefore, there is a threefold way of distinguishing between all forms of existence. For each thing that exists has being either from eternity and from itself; or, on the contrary, neither from eternity nor from itself; or mediately between these two, from eternity, but nevertheless not from itself. However, a fourth way of being, which seems to respond to this [last option] as its contrary, is absolutely impossible by nature, for absolutely nothing is able to exist from itself, but not from eternity. For there was a time when all that began to exist in time did not exist. But as long as it did not exist, it possessed absolutely nothing and was capable of absolutely nothing. Thus, it did not give being nor the ability to do something to itself or to anything else, otherwise, it [would have] given what it did not have and made what it was not able to make."

It remains, therefore, that if something exists in time, it is not from itself, but from another. Therefore, the faulty consequence shows that if something is from itself, it is not from time but from eternity; therefore, the fourth option is impossible, namely, that something that derives its existence from itself nevertheless does not exist from eternity.

[In addition] to positing these things, Richard argues as follows [*On the Trinity* 1.7–8]: "every day experiences show plainly the innumerability of those things which did not exist from eternity. Superior reasoning, however, finds that whatever did not exist from eternity is not able to derive its existence from itself. But if nothing came from itself, there would have been absolutely nothing from which those things would have been able to exist, which do not have nor can have their own existence from themselves. Therefore, it is clear that something exists from itself, and for that very reason, as has just been stated, it exists from eternity." And we call this the divine substance.

Richard further argues [*On the Trinity* 1.9]: "the existence of something from eternity, that nevertheless did not derive its existence from itself"—which is the intermediate variation—"should seem impossible to no one, as if a cause always had to precede its effects, and everything which is from another always had to be subsequent to its principle or origin. Certainly, a ray of the sun proceeds from the sun and originates in the sun; nevertheless, it exists for as long as the sun does. If therefore that physical light has a ray which is always simultaneous with itself, why should that spiritual and inaccessible light not have a ray that is coterminous with itself?"

II. John Damascene [*On the Orthodox Faith* 1.3] also proves the same point through the notion of causality: "all that is, is either causable or uncausable [created or uncreated]. But all that is causable is changeable, either according to choice, as in the case of a spiritual substance [i.e., angel], or according to generation and corruption, or alteration, or according to locomotion, as with bodily things. Therefore, [changeable things] departed from nonbeing into being. For those things whose existence begins from change are subject to change and mutability; conversely, things that are subject to change began from change." Since all substances of this world are changeable, consequently, they moved from nonbeing into being. Therefore, they are causable; but nothing is causable by itself; it remains, therefore, that there is an uncaused substance, from which other causable things derive their existence.

It is clear that the universe of created things, whether it is posited as finite or infinite, is entirely caused; since therefore nothing is its own cause, it is necessary that it should have a cause that is not caused. [Indeed,] a circle of efficient causes cannot be posited, because it would follow that the same thing would be both prior and posterior to itself in being. For instance, if A were posited as the cause of B, and B as the cause of C, and C likewise as the cause of A, then in [the order of] causation, A would be before B and C. Therefore, A is prior to that, to which C is prior; but C is before A, of which it is the cause; therefore, A would be before A, which is impossible. It remains, therefore, that a circular argument cannot be posited. The preceding [line of] reasoning therefore follows of necessity.

Also, Wisdom 13:4–5 [states]: *"if they marvel at the power and works of creatures, let them understand from them that he who made these things is greater than them; for by the greatness of the form and of the creature, the Creator of those things can be discerned."*

Hugh of St. Victor [writes], in *On the Sacraments* 1.[8–9]: "since the soul naturally is not able to doubt that it exists, because it is not able to be unaware of itself, it is also naturally compelled to believe that it has not always existed, because it remembers itself to have begun at some point. As therefore it sees that it did not begin and have a beginning through itself, it is not able to be unaware of the fact" that it was not its own beginning. "Therefore, the beginning of something that did not exist requires another maker who existed." And this we call God. So it is said in the Psalms [99:3]: *"Know that the Lord himself is God, the one who made us,"* etc.

III. Furthermore, with reference to the notion of truth, the same point is proved by Anselm in his book *On Truth* [1]: "Try to imagine that something that was later to come true was not true earlier, or that something [true] will cease to be true in the future once it has slipped into the past. Now if neither of those things can be conceived, and if neither of them can be true without truth, it is impossible to think that truth has a beginning or an end." Therefore, truth is eternal: and this we call the divine essence.

In the same place, Anselm also writes: "if truth had a beginning or will have an end, then the statement 'there is no truth' was true before it began. And after truth comes to an end, the statement 'there is no truth' will [still] be true. But true statements cannot exist except by truth; therefore, there was truth before there was truth, and there will be truth after truth ends; which is most incongruous." Therefore, truth exists eternally.

From the negation of truth, the affirmation of truth follows, as Augustine argued in the *Soliloquies* [2.15]: if there is no truth, then there is truth, because it follows that the statement "truth does not exist" is true. If the statement "it is true that truth does not exist" is said to imply that truth is posited in a qualified sense, not simply or without qualification (*simpliciter*), nevertheless, [the consequence] still follows, because everything that is in a qualified sense stands in relation to something that is [predicated] in an unqualified sense. If therefore there is truth in a qualified sense, it necessarily follows that something is true without qualification, and that some truth is [predicated] in an unqualified sense.

IV. Some [Boethius, *The Consolation of Philosophy* 3.10] prove [the necessary existence of God] through the idea of goodness, [affirming that] "the best is the best." Therefore, the best exists, because "to exist" is implied in the understanding of what is best. One can respond by saying that this does not follow, because this word "is" [in this context] does not refer to the act of existing, but only to the essence or disposition for being, as in this example: "Caesar is Caesar," from which it does not follow, "therefore, Caesar exists."[1]

On the other hand: the notion of what is "best" implies actual existence by necessity, because the meaning of that which is "best" is "that than which nothing is better." But existence in act [reality] is better than existence in potency, and both are better than something that does not have existence [in either way], if one may say so. If, therefore, a being "than which nothing better exists" implies actual existence by necessity, then "the best" also denotes existence in act. If, therefore, no intellect is able to deny that what is best is best, it necessarily has to concede that the best exists in act.

In *Proslogion* [2], Anselm [writes]: "we believe that you, God, are something than which nothing greater can be conceived. Or is there not anything of such a nature, since the fool has said in his heart, 'there is no God' [Psalms 13:1]? But certainly, the same fool, when he hears my statement about 'something than which nothing greater can be conceived,' understands what he hears, and what he understands is in his intellect, even if he does not understand that it exists." Thus it follows, "certainly that than which a greater cannot be thought is not able to exist only in the intellect. For if it only exists in the intellect, it is able to be thought to exist also in reality, which is greater. If, therefore, that than which a greater cannot be conceived is in the intellect only, that very thing than which a greater cannot be conceived is that than which a greater can be conceived; but this certainly cannot be [the case]. Therefore, there exists without doubt something than which nothing greater

---

1. That is, existence is not a predicate.

can be conceived both in the intellect and in reality." And Anselm himself clarifies the necessity of this reasoning in many different ways in his book *On Behalf of the Fool* [1].

V. A similar point is proved through the notion of eminence. As Anselm says in the *Monologion* [4], "Although it cannot be denied that the nature of some things is superior to others, nevertheless, reason persuades that a certain nature among these is so super-eminent that it does not have one superior to itself. For if the distinction of degrees is infinite to such a degree that no superior grade can be found, to which there would be no other superior, this conclusion must be deduced, namely, that the multitude of natures themselves is not limited by any bounds. But this is absurd." Therefore, there is of necessity a certain nature, which is so superior to some nature or natures, that there is no other nature to which it could be ordered as inferior. It remains, therefore, that the highest nature exists.

Richard in *On the Trinity* [1.11] writes, "I believe that no one is able to doubt that which is most certain: that the whole multitude of existing things and the multiplicity of different grades requires something that is highest. However, we call the highest of all things that than which nothing is greater, nothing is better."

By these reasons, it has been demonstrated that God exists by necessity.

IS THE DIVINE ESSENCE NECESSARILY KNOWN IN SUCH A WAY AS TO PRECLUDE THINKING OF IT AS NONEXISTING? [CAN GOD BE THOUGHT NOT TO EXIST?]

SH 1, P1, In1, Tr1, Q1, C2, Ar1 (n. 26), 42–44

In order to adumbrate the necessary existence of God, it must be shown that the divine essence is known in such a way that it is not possible to think that it does not exist.

a. As Anselm has argued in the *Proslogion* [3], "if something can be thought to exist that is not able to be thought not to exist, it will be greater than that which can be thought not to exist. If, therefore, that than which nothing greater can be conceived, can be conceived as not existing, then that than which a greater cannot be conceived, is not that than which a greater cannot be conceived, which is self-contradictory. So truly, therefore, is there something than which a greater thing cannot be thought, that it cannot be thought not to exist. And this is you, our Lord God. For if some mind was able to think of something better than you, the creature would ascend above the Creator, which would be completely absurd."

b. Natural impressions, while nature remains, are immutable and universal and the same for all. But "the knowledge of God's existence is naturally impressed upon us," as John Damascene says [*On the Orthodox Faith* 1.1 and 3]. Therefore, because nature always remains, it is clear that this [naturally impressed] knowledge is universal and the same for all. Therefore, concerning the existence of the divine essence, no one is able to doubt. Therefore, a rational creature cannot be unaware of the existence of this essence.

c. "Essence" (*esse-ntia*) in the truest sense is that which can neither not exist (*esse*), nor be thought not to exist, namely, when it exists truly and perfectly, such that it is not able not to exist either in reality or in thought. If, therefore, the divine essence is [essence] in the truest sense, it is therefore not able not to exist, nor to be thought not to exist.

d. Next, imagine a distinction is drawn, as some have done, between *ratio* as reason [i.e., knowledge inasmuch as it pertains to the knower] and *ratio* as a nature [i.e., knowledge inasmuch as it pertains to the nature of the object known]. [And what if one claims that] God cannot be ignored nor thought not to exist by *ratio* as nature, but by *ratio* as reason he can be? To this it might be objected that no one can be unaware of their own existence, if moved by *ratio* as reason to thinking about themselves, because they are always present to themselves [i.e., "I think, therefore I am"]. Additionally, they are not able to be unaware [of the fact] that they did not always exist; but if they know themselves as existing and as not always having existed, it is necessary that they know themselves to draw their existence from some other thing that is the principle of their own being, according to the Psalm (99:3): "*know, because the same Lord is God; the same made us,*" etc. Therefore, it is not possible to be unaware of God if one is moved by *ratio* as reason.

On the other hand: 1. John Damascene [*On the Orthodox Faith* 1.3]: "although the knowledge of God's existence is naturally impressed in us, nevertheless, the pernicious evil of human beings has prevailed to such an extent, that they say that God does not exist, according to what David says (Psalm 13:1): 'the fool has said in his heart, there is no God.'" Therefore, the divine essence is able to be ignored and to be thought not to exist by the fool.

2. Related to this, Anselm objects, in *Proslogion* [4]: How has the "fool said in his heart, there is no God"? For he has either said what he was able to think or what he was not able to think. If he said what he was able to think,

God is therefore able to be thought not to exist. If he said what he was not able to think, to the contrary: "it is the same thing to say in the heart and to think; if therefore [the fool] has truly thought what he said in his heart," that God does not exist, he was therefore able to think that God does not exist.

3. The idolater says about the God of the faithful that he is not God; but the God of the faithful is the only true God; therefore, about the true God he says and thinks that he is not God, nor even anything; therefore, it can be thought that God does not exist.

4. 1 Timothy 6:16: "*He alone possesses immortality and dwells in light inaccessible, which no human being has seen nor is able to see.*" From which it is accepted that the divine being is the least knowable thing. If, therefore, we are able to think concerning any created being that it does not exist, therefore, it is even more possible to think that the divine being does not exist.

5. Boethius, in his book *On the Seven Days:* If we admit for the time being and for the sake of argument that the highest good does not exist, things would still be understood to be white, or to be large, but nevertheless nothing would be understood to be good. Therefore, our intellect is able to accept of things that they exist, without the highest good being understood to exist. From this it seems to remain: the highest good can be thought not to be.

Solution:

It must be said that the cognition of God is twofold: there is a cognition in act and a cognition in habit. The habitual cognition of God is naturally impressed in us, because this [knowledge] in us is a naturally impressed habit, namely, a likeness of the first truth in the intellect, by which [the intellect] is able to infer that God exists, and God cannot be ignored by the rational soul. As for cognition in act, it is twofold. One type occurs when the soul is moved according to the superior part of reason and the habit or likeness to the first truth impressed on the superior part of reason, in such a way as to recall its principle of origin through the fact that it sees itself not to be from itself. And in this way, by thinking of its origin, the soul also is not able to be unaware that God exists. The other [type of cognition] occurs when the soul is moved according to the inferior part of reason, which contemplates creatures. And in this way the soul is able not to recognize that God exists, namely, when turned aside from God by sin and error, it is in darkness, in the way that the Apostle says in Romans 1:21: "*When they knew God, they did not praise him as God, but rather strayed in their own knowledge, and their foolish hearts were obscured and served creatures more than the Creator.*" And this is the way in which the fool has said "there is no God": however, not in the other ways.

Replies to the objections:

1. Through the preceding, the reply to the first objection is clear.

2. Anselm responds to the second objection in the *Proslogion* [4]: There are two ways in which "something is said or thought in the heart. For it is one matter for a thing to be thought when the word signifying it is thought; it is another, when that, which the thing itself is, is understood. Therefore, in that way, namely, the first, God is able to be thought not to exist. In the second way, not at all. For no one understanding what God is, is able to think that God does not exist, even though they may say these words in their heart either without any or with some extramental signification. For God is that than which nothing greater can be conceived; the one who really understands that understands indeed that God exists such that not even in thought is he able not to exist; nor therefore is [the knower] able to think that God does not exist."

3. To the third objection, it must be said that the cognition of something can be through one of two ways: according to a general nature or a proper nature. It is possible, therefore, for something to be known in terms of its general nature, but not to be known in terms of its proper nature: as when someone knows honey in terms of its general nature, namely, that it is something soft and reddish, but is ignorant of its proper nature. Thus, when this one sees bile to be a soft, reddish substance, he is deceived and believes it is honey. Similarly, the cognition of happiness and the desire for it is innate to us in terms of its general nature: it "is the state of all good things gathering together perfectly." Nevertheless, its proper nature is unknown to some. Thus different people understand and reckon happiness in diverse ways: some place it in pleasures, some in wealth, some in honors. From this it is clear that these persons are ignorant of the proper nature of happiness. Similarly, it must be said that the idolaters are not ignorant of God with respect to his general nature, that he is a being, the origin, omnipotent. Nevertheless, they are ignorant of the proper nature of God and therefore say of God, who is three and one and true, that he is not God, and of an image [i.e., idol], that it is God.

4. To the fourth objection, the reply is clear through the preceding [statements] about the knowledge of God: because by a knowledge "that he is" and not "what he is," which is according to an infused or innate habit, God

is quite knowable, as was said above, in the last chapter inquiring about the cognition of God.[2]

5. To the fifth and last objection, it must be said, as Anselm stated earlier, that when we apply the cognition of the type "when the word signifying a thing is thought," the highest good is able to be thought not to be; this is not at all the case, however, when we apply the cognition or thought by which "that, which the thing itself is, is understood."

IS IT A PROPERTY OF THE DIVINE NECESSITY NOT TO BE ABLE TO BE THOUGHT NOT TO EXIST?

SH 1, P1, In1, Tr1, Q1, C2, Ar2 (n. 27), 44–45

It remains to be inquired if it is a property of divine necessity, not to able to be thought not to exist, such that this property does not befit any other thing.

1. As Gaunilo objected, responding to Anselm on behalf of the Fool [*On Behalf of the Fool* 7], "I do not know whether I am able to think of myself as not existing, as long as I know myself to exist with absolute certainty. Now if I can [think of myself as nonexistent], why [can I not do the same with] something else that I know with the same certitude?" But then, although it is certain to me that God exists, I will be able to think that he does not exist. If, however, I cannot [think of myself as nonexistent], then it is not a property of God [alone] not to be able to be thought not to exist [but also of myself].

2. If by definition falsities cannot be understood, then nothing that exists can be understood as not existing: for it is a falsity for a thing that exists not to exist. Therefore, it will not be a property of God [alone] not to be able to be understood not to exist [but also of any existing thing].

On the other hand: a. Anselm objects in "Against the One Responding on Behalf of the Fool" [1]: "Without doubt, something that does not exist at some place or some time, even if it exists somewhere and at some time, is nevertheless able to be thought of as existing never and nowhere, just as it does not exist at some place and time. For example, what did not exist yesterday and exists today is able to be understood as never having existed, just as it is understood not to have existed yesterday. And that which does not exist here and does exist elsewhere can be thought not to exist anywhere, just as it does not exist here. As regards a thing, some of whose particular parts do not exist in the place and at the time its other parts exist, all of its

2. SH 1, Tr Int, Q2.

parts and therefore the whole thing itself can be thought to exist at no time and in no place. For even if time is said to exist always, and the world everywhere, nevertheless, [time and the world respectively do not exist] always in entirety or everywhere all at once. And just as the single parts of time do not exist when others do, so they are able to be thought never to have existed; and the single parts of the world are able to be understood not to exist anywhere, just as they do not exist where others do. Furthermore, that which is comprised of parts can be taken apart in thought, and thus cease to be. Therefore, whatever does not exist entirely at some place or some time, and yet exists, is able to be thought not to exist." However, such is every creature. "However, that than which nothing greater can be conceived, if it exists, is not able to be thought not to exist," as was proved before. Therefore, it is a property of the divine essence alone to exist in such a way that it cannot be thought not to be. This is to be conceded with the distinction that was posited [in the solution] earlier.

It must be said according to Anselm [*Against the One Responding on Behalf of the Fool* 4]: "although no things which exist, inasmuch as they exist, are able to be thought not to exist, because we are not able to think that things simultaneously exist and do not exist, nevertheless, all things are able to be thought not to exist except that which supremely exists. Therefore, all and only those things can be thought not to exist, which have a beginning or end or combination of parts, and, as I have said, did not exist completely at some place or time. At the same time, that only is not able to be thought not to exist, in which neither beginning nor end nor a combination of parts can be posited, and which no cognition discovers except as always and everywhere complete."

Replies to the objections:

1. To the first objection, therefore, Anselm responds [in *Against the One Responding on Behalf of the Fool* 4]: "Know that you are able to think that you do not exist, although you know most certainly that you exist. For we think of many things as not existing, which we know to exist; and [we think of] many things that we know not to exist, as existing—not judging but imagining things to be as we think." Not, however, inasmuch as [a being] is regarded as existing, is it able at the same time to be thought not to exist.

2. From the things already stated the reply to the second objection is clear. Thus ends the question about the necessary existence of God.

CHAPTER 4

THE DIVINE NATURE

IS THE DIVINE ESSENCE FINITE OR INFINITE?

SH 1, P1, In1, Tr2, Q1, C1 (n. 34), 54–57

Objections related to the first point [that God is finite]:

1. Finitude and infinitude pertain to quantity and are always referred to in terms of quantity, whereas simplicity and composition [are always treated] in relation to substance or essence. Now, we do not ascribe quantity to the divine essence with the exception of his power (*virtus*), which can be quantified in a way by using the distinction between either virtual or dimensional quantity posited by Augustine in *The Greatness of the Soul* [3]. Therefore, we cannot say that the divine essence is finite or infinite, but only his strength or power.

2. Finitude is the same as completeness. But the divine essence is supremely complete; therefore, it is eminently finite.

3. Also, just as a power (*potentia*) is defined by what it is able to do (*posse*), so an essence (*essentia*) is defined by what it can be (*esse*); however, the power that is able to deal with a certain number of things, and no more, is called finite; therefore, it is similar in the case of existence (*esse*) and therefore essence: the essence that is merely "this essence" in such a way that it is not another, is called finite; however, the divine essence is this [i.e., divine] essence in such a way that it is not another; therefore, it is finite.

4. Among the [specific] differences of being, what is most noble is always attributed to God. Therefore, because being in act is more noble than being in potency, God is called "being in act" and not "being in potency"; but finitude is a more noble condition than infinitude. Therefore, the divine essence will be referred to as finite and not infinite.

5. Finite [things] better lead to God than infinite things, for creatures lead to God precisely on account of their finitude, because they are described as finite due to being ordered to an end. What is infinite, however, does not lead us to [the idea of] order [to an end].[1] Thus, what is finite is a better likeness and expression of God in [created] beings than infinite [things]. If,

---

1. This was Aristotle's view of infinity.

therefore, we should attribute to the exemplar what best expresses him, then God should be described as finite, not infinite.

On the other hand:

a. Power and essence are the same in God. But his power is infinite, so his essence must be also. The confirmation of this argument is that in the supremely simple being, power and essence do not differ, otherwise it would not be the supremely simple being. For this reason, the scope [or extent] of his power is equal to the scope of his essence. Since "infinite" implies extension beyond the finite, it would have to be said that [God's] power extends beyond [his] essence unless the essence is also infinite.

b. The divine essence can be considered absolutely and in itself, or without regard to any relations. If, therefore, finitude and infinitude imply relative notions, they are not in the divine essence absolutely but insofar as we understand it in the sense of extension, when we say that the divine essence extends itself in every [sort of] being, just as his power [is extended] in all that can be done; but in this way, his essence is infinite. The proof that his power is infinite is that doing—or being able to do—a certain number of things does not preclude him from doing still more things. Similarly, therefore, if we cannot say of the divine essence that it is—or can be—in the essences of things, in such a way as to not be able to be yet in more [essences of things], it is clear that it is infinite.

c. That goodness is called infinite from which all goods come and than which a greater cannot be conceived; similarly, that power is infinite from which all power [derives] and than which a greater cannot be conceived. Therefore, also, that being will be called infinite from which all being derives and than which a greater cannot be conceived. But such is the being of the divine. Therefore, he is infinite. I say, however, that that one is the highest being, as Anselm says [in *Proslogion* 22], who is maximally removed from nonbeing, namely, who neither has nonbeing after being nor being after nonbeing, nor can be thought of as nonexistent.

d. Also, to use an impossible hypothetical, if the divine power were considered separately from the divine essence, still I could say that God is everywhere, and one could not think of him as being in a certain place without also being able to say that he is beyond that place. Therefore, just as a body would be called infinite if it could fill the entire world and beyond—if there were infinite worlds—in the same sense the divine essence should be called infinite.

e. 1 Kings 8:27: "*The heavens, even the highest heaven, cannot contain you.*" This suggests that if there were multiple heavens, they would not be able to contain [God], but he would fill all of them. Therefore, God himself in his essence is infinite.

f. God is the first efficient, formal, and final cause. Thus, if we cannot say of him as the first efficient cause that he is an effect, and if we cannot say, insofar as he is a formal cause, that he is formed, nor can we say that as a final cause he is finite. For if according to his essence he is the end or final cause [of all things], it is clear that his essence is infinite. But what if it is said that the divine essence can be called finite not because he has a goal or end by which he is completed or finished, but because he has this essence and not that one? This is one mode of finitude. But that he should not be called finite in this way is clear, namely, because before another essence was created, one could say that the divine essence existed, but one could not say that it was limited in relation to other things, because those things did not yet exist. But its being is the same before and after the creation of things. Therefore, if it could not be said to be finite with regard to [created] things then, neither can it be said to be finite now.

g. If the [divine] essence were called finite because it is this essence and not that [one], in a similar way, his power could be called finite, as it would be this power and not that one. This, however, is unfitting to say. But what if it is said that the divine power is (1) being and (2) operation, and it is true that insofar as it is a being, it is finite nevertheless, insofar as it is an operator it is infinite, because his power does not extend to a certain number of things without being able, at the same time, to extend to more things? Against this, it still seems, according to this way [of arguing], that [the divine power] is finite insofar as it operates, because just as one can say that "the divine power is this and not that power," so one can say that "the divine power acts on these things and not those." Therefore, using this reasoning—if that really amounts to finitude[2]—his power [also] can be called finite insofar as it operates. Nevertheless, it is not fitting to say [that God's power is finite].

h. Damascene [*On the Orthodox Faith* 1.8] says, "it must be believed that the one God is immortal, eternal, infinite, and uncircumscribed." But when I say, "one God," I speak of God's essence. Therefore, the divine essence is infinite.

---

2. That is, being "this" and not "that."

i. Exodus 33:20 says, "*no one will see me and live.*" In this regard Augustine disapproves of the opinion of those who say that God will not be seen in his essence, but in his light. And he objects as follows: his light is nothing other than his essence, therefore, seeing him in his light is nothing other than seeing him in his essence. Because his power is nothing other than his essence, he is just as infinite in power as he is in essence.

Solution:

One should side with Dionysius, who says [in *The Divine Names* 1.1], "we should not dare to say something universally of the unsurpassable and hidden divinity, apart from those things which God himself in the Sacred Scriptures makes clear to us." Since nothing can be found in Sacred Scripture about the finitude of the divine essence, we should not assert that his essence is finite unconditionally but [must say] that it is infinite. Strictly speaking, therefore, he must be called infinite according to substance and not finite, unless finite means "complete." Hence, Damascene says [in *On the Orthodox Faith* 1.8] that "God is uncircumscribed, uncreated, infinite." And in the same place [1.9], he says that "it seems that of the names that are said of God, 'he who is' is primary. For God includes everything in himself and has being as a certain infinite and indeterminate sea of substance." Therefore, according to Damascene, God is infinite according to essence.

However, infinity can be defined in three ways, namely, negatively, privatively, and disparately. Negative infinity involves the abnegation of an end. In this sense, infinite is the same as "not finite," and in this way, the infinite is what is not naturally meant to be completed or terminated.

Privative infinity refers to what is naturally meant to be completed but is not yet completed. Contrary or disparate infinity is that which has a disposition that is contrary or disparate to being terminated.

In the first way, the divine essence is infinite, because it does not have an end but is the one that completes all things. Nor is God's nature meant to be completed. Similarly, if we speak of disparate infinity, then God is also infinite, because he has a disposition that is disparate or contrary to finitude. For we say that something is finite when it cannot exist in more things that it is in [already]. In God, however, there is a disposition that is opposed to this, because the divine essence is both in all things and beyond all things; in addition, if these things themselves were infinite, he would nonetheless fill them. Thus, we speak of a disposition contrary to finitude, and therefore of infinitude, when we say that "he is in all things and not included in them and fills them, even if they were infinite." If we speak of privative infinity, then God cannot be called infinite, because he is not naturally meant to be limited, but is the one who limits or defines all things.

Replies to the objections:

1. To the first argument to the contrary, we say that as finitude is defined by positing an end, so infinitude is defined through the removal of an end. However, there are three kinds of ends, and similarly, there are three kinds of finitude and infinitude. An end can be a terminus, and thus finitude and infinitude, defined in relation to an end, pertain only to quantity, because they are understood quantitatively by reason of an [end taken as a] terminus or limit. Since there is no limit to the divisions that can be made in continuous things, we say that such things are divisible unto infinity or infinite in division. Similarly, because there is no limit to how many numbers can be added one to another, we say that number is infinite in addition. Also, just as place is said to be finite or infinite with regard to circumscription, so time is finite or infinite in duration. In another way, an end is said to be the same as a completion, and thus we speak of what is finite and infinite in substance. Thus it is said that matter in itself is infinite because it lacks completion. In the third way, an end is defined according to its proper meaning, which is "to be that, for the sake of which something is." And so finitude is referred to an end on account of its ordination to an end, and infinitude through a lack of such ordination. Thus, the evil of sin is described as infinite.

In the first sense, according to which finitude and infinitude are described quantitatively, God is infinite. But there are two kinds of quantity, as Augustine says [in *The Measure of the Soul* 3], namely, dimensional and virtual (*virtualis*). Insofar as finitude and infinitude pertain to dimensional quantity, neither is in God, because there is no such quantity in him. In terms of virtual quantity, however, which is present in God, he is called infinite. But because power (*virtus*) and essence are in all respects indivisible in God, he cannot be infinite in power without also being infinite in essence. Where power and essence differ, however, what belongs to one does not belong to the other.

2. To the second objection, one can reply that completeness can be defined in two ways, namely, through itself or through another. What is complete through itself is called an end because an end is that which completes. What is complete through another, however, is attributed only to those things which are oriented toward an end. For an end is completed not from another but from itself. Therefore, since "finite" or "finished" (*finitum*) implies that

something is finished or completed with the help of something else, because it is a passive form,[3] for this reason it does not follow that "it is an end; therefore it is not infinite," or "therefore it is finite" but "therefore, it is the one that finishes [or completes something else]." Thus, it does not follow that if God is complete or perfect, as he is perfect in himself, as the end of all things, that he himself is finite but only that he is the one who finishes [or completes] all things.

3. To the third objection, it must be said that something should not be called finite because it is this and not that, but because it is terminated in something or because it exists on account of something else or because it is perfected by another. And this is assumed on the basis of the threefold meaning of an "end" (because "finite" is derived from "end" [*finis*]): indeed, a "term" is an "end"; "that for the sake of which something is" is an "end"; and "perfection" is an "end." But these kinds of ends do not pertain to the divine essence. Indeed, it is not terminated by another, and there is no essence in which it does not exist essentially, even if [those essences] were infinite—in fact, he is the end of all things and not the other way around. Similarly, he does not exist for the sake of other things, but all others exist for his sake. Similarly, he is not perfected by another but perfects other things. Thus it is clear that he cannot be called finite. Indeed, that argument misunderstands the nature of what is finite, as was also demonstrated in the arguments for the affirmative.

4. To the fourth argument, it must be said that as in a thing that is ordered to a formal cause, excellence consists in being formed, so in a thing that is ordered to an end, excellence consists in being completed; and because all creatures are ordered to an end, therefore, in all creatures excellence consists in being finite. Similarly, in those things that have order to an efficient cause, excellence consists in being effects, but in the one who causes, this is not excellence but deficiency. Also, in a form it would be ignobility that it would be formed and in an end that it would be completed. Therefore, to be an effect, to be formed, to be finite—all these things are signs of excellence in creatures, because they are ordained to an efficient, formal, and final cause. In God, however, who is the first efficient cause and first exemplary form of all things, these things would pertain to ignobility, and therefore those things that are contrary to them are signs of excellence in him.

---

3. That is, a past passive participle in Latin.

5. To the fifth objection, it must be said that God is the efficient, formal or exemplar and final cause. According to the first two types of causality, creatures are related to God as to that from which they are, or as to their principle. However, insofar as he is a final cause, creatures are ordered to him. Therefore, although finite things lead to God to a greater degree insofar as he is the end, nevertheless, [they do not lead to him] insofar as he is the efficient or exemplar cause: in fact, it is the infinite that better leads to him in these ways, when he is considered in terms of efficient and exemplary causality. Thus prime matter, which is infinite in passive potency, tends to the infinite power of God, not because it is ordained to him as to an end but because it is ordained to him as its efficient and exemplar cause. And in this mode, it better leads to him than it would if it were finite in potency. Similarly, rational creatures which have an infinite potential to know things, because they are always able to understand more things [than they do already], tend to God more as their efficient and exemplar cause than if they were finite. Similarly, the infinite duration of rational creatures better leads to God insofar as he is eternal than finite duration, because this [infinity] is his image, and that [finitude] is not, "for it would not be his image, if it faltered at the end of death," as Cassiodorus says [in *De anima* 2]. Therefore, although finitude in a certain way better leads to God than infinity, [it does] not [do so] unconditionally, and is even a worse conduit under other conditions. . . .

DOES GOD KNOW THROUGH ONE OR THROUGH MANY?

SH 1, P1, In1, Tr5, S1, Q un., M2, C3 (n. 166), 248–49

1. It seems that he knows through many, [as noted in] Augustine's *83 Questions* [46.2], "the things existing in divine knowledge are nothing other than the reasons of things existing in the divine knowledge." However, as he says in the same place, "all singular things are created according to their proper reasons; the human being is created according to one reason, a horse, another." Therefore, singular things have their proper reasons; but God knows these things through reasons; therefore, he knows them through many.

2. Every kind of being has existence in God. But being is distinguished according to one and many. Thus, in God there is an exemplar of unity and one of multiplicity. As God therefore knows one thing through one exemplar, so he knows many through many exemplars.

3. Either God knows one through one or one through many. If he knows through many, then our case is made. But if he knows through one, then, since he knows all things through their own mode, and since in him all things are one, he only knows one thing.

On the other hand:

a. Dionysius, *The Divine Names* [5.7] says that "in the whole cause of all things," that is, in the perfect cause of all, "all natures of singulars are brought together through one unconfused unity." Here he posits the example of the unity of a center. Therefore, all singular natures are known through such a united one.

b. Also in *The Divine Names* [7.2], "God universally knows many as one." As he says, "the divine wisdom, knowing himself, knows all things and universally knows many as one."

Reply:

God knows all things through himself, and he knows all things through one. And the reason for this is that it is more perfect to know many things and one through one thing than many through many or one through one. Since whatever is more perfect must be attributed to God, he knows both one and many through one. An example of such oneness is if we granted unity an ability to understand its essence, power, and relations—which is similar [to granting comprehensive understanding] to a [geometrical] center or point. If this were to be granted, then the unity that comprehends itself would understand its unity as well as its power. And since its power consists in the fact that from its multiplication every number arises, it would know every number by knowing its own power. Likewise God, understanding himself, understands all things. The same is true of a center: if it were to understand itself and its power, by one simple [act of] intellection it would understand the infinite number of lines that can be drawn out from it.[4]

Replies to the objections:

1. To the objection that "singular things are created according to their own proper reasons," it must be said that this argument is invalid, namely, that "reasons are many, and God knows through reasons; therefore, he knows through many." For [we can think of] the reasons as both multiple and as

---

4. This example is taken from Pseudo-Dionysius's *The Divine Names*, chapter 5, section 6.

one. When we think of them in terms of the one to whom they belong, [namely, God,] there is only one reason. When we think of them in terms of those things of which they are reasons, then there are many. A good example of this can be taken from the relationship of a point to lines. While the point considered in its own right is simple and one, when we think of it in terms of the multiple lines that come from it, it is many.[5] Thus, the fallacy of accident is committed by the one who argues that [God knows through many]. For insofar as he knows things through himself, there are not many reasons but only one.

2. To the other [objection], we must reply that God as one knows both one and many; indeed, "one" is the exemplar of unity and multiplicity. Insofar as it is in act, "one" is considered the exemplar of unity, but when it is considered in potency, it is the exemplar of multiplicity.

3. To the one who objects that God "knows things as they are in him, and in him, they are one; therefore, he knows only one thing," it must be said that this is invalid. It is not the case that he only knows one thing. Rather, it should be inferred that he knows things as one. . . .

DOES GOD HAVE KNOWLEDGE OF SINGULARS?

SH 1, P1, In1, Tr5, S1, Q un., M3, C6 (n. 173), 256–57
That he does:

1. The human intellect does not consider singulars but only universals. The reason for this is that the human intellect is immaterial and not located in place and time, but singulars pertain to the here and now. Since the divine intellect is supremely immaterial and abstracted from space and time, it cannot have knowledge of singulars.

2. Aristotle shows in *Metaphysics* [11.9] that God does not know any other than himself, because his intellect would otherwise become degraded.

3. Augustine says in *Enchiridion* [17], "it is better not to know some things than to know them," for example, inferior or base things. If, therefore, [singular] things are inferior with respect to the divine knowledge and goodness, it is better to ignore than to know them.

On the other hand:

a. Augustine says in *City of God* 11.[22], "From the earth to the heavens, from visible to invisible, there are some things that are good and others that

---

5. That is, each line would have its own point when passing through this one point.

are better, and things are unequal in order to make a whole. However, God is the artificer of great things in such a way that he is no less of the artificer of small things." Therefore, God is equally skilled at making great and small things, and in his art he equally knows great and small things.

b. Further, that which creatures can know, God cannot fail to know. If, therefore, creatures can know singulars, God cannot be ignorant of singulars. And this must be conceded.

Replies to the objections:

1. In response to the first objection, some say that our inability to cognize singulars derives from an imperfection in our intellect, not from its immateriality. However, another position—the more accurate one—is that the human intellect does understand singulars. For the intellect receives the species of a thing and [thus] understands that thing: "for a stone is not in the soul, but the species of the stone" [Aristotle, *On the Soul* 3.8], by which, however, the stone itself is understood. As for Boethius's statement that it is not the singular but the universal that is understood, this refers to the species received by the intellect. The species, as such, has the nature of a universal. At the same time, it is the thing whose species it is—that is, something singular—that is understood through the species.

Note, therefore, that the human intellect understands singulars through their species or likenesses, which are received through the support of the senses; the angelic intellect accepts a singular through its species or likeness, which is not received through the assistance of the senses. For the intellectual power of the angel is just as capable of cognizing universals and singulars through the intellect as the cognition of the rational soul is capable insofar as it is divided according to the senses which cognize singulars and the intellect which cognizes universals. Therefore, both the human and the angelic intellects understand singulars through a species or a likeness, which is in the intellect but which is not the one who understands. But they do this in different ways, for the human intellect does this through the guidance of the senses, the angel, through itself. The divine intellect does not understand singulars through the support of the senses or through a species or likeness that is other than the one understanding, but by himself or through a likeness that is himself.

To the objection, then, that the "human intellect does not cognize singulars, because it is immaterial," one must respond through negation and by adding that immateriality is not the reason why singulars are not understood, because then angels would not understand them. Rather, immateriality is the reason why a species or likeness of a thing that is received by the intellect, as such, is not a singular but rather a universal, insofar as it is a likeness or exemplar of many similar things.

2. To the second objection, where the philosopher says that "God cannot know anything other than himself, lest he become worthless," we must reply that this does not mean that God does not know anything other than himself, but that he does not know things outside himself, but rather knows them in himself, the cause of those things. For in knowing himself as the cause of all, he knows all things, and therefore his cognition of them does not depend on knowable things in the way of the human intellect. For if a point or center from which were drawn out many lines had an understanding of itself, in knowing itself, the cause and beginning of all lines, it would know all those lines.

3. To the third objection, one must reply that Augustine in his authoritative statement in the *Enchiridion* takes "ignore" to mean "not to approve," and so it can be said that God ignores sin. Thus, what I call "worthless or vile things" in this case mean sins, not the least or least noble creatures. . . .

IS DIVINE POWER PRIOR TO OR DOES IT EXTEND FURTHER THAN THE DIVINE WILL?

SH 1, P1, In1, Tr4, Q1, M2, C2 (n. 135), 206–7

We will now compare the meanings of "power" and "will" as regards both order and extension.

I. As regards order, it is objected: 1. Anselm in the book *Cur Deus Homo* 2.[10], "every power is the consequence of will."

2. Wisdom 13:18, "*Lord, if you should will [something], your power is subject to you.*"

3. As Hugh of St. Victor says in his *On the Sacraments* [1.6], "the will moves, knowledge organizes, and power operates." Thus, it remains that will is prior to knowledge and power.

On the other hand:

a. As willing relates to being able to do something, so will to relates to power, but being able to do something always precedes willing; therefore, power precedes will.

II. Further, we will inquire about the reach or extent [of power].

a. Now, Augustine says in his *Questions on the Old and New Law* [q. 97], "God surely can do all things, but he does only that, which befits his truth and justice," that is, his will which is true and just. Therefore, his power extends further than his will.

b. Augustine in the same work [q. 106] says, "God was able to make everything collectively at once, but reason prohibited it," "that is, his will," as Master Lombard explains in his *Sentences* 1.42.

c. Power is related to all possibilities but the will [merely] to all goods. However, there are more possibilities than there are goods. Therefore, power extends further than the will.

On the other hand:

1. Whatever God does, he wants to do, and whatever he is able to do, he wills to be able to do. Therefore, he wills those things to be possible for himself which are [in fact] possible for him. Therefore, his will extends not only to actual goods but even to all things that are possible for God.

2. The will also extends both to the divine being and divine activity, as when it is said that "God wills himself to be, God wills to act." In addition, he is said to will the action that is eternal, as when it is said, "God wills to understand," as well as temporal action, as when it is said that "he wills to create." Since everything within his power can also be subject to his will, his power does not extend beyond his will.

3. Ambrose in his *Commentary on Luke* 5:12 says, commenting on the phrase, "*Lord, if you will, you can make me clean*": "Here you see beyond any doubt that God's will is his power." Therefore, the will and power of God are coequal.

4. It is objected: since God makes many things according to his mercy, Augustine seems to say something false when he says, "God makes only that, which befits his truth and justice" [*Questions on the Old and New Law*, q. 97].

5. It seems false to say, with Augustine, that "God was able to make everything at once, but his reason prohibited it" [*Questions on the Old and New Law*, q. 106], because what prohibits is contrary to that which it prohibits. If, therefore, reason were to inhibit power, then will would be contrary to power. Furthermore, "reason" either refers to something created or uncreated. It is not created because nothing created can inhibit the divine power; if it is uncreated, namely, if it is the divine will, then the will is contrary to divine power.

Reply:

I. With regard to the initial inquiry regarding order, we must say that there are two kinds of power, namely, the power of being able and the power of executing, or power in habit and power in effect. When we speak of the power of being able or power in habit, then power is understood to be prior to the will. But when we speak of the power of executing or power in effect, then will is prior. For the will is the cause of the execution of an act which is elicited immediately from power.

Replies to objections 1–3:

1–2–3. We should not take the objections of the authorities to signify that power is subject to the will or that it follows it as such. Although willing derives from being able, in God, however, these two things are understood to be the same. But because the execution of power in act is from the will, therefore, it is said that power follows will by virtue of its object, but not in itself. This is what Anselm means in *Why God Became Man* [2.10] when he says that "every exercise of power follows the will. For when I say that 'I am able to speak or to walk' this implies 'if I will to do so.' For if my will is not presupposed, then there will not be an ability but necessity." And this makes clear the reply to the objections.

II. To the objection regarding the matter of extension, we must say that these notions of power and will are coequal and interpenetrate one another if they are defined in relation either to being or acting, and if through acting, according to an eternal or a temporal act, and if according to a temporal act, insofar as that concerns the eliciting or ordaining of an act. Nevertheless, when we consider absolute power in relation to the will, power extends further than the will. As regards ordained power, understanding ordination in the sense of preordination, power and will are coequal. Thus, we must distinguish absolute from ordained power. Absolute power extends to those things that were not preordained by God. Ordained power pertains to those things which are preordained by God, that is, those things which are disposed by God. And this makes clear the reply [to the objection]. This will be made clear more amply below in the section on God's knowledge.

Reply to the objections:

4. To the one who objects against Augustine that "God does many things from his mercy and therefore not from his justice," we must say that justice can be defined in two ways. One mode involves retribution for each and every person according to their merit; and in this sense God does not do all things from his justice. The other mode involves what befits his goodness, and in this way he does all things from justice, nor does he do anything unless it befits justice.

5. To the one who objects that "reason prohibits" God, we reply that *ratio* refers principally to the divine will, but it connotes order in creatures with respect to things that will come into existence, above all, the ordering of merit to reward and guilt to punishment. For it would be contrary to order if one were punished prior to committing a crime or rewarded without prior merit. When, therefore, it is said that "*ratio*, that is, the will, has prohibited" something, this does not mean that the will prohibits power as such but only the exercise of power. Further, prohibition does not refer to the principal [referent], which is the divine will, but to that which is connoted together with it. Moreover, "prohibition" is used in this case [i.e., for God] catachrestically, namely, for that which is the cause or the principle that prevents something from happening....

IS DIVINE POWER LIMITED BY GOD'S GOODNESS AND JUSTICE?

SH 1, P1, In1, Tr4, Q2, M2, C2 (n. 141), 219–21

I. One can argue that [God's power can be limited] by his goodness and justice along the following lines:

1. "God can only do what is good and just for him to do; therefore, nothing is good and just for him to do except what he [actually] does—otherwise he would not have done *all* that is good and just for him to do." Therefore, he can only do that which he [actually] does.

2. "God can only do what his justice demands; but his justice does not demand that he do anything other than what he does. Therefore, he is not able to do anything other than he does."

3. God is not able to do or omit anything unless he ought to do so; but he is not required to do or omit anything except what he actually does or omits. Thus, he is able to do only that which he does or omits.

II. Next we consider whether God is able to do only what is just or if he is able to do by his power what he is not able to do by his justice.

1. Galatians 4:15: "*if it were possible, you would have torn your eyes out and given them to me.*" The Gloss says: "What cannot be done justly, cannot be done." Therefore, God is not able to do anything unless it is just.

2. Also, if he can potentially [do] something due to his [absolute] power that justice [i.e., his ordained power] would not allow him [to do], [and if]

this potential were to be actualized, then the [result] would be either just or unjust. If it is unjust, then God can do what is unjust; if just, then he can only do what is just.

III. Next we consider if God can damn Peter and save Judas.

1. 2 Timothy 2:13, "*he cannot deny himself.*" Augustine's gloss says: "Since he is just, he cannot deny his justice." Thus, the Gloss says that "the fact that he cannot deny himself speaks to the glory of the divine will, just as the fact that some cannot believe is the fault of the human will." On this basis, we argue that his inability to deny Peter glory and Judas punishment speaks to the glory of the divine will.

IV. Further, we consider whether it is possible for the damned to be liberated by God.

a. Now eternal punishment is justly owed to every damned person, and it is just to give everyone what is owed them, for if the damned were liberated, they would become so unjustly.

b. Also, the following confirms the same: "in hell there is no redemption," and Wisdom 2:1, "*the one who is brought back from the flames is not recognized.*"

On the other hand:

1. Genesis 19:22, "*I am not able to do anything before you come out.*" And in the Gloss, attributed to Augustine, "without doubt he could do something through his power but not through his justice," namely, to destroy Lot with the Sodomites. Therefore, he is able through his power to damn Peter and save Judas and whoever else is damned, although he cannot do so through his justice.

2. Similarly, he is able to bring Peter back from Paradise to this life, just as he can bring Judas back from hell. As, therefore, in this life we are able to endure in grace and to sin, Peter is able finally to sin and Judas ultimately to remain in grace, such that God is able to damn Peter and even save Judas justly.

3. Are not many brought back from death even though they were justly damned? Thus, it remains that God did something from power that was not from his justice.

Reply:

I. According to Hugh of St. Victor [*On the Sacraments* 1.2.22], "as time does not equal the eternity of God, nor place his immensity, nor the senses his wisdom, nor virtue his goodness, so neither his works can compare to his power." For this power exceeds his work to an infinite degree.

Replies to the objections:

1. In reply to the first argument, which says that "God is able to do only what is good and just," we must distinguish between different uses of the copula "is" which can signify either the "present indefinite," or a habitual state, or the "present continuous," namely, something that is actually happening now. The first use is true in this sense, "God is able to do only what would be good and just, if in fact he were to do it." The second use is false in this sense: "God is able to do only presently existing good and just things."

2. To the second argument, it must be said that this verb "to demand" is strictly speaking a verb of requirement, but no verb of requirement befits God. Nevertheless, accepted improperly, it signifies something that is congruent with God. Thus, we must draw the following distinction: when we say, "God is able to do only what his justice demands," if the verb "demand" implies habitual congruence, it is true, as if the sense were, "if he does anything, he is able to do only what would be consistent with his justice." If it implies congruence that actually exists now, however, it is false to say that "he is able to do only what currently befits his justice."

3. In response to the third argument, we must say that the word "ought" does not befit God in its proper sense because it is a verb of obligation; but considered improperly, insofar as "ought" means "to befit," we can draw the same distinction as before, because if we speak of what befits God habitually, it is true, but if we speak of [what befits God] actually now, it is false.

II. In reply to the objection that deals with "whether he can do by his absolute power what he cannot do by his justice," it must be distinguished that the justice of God in one sense connotes what befits the divine goodness. And in this sense, whatever he can do from power, he can do from justice, or what befits his goodness; for it befits the highest goodness to be able to do whatever is possible for its power. In another sense it connotes what is congruent with merit; and in this sense he is not able to do by his justice, which is given to us according to what is consistent with our merit, whatever he is able to do by his power.

1. To the one who objects that "God cannot do anything unless it is just," we understand this to mean that "he is not able to do anything [unless it is just] in the sense of his ordained power only." For although humans are said

to be capable of acting by right (*de jure*) and in principle (*de facto*), from a legal standpoint we say that we are only able to do what we are able to do by right. For God, however, what is possible in principle and by right is the same, insofar as what is "right" refers to what befits the divine goodness. Thus, "to do what is just" is understood one way with respect to human beings and another way with respect to God. With respect to human beings, justice is done when a human does something that is just.[6] On the part of God, however, justice is done by the mere fact of God acting. Thus, it follows that "he cannot do anything unless it is just" in the aforementioned sense, namely, that "if he does it, it is just."

2. The reply to the subsequent objection is clear.

III. To the one who inquires "whether God can damn Peter," we must say that the power of God can be understood in two senses: in one sense as absolute and in the other as ordained in accordance with the divine preordination of justice, which is distributed to each one according to merit. By his absolute power, God can damn Peter and save Judas; but by his ordained power, insofar as it is preordained to give recompense according to merit, he cannot. That is not to derogate his power, but to demonstrate the immutability of his ordained power according to what is preordained and just. In a similar way, we must say that he could bring Peter and Judas back to life, etc.

IV. To the one who inquires about the damned, it must be said that Hugh of St. Victor in his *On the Sacraments* [1.8.8] makes the following distinction: "justice is one thing so far as it concerns the responsibility of the one doing it, and another thing so far as it concerns the merit of the recipient. In the first way, it concerns power, in the second, fairness." "Thus, God receiving to salvation some of the whole mass of the human race, deploys the justice that he should [deploy] by his power; and in deserting some to perdition, he deploys his justice [to accomplish] what is permitted by fairness: he does the former on the basis of what is owed, the latter on the basis of our merit. However, if he were to desert those he now receives to salvation, that would not be an injustice, because they would [then] receive what they deserve according to the justice of fairness. If, however, he were to save those whom he now deserts, likewise, it would not be an injustice, because he would deploy in their salvation the justice of his power."

---

6. That is, something that is defined as just prior to the act.

3. To the one who objects that liberty can be obtained through the prayers of the saints, we must reply that liberty cannot be achieved through one's own merits, but rather that some may be liberated through the [accumulated] merits of the Church. Nevertheless, we must note that hell is an eternal and most bitter punishment; no one, therefore, who is enslaved to infernal punishment for eternity can be liberated, but only those enslaved to infernal punishment with regard to its bitterness, and this not according to their own merit, but according to that of another, as in the case of those who are resurrected by the prayers of the saints.

CHAPTER 5

THE TRANSCENDENTALS

THE ESSENCE OF "ONENESS"

SH 1, P1, In1, Tr3, Q1, M1, C1 (n. 72), 112–13

I. The first matter for discussion is the definition of "one" proposed by the Philosopher [*Physics* 3.7; *Metaphysics* 9.3]: "One" refers to a being that is undivided in itself but separated from other [beings], and unity refers to the lack of division in a being.

Objection:

1. Every definition must be given based on what is prior and better known; however, this definition is given based on what is posterior and less immediately known (because it is based on "being undivided," which is the same as lack of division; however, division is posterior to and less immediately known than unity, because it becomes known through unity; by the same token, being undivided is less immediately known than unity); therefore, the aforesaid definition is faulty.

II. Also, one asks whether "one," which belongs to first intentions,[1] can be clarified through something prior [to it].

Arguments in favor:

1. "One" posits the notion of "being" and over and above ["being"] adds another notion that is defined by a type of positing; therefore, "one" could be clarified through "being" and that superadded notion as through something that is prior to it: indeed, both "being" and that notion that is added to being are understood to be prior to "one."

2. "Good" characterizes being in relation to the final cause, "true" characterizes being in some respect in relation to the formal cause, and "one" characterizes being in some respect in relation to the efficient cause; therefore, [all] these [i.e., good, true, and one] can be clarified through "being" and those [additional] notions as through something prior [to good, true, and one].

---

1. In Western medieval philosophy, first intentions are natural signs in the soul that refer to things, whereas second intentions refer to first intentions or concepts in the mind.

To the contrary:

a. Suppose that those things that are of first intention could be clarified by a notion added to "being." Then, since this includes the notion of "being" and in addition to that something added over and above ["being"], [this first intention] can be defined through "being" and that added notion; but then either we must, in turn, inquire about that notion, and so forth ad infinitum, or we should not move beyond the first stage. Therefore, first intentions cannot be defined through something prior [to them].

Reply:

II. One must say that because "being" is the first intelligible, its meaning is familiar to the intellect; therefore, the first determinations of being—which are one, true, and good, as will become clear later—are the first impressions of the intellect; therefore, there could be nothing prior to them specifically for the purpose of making them known. Therefore, if they do become known, this can only be through something posterior, for example, through a negation or a consequent effect. This is why the recognition of "one" goes both by way of negation and by way of consequent effect. The negation is of the opposite meaning, which is "division" or "multitude," when we refer to a being as "undivided." The consequent effect is to distinguish [this being] from other [beings]: indeed, unity distinguishes "one" from another, and therefore [that one] is referred to as "separated from other [beings]."

Replies to the objections:

I. 1. To the objection that [every] "definition must be given based on what is prior and better known" one must reply that "prior and better known" can be taken in an unqualified sense or in relation to us. Now since there is nothing "prior and better known" to the first impressions of the intellect in an unqualified sense, these [first impressions] cannot become known through something prior in an unqualified sense, but they can become known through something "prior and better known" in relation to us. And what is better known to us is that which first occurs to our senses; but what first occurs to our senses is separateness and distinction; however, multitude or division are opposites of unity, and distinction is its consequent effect.

II. 1. To the objection that [unity] "can become known based on the notion added over and above being, which [notion] is, however, prior," one must reply that the notion that is added to being is not different from unity, because unity is [one of] the first determinations of being, and therefore "to make [something] known through this [notion of unity]" amounts to "one and the same thing becoming known through itself." Therefore, if it does become known, this can only be through something posterior, that is, either by means of negating an opposite meaning or by means of positing a consequent effect.

2. This clarifies how to respond to the rest.

HOW DOES "ONE" RELATE TO "BEING," "TRUE," AND "GOOD"?

SH 1, P1, In1, Tr3, Q1, M1, C2 (n. 73), 113–16

I. The first objection concerns the perception of the relation between "one" and "being" as one of difference.

1. According to Dionysius [*On the Divine Names* 12.2, who says that] "no being is deprived of unity," "one" is interchangeable with "being." But then the meaning of "one" would not seem to add anything to "being"—because if it does add something, this added determination would contract the intention "being" and restrict it to fewer supposits than the intention "being" in its absolute sense. But then "oneness" would not be interchangeable with "being" in an unqualified sense, which is false. It remains, then, that it does not add [anything to being].

2. When vestiges of the Trinity are attributed to creatures using the intentions "unity," "truth," and "goodness," the intentions "one" and "being" are used interchangeably and are predicated of one and the same thing, which is attributed to the Father, just as truth is attributed to the Son and goodness to the Holy Spirit; therefore, the intentions "one" and "being" are not separate. . . .

The following makes it clear. Augustine says in *83 Questions* [18]: in everything "that exists, that which constitutes it, that which makes it detectible, and that which makes it fitting are different things"; "that which constitutes it" is entity; "that which makes it detectible" is truth; "that which makes it fitting" is goodness. And in *On the Trinity* [6.10.12] he presents [vestiges of] the Trinity differently by saying: "all things produced by divine art display some unity, shape, and order." If we align [the two characterizations], "order," as something through which a thing fits in, corresponds to goodness; "shape," through which a thing is detectible, corresponds to truth; but then "unity," which constitutes a thing, corresponds to entity.

Also, [Augustine says] in *On the City of God* [11.28]: "We detect vestiges of the Trinity in those things that are positioned below us through the fact that they exist, that they have some shape, and that they either have or desire order." So just as shape is the vestige of the Son, and order of the Holy Spirit, so being is the vestige of the Father. But in *On True Religion* [7] he also says: "Every substance, essence, or nature, or whatever you may call it, if you find a better word, has these three: it must be something one; it must have its own detectible shape; and it must fit into the order of things." But then it is "one" that is the vestige of the Father. Therefore, the intention "one" is the same intention as "being," and it does not add anything to being.

To the contrary:

a. "Many" is not opposed to "being," because "many" are contained under "being"; however, "many" is opposed to "oneness"; therefore, to say "one" signals some addition to "being."

II. Another set of objections opposes the distinction between "one" and "true":

1. "True" refers to how one thing is distinguished from another. This is clear, for the truth of a thing is associated with its shape, and, as the book *On True Religion* [31] says, shape is what distinguishes one thing from another. But the whole point of the intention "unity" is also to distinguish [one thing from another] (which is clear from the nature of [something] "one," which is "undivided in itself, but separated from other [beings]"); therefore, the intentions "unity" and "truth" will not differ.

2. As some proposed, following the philosophers, truth is the absence of division between existence and that which exists; however, the absence of division of being is unity; therefore, the essence of unity and truth is the same.

To the contrary:

a. Multitude and falsity are not the same thing; moreover, multitude contains truth, as in the case of multiple true things; therefore, the essence of unity and truth is not the same.

III. There are also objections as regards the relation between "one" and "good":

1. Boethius says in *The Consolation of Philosophy* [III, pr. 11]: "Everything that craves subsistence and persistence, desires to be 'one'; therefore, all things desire oneness." But since the same author defines the essence of the good as "that which all desire," it remains that "one" and "good" mean the same thing.

To the contrary:

a. "One" is understood even when one fails to understand "good"; moreover, oneness is predicated of something evil, when one says, "one evil thing"; therefore, "one" and "good" do not mean the same thing.

Thus far the questioning has concerned how things are relatively different.

IV. In addition, one can pose questions about how things are relatively ordered:

1. As Boethius says in *On the Trinity* [2], "Everything beyond the first is constituted of this and that"; but then, in order for a thing to exist, it is necessary for the unity of those [parts] that constitute it to precede [this thing] as [its] cause; therefore, unity would be the cause of entity; therefore, "one" is prior to "being." By the same token [unity] will be the cause of truth, because truth follows this unity.

2. Boethius says in *The Consolation of Philosophy* [III, pr. 11]: "If you take away unity, there will not be any existence in anything"; similarly, there will not [be any] true existence; therefore, unity is the cause of entity and truth.

3. Boethius says in *The Consolation of Philosophy* [ibid.]: "As long as there is disagreement in things, they are minimally good; however, when they acquire unity, they become good; therefore, it is the acquisition of unity that is responsible for their goodness." Therefore, unity is the cause of goodness.

Reply:

One must say that "being" is the first intelligible; however, the first determinations of being are "one," "true," and "good": indeed, they delimit being insofar as the being of things is considered in their own kind; also insofar as their being is related to the divine cause; finally, insofar as things are related to the soul, which is an image of the divine essence.

Now, insofar as the being of things is considered in their own kind, there are three determinations of being. Indeed, being is considered either as absolute or as relative. In its turn, relative being is considered either as far as difference is concerned or as far as agreement is concerned. Insofar as a being is considered as absolute, undivided in itself, and separated from other [beings], it is delimited by "oneness." However, insofar as a being is considered in relation to another [being] in terms of its distinctness, it is delimited by "truth," for "true" stands for the ability of a thing to be detectible. However, insofar as [a being] is considered in relation to another [being] in terms of agreement or order, it is delimited by "goodness," for "good" stands for the ability of a thing to fit into an order.

Similarly, insofar as the being of things is taken in relation to the divine cause, it has three determinations. For the divine cause causes in three ways: as an efficient cause, as a formal or exemplary cause, and as a final cause. And although all this causality is common to the entire Trinity, its efficient aspect is appropriated to the Father, exemplary to the Son, and final to the Holy Spirit. In accordance with this [triple causality] the being of creatures, which emanates from its cause, is impacted in three ways, in conformity with the [three types of] cause. The impact that results from conformity to efficient causality in creaturely being is unity: as the efficient cause, which is one and undivided, impacts a multitude of creatures, each acquires, to the extent of its ability, undivided being. Next, the impact that results from conformity to formal or exemplary causality [in creaturely being] is truth: as the exemplary cause is the primary art of truth, so every creature, to the extent of its ability, receives an imprint of this art, which amounts to possessing truth. In addition to that, the impact that results from conformity to final causality [in creaturely being] is goodness: as the final cause is the highest goodness, every creature has a proclivity and conformity to the highest goodness, which is the goodness of creatures. Thus, the unity of being of creatures demonstrates the unity of the efficient cause; the truth [of being of creatures demonstrates] the truth of the exemplary cause, and the goodness [of being of creatures demonstrates] the goodness of the final cause.

Also, insofar as [the being of things] is taken in relation to the soul, it has three determinations. Indeed, the being of things is related to the soul in three ways: namely, as things are ordered in the memory, as they are perceived by the intellect, and as they are desired by the will. Every being possesses unity from the efficient cause, which allows it to be ordered and saved in the memory—for the memory organizes the things that it retains according to a pattern of unity and difference among them. Also, every being possesses truth from the exemplary cause, which allows it to be perceived by the intellect. Finally, [every being possesses] goodness from the final cause, which makes it desirable to or approved by the will.

I. To the first inquiry, as to whether "one" adds anything different to "being," I say that it does. And this addition is a determination of the being of a thing that allows it to have independent existence, to conform to the first efficient cause, and to be able to be ordered in the memory. None of this is implied by what "being" means but is communicated by what "one" means.

Replies to the objections:

1. To the first objection, that "this determination will contract 'being,'" one must reply that "contracting" is taken in two senses: insofar as [contracting] the conceptual range [of a thing] is concerned, and insofar as [contracting] the existential range of the supposits is concerned. One must say, then, that when the determination of unity is added to "being," it contracts the latter as far as its conceptual range is concerned. Indeed, when I say "one," I do not imply "being" in any sense whatsoever, but only in the limited sense of being undivided. However, as far as the [existential] range of the supposits is concerned, ["one"] does not contract ["being"], because no being exists without participating in unity, as Dionysius says [in *On the Divine Names* 13.2]: "Just as every number, whether it be one half, a pair, or a dozen, is referred to as "one" and therewith participates in unity, in the same way every thing, and every little part of every thing, participates in unity, and the existence of every being consists in being a unit."

But what if one objects: therefore, what it means to be "one" contains "many"? One must reply that this is true insofar as "one" is taken in its common sense and "many" implies an act of existence—for they have their act of existence through their relation to "one." However, insofar as the meaning of "one" is contracted to "oneness" in an unqualified sense, a difference and opposition to "many" emerges.

2. To the second objection, that "'one' and 'being' mean one and the same thing when speaking of vestiges of the Trinity," this must be conceded. However, it does not follow from this that there is no difference in meaning between the two. Take the case when our intellect thinks of some being. Indeed, it is thought of as undivided together with [being thought of as a being], and therefore [both "being" and "one"] are understood to refer to one and the same thing. And yet this sense of undividedness is not communicated by "being" but by "one." However, the situation is not the same in the case of the meanings "true" and "good." Indeed, our intellect can think of "being" without thinking of "good." Similarly, as far as the thing itself is concerned, it can be thought of as existing without also thinking of it as true—unless

the nature of the understanding, which is incapable of understanding anything apart from what is true, disallows this.²

II. To the question about the distinction between "one" and "true," the difference is clear from what has been said.

Replies to the objections:

1. To the objection that "of themselves, both one and true distinguish [one thing from another]," one must reply that two things are distinguished insofar as they are separated from each other in their real existence or insofar as they are separated as two objects of the intellect when they become known. The first type of distinction is brought about by unity, the second, by truth.

2. To the other objection, one must reply according to an opinion voiced by a number of people. All three—"one," "true," and "good"—have to do with undividedness. However, if we consider "one," undividedness in this case means undividedness of being (*ens*): something "one" is an undivided being. If we consider "true," [undividedness in this case means] undividedness of existence (*esse*), because truth is the absence of division between existence and that which exists. If we consider "good," [undividedness in this case means] undividedness of completeness from the potential of becoming complete, when it reaches its end: hence, goodness is the absence of division between act and potency, and act is called the perfection or completeness [of potency]. For in the case of the absence of division between the principles as they constitute a thing in its being in an unqualified sense, this [absence of division] gives things their unity. And in the case of the absence of division insofar as [the principles] constitute this thing in its being-known, this type gives [things their] truth. Finally, in the case of the absence of division between the principles as they constitute a thing in its ordering toward its end, this type gives [things their] goodness.

III. To the third question,³ about the relation between "one" and "good," one must reply that the relation between "one," "true," and "good" is one of circumincession, or reciprocal existence in each other. Hence, as far as "true," "one," and even "good" itself become objects of desire, they put on the trappings of the final cause and are all desired as "good." Similarly, insofar as they

---

2. Because "truth" can always be understood in terms of the relation between the thing and the intellect, that is, as far as this thing is understood by the intellect, whether it is true or not in itself.

3. This paragraph has been paraphrased instead of translated in order to avoid repetition.

are perceived by the intellect, they put on the trappings of the true and are understood insofar as they are all "true," including truth itself. Similarly, insofar as they are ordered in the memory, they put on the trappings of unity and are all ordered in the memory as "one," including unity itself. Consequently, one must say that something is principally desired not by virtue of its own nature, but as something good, and not in any other way.

IV. To the fourth question, about order, one must reply that the meaning of "being" naturally precedes the meaning of "one," and the meaning of "one" [naturally precedes] the meanings of "true" and "good." Indeed, "being" is more absolute than "one," as has been shown. In addition, "one," which characterizes a being insofar as it is considered as something absolute, is more absolute than "true" and "good," which characterize a being in relation [to something else]. Also, "true" is more absolute than "good," for the former [characterizes] the being of a thing considered apart from its utility or [place in the] order [of things], and the latter [characterizes] the being of a thing [considered] together with its utility and [place in the] order [of things].

Replies to the objections:

1–3. To the objection that "unity is the cause of entity," one must reply that if one considers unity and entity in relation to one and the same thing, entity always precedes unity. However, if one considers unity and entity in relation to different things, on occasion unity could precede entity. For example, the unity of the principles that constitute a thing precedes the entity of the composite [that is this thing]. However, if [unity or entity] are considered in relation to one and the same thing, entity in principles precedes unity in principles, and entity in a composite precedes unity in this composite....

DOES THE UNITY OF THE DIVINE BEING ALLOW FOR A PLURALITY OF IDEAS?

SH 1, P1, In1, Tr3, Q1, M2, C4 (n. 80), 130–32

It is shown that it does:

a. Augustine says in *83 Questions* [46.2]: "Ideas are some foundational, stable, and unchangeable forms of things that are contained in the divine intellect. They themselves have not been created, and therefore they are eternal and always in the same state. And while they themselves neither come into being nor perish, nevertheless, they are said to give shape to everything that can come into being and perish." Therefore, if ideas are eternal, foundational forms in the divine being—and by saying "ideas" in the plural I do imply plurality—it is clear that from all eternity there is a plurality of ideas in the divine being. Therefore, the unity of the divine being does allow for a plurality of ideas.

b. If one should object that although "ideas" is said in the plural, yet they are not multiple, Augustine's words in the same work state to the contrary: "It is not absurd to believe that distinct things are created based on their own distinct reasons (*rationes*); indeed, the human being is created based on a different reason than that of the horse"; and by "reasons" he means "ideas." Therefore, ideas are multiple, and they exist from all eternity together with the divine being. Hence, Augustine says [ibid.]: "And where should one think those reasons are except in the mind of the Creator?"

To the contrary:

1. Ideas are reasons that are eternal and unchangeable; therefore, if there are multiple ideas, there are multiple eternal things, and therefore multiple gods, which is false. Therefore, it remains that the unity of the divine being does not tolerate a plurality of ideas.

2. The primary material cause, to which all other matters are reduced, is one. Similarly, there is only one efficient and one final cause. Therefore, similarly, there is only one formal cause, to which all other forms are reduced. However, an idea is a formal and exemplary cause of all, to which all other forms are reduced; therefore, there is only one idea; therefore, there is no plurality of ideas in the divine being.

3. If there are multiple ideas in God, this plurality is either on the part of the thing itself or merely on the part of the intellect. If on the part of the thing: multiple ideas exist in God from all eternity; therefore, multiple [real] things would exist in God from all eternity; therefore, a plurality [of things] exists from all eternity. If on the part of the intellect, then once one prescinds from the intellect, there will be no plurality of ideas.

4. All multiplication comes either from the subject, or from [the passing of] time, or from the final product. However, in the divine being no plurality of ideas can come from the subject, because there is only one substance there—namely, the divine substance—which is completely simple. Similarly, it cannot come from [the passing of] time, because then something temporal would be a cause of something eternal, which is incongruous. Similarly, it cannot come from the final product, that is, from creatures that are modeled on the idea, because then it would follow that the divine being depends on

creatures, which is incongruous. Therefore, if no plurality of ideas can arise in God in any of these multiple ways, it remains that the unity of the divine being does not permit a plurality of ideas.

Solution:

One must reply following the words of Dionysius in *On the Divine Names*, chapter [5.6–7] "On Being": "every number subsists unitarily in the monad. ... However, insofar as [any number] emanates from the monad, it becomes distinct and multiple. In the same way all the [straight] lines of a circle[4] are constituted in its center according to primary unity.... Those [lines] that extend only a short distance [from the center] are separated by short distances, and those that [extend] a long distance exhibit greater separation.... It is the same in the entire nature of all things," that is, in God: "all the reasons of singular natures are brought together [there] by way of a single unmixed unity." Therefore, the situation with [divine] ideas is the same as with the point and unity: if one asks if the latter two are one thing or multiple, one would say that they are one thing in reality, but multiple [distinct things] conceptually. The same should be said about ideas: they are only one thing in reality, but multiple conceptually. Indeed, it is clear from the words of Dionysius that the divine unity is only one, in which all unities created by way of exemplarity are brought together. Therefore, one must reply that an idea in God is the same as the divine essence—however, it signifies the divine essence in a different way. For the divine essence can be signified in an absolute sense: in this sense it is signified by the term "essence." Also, it can be signified as a cause: efficient, final, or formal-exemplary. "Idea," then, signifies the divine essence insofar as it is the formal-exemplary cause, because the [divine essence] is the exemplar of all things. Thus, "idea" signifies two things: first, the divine essence, which is its principal signified, and in this respect "idea" refers to only one thing; also, "idea" has a connotation, and what it connotes is a relation to multiple things, which are modeled on the divine exemplar. In this respect [divine] ideas are multiple, because there are multiple and diverse reasons according to which [things] have been created.

---

4. Dionysius certainly means "all lines that intersect both the circumference and the center of the circle"; otherwise his analogy is false. He might have had in mind the method of finding the center of a circle by drawing any number of chords, finding their middle points, and drawing perpendicular lines from those points, which all intersect at the center of the circle. Obviously, he fails to formulate it correctly.

However, there is an objection: just as "idea" refers to an exemplar, in the same way does "life," as in John 1:3: *"That which was made, in him was life."* However, one does not say that in some sense there are multiple lives in him; therefore, neither [should there be] multiple ideas—for why would one say there is only one life [in him] but multiple ideas?

To this one must reply that the connotations here are different. Indeed, life, idea, and reason (*ratio*) are consonant in terms of being part of God's exemplarity, which is responsible for the formation and existence of creatures; however, [they are all part of God's exemplarity] differently. Indeed, in a being that is being formed "being/existence" comes first, then "being-distinct," and then "being-ordered": this is the way the works of original creation in Genesis 1 are distinguished. Therefore, the divine exemplar can be signified by connoting merely a relation to being: it is in this sense that "life" signifies the divine exemplar, because life implies existence. Or [it can be signified by connoting merely] a relation to "being-distinct": this is how "idea" signifies it. Or [it can be signified by connoting merely] a relation to "being-ordered": this is how "reason" signifies it. Now, because "life" signifies the divine exemplar insofar as it is related to being or existence, and because by saying "being" or "existence" I do not refer to anything that might lead to inferring number in creatures (in fact, all are united in being); therefore, "life" does not connote anything further that might imply multiplicity in it. And because plurality in these [divine] things comes on the part of that which is connoted, and not on the part of the principal signified, which is always one, on this account one cannot refer to multiple lives in any sense—rather all are one life in the Creator, nor is there plurality [in this sense] in relation to things. However, what is connoted by "idea" is something that can be multiplied, because what is connoted here is the distinction of one thing from another, and this is where plurality of ideas comes from. Similarly, "reason" connotes a relation to ordered being in creatures; however, ordered being implies distinction in creatures, because corporeal, spiritual, etc., beings are ordered to different things; therefore, in this respect, there is a plurality of reasons.

Answers to objections:

1. To the first objection, that "if there were multiple ideas, there would be multiple eternal things," one must reply that the term "idea" can be used directly, to signify its primary signified, which is the divine essence or exemplar. "Idea" can also be used indirectly to connote something, such as relations to creatures. Therefore, the expression "multiple ideas" merely

amounts to saying, "an exemplar of many [things]." Therefore, no plurality is implied on the part of the primary signified, but only on the part of that which is connoted. And it does not follow on this account that "there would be multiple eternal things"—rather it follows from this that there would be one eternal exemplar for all things.

2. To the second objection, one must reply that insofar as by "idea" one means exemplary form or exemplar, there is only one such "idea." In this sense "idea" stands for the exemplar of all things: modeled on this exemplar, all things are like life, as has been said, and things are not different as far as their existence[5] is concerned. However, insofar as "idea" refers to an idea [proper], then it is multiple—to wit, as far as what it connotes is concerned—because distinctions between things are multiple. For insofar as "idea" stands for an idea [proper], it refers to the exemplarity of distinct existence and to multiple reasons and multiple orderings. Thus, one must concede that there is only one exemplar or exemplary form, just as there is only one efficient [cause].

3. To the third objection, one must reply that this plurality is on the part of the thing itself. However, "thing" can be taken in two senses, absolute and relative; in the latter case, "thing" will stand for a "relation to a thing." Therefore, one must say that the plurality of ideas stems from relational plurality.

4. To the fourth objection, one must reply that this sort of multiplication comes from the final product. However, it does not follow from this that there is a dependence on or relation to creatures in God. In fact, it follows that it is creatures that have a dependence on or relation to God. Therefore, when I say that "'idea' signifies the divine essence as the exemplary form of a certain thing," by this I connote this created thing's dependence on and relation to the divine exemplar, and not vice versa. And although this manner of speaking and thinking does suggest some relation of the Creator to creatures, this does not mean that the Creator depends on creatures or [in fact] has a relation to them. This suggestion appears only due to the deficiency of our intellect, because we do not understand God other than through creatures, and on this account our manner of signification implies that he connotes a relation to creatures. However, what this signifies is

---

5. In the solution, "life" was equated to "existence."

rather the dependence of creatures on God, because creatures are from him, toward him, and through him. Hence, Augustine says in *On the Trinity* [5.16]: "No change is posited in God on account of positing a relation of God to creatures; instead, [a change] is posited in creatures in relation to God." . . .

DOES TRUTH NECESSARILY HAVE ETERNAL EXISTENCE?

SH 1, P1, In1, Tr3, Q2, M1, C1 (n. 87), 138–39

a. First, it is argued based on Augustine's *Soliloquies* [2, c. 2]: "If this world will remain, it is true that it will remain forever; if it does not remain, it is true that it does not remain; if this world is to perish, when it will have perished, it will still be true that the world has perished; but it could not be true unless truth continued to exist." Therefore, even if the world were to perish, truth would still exist.

b. Anselm proves in his books *On Truth* [10] and *Monologion* [18] that truth exists eternally in such a way that one cannot even think of it as nonexisting. First he demonstrates it in this way: "Let him who is able to do so imagine when [exactly] something that was going to happen in the future had begun to be true, or think of the time when it was not true; or [let him imagine] when something that is past will cease to be true. And if neither of these can be thought and neither can be true without truth, it is impossible [even to think] that truth has a beginning or an end."

c. Anselm says in the same book [*Monologion* 18]: "If truth had a beginning or has an end, most absurd consequences follow [such as]: before truth began, it was [already] *true* that it did not yet exist; after truth ends, it will [still] be *true* that it does not exist; thus, truth would exist both before it began to exist and after it has ceased to exist. Therefore, whether one says or thinks that truth has, or does not have a beginning or an end, it cannot be limited by a beginning or an end." It remains, therefore, that truth necessarily has eternal existence and that it is not possible [even] to think of it as nonexisting.

To the contrary:

1. Just as the true is interchangeable with being, because every thing is related to truth in the same way as it is related to being, in the same way the good [is interchangeable with being], because "every thing, insofar as it

exists, is good."[6] But since one can [certainly] think of something as existing without thinking of its goodness, in the same way one can think of something as existing without thinking of its truth. And it is even easier to think of something as nonexisting without thinking of its truth. Therefore, "thinking of something as true" does not accompany "thinking of something as existing"; nor does "something not being true" accompany "something not existing."

2. The following argument appears to be sophistical in [the sense of confusing] the qualified and unqualified senses: "it is true that something does not exist (for example, that the world has perished and such)" or "it is true that the world will exist"; therefore, some truth exists. Indeed, here one infers "truth" in an unqualified sense from "truth" in a qualified sense.

I reply following Augustine's statement in *On True Religion* [34]: "No one understands falsehoods: for that which I contemplate with my intellect must be true."

Replies to the objections:

1. To the first objection, one must reply that the essence of a thing moves the mind in two ways: the aspect of truth moves the intellect, and the aspect of goodness moves the affective faculty. This means that, just as the essence of a thing is loved on account of its goodness, in the same way it is understood on account of its truth. And just as it is impossible not to love goodness, when the essence of a thing is loved, in the same way it is impossible not to understand the truth of the thing when its essence is understood. It is clear from this that truth in thought is not separable from existence.

2. To the second objection, one must reply that since everything that is predicated in a qualified sense is [also] predicated of something in an unqualified sense, if one posits truth in a qualified sense, truth in an unqualified sense will necessarily be posited [as well] (although not in relation to the same thing, but in relation to different things), because everything that is [predicated] in a qualified sense is reduced to [predication] in an unqualified sense.

---

6. Boethius, *On Seven Day Cycles*. The point of this initial statement seems to be simply to equate the true and the good as transcendentals, in order to make sure that one can speak of the true as being interchangeable with the good and behaving in the same way. Otherwise, equating both the true and the good with being seems to go against the argument that is outlined in the next few lines.

DOES "TRUTH" MEAN SOMETHING DIFFERENT FROM "ENTITY," "UNITY," AND "GOODNESS"?

SH 1, P1, In1, Tr3, Q2, M1, C2 (n. 88), 139–41

I. 1. Indeed, Augustine gives the following definition in *Soliloquies* [2.5]: "The true is that which exists." Therefore, truth by definition is entity; therefore, the two do not mean different things.

2. Augustine says in *On True Religion* [36.66]: "True things are true to the extent that they exist."

To the contrary:

a. Augustine in *On True Religion* [ibid.]: "The person to whom it is clear that falsity is that which makes one assume that which does not exist should understand that truth is that which demonstrates that which does exist." However, "that which makes a thing exist" does not mean the same as "that which demonstrates the thing's [existence]"; entity or essence is that which makes a thing exist, and truth is that which demonstrates [the thing's existence]; therefore, truth and entity mean two different things.

II. 3. Augustine says in *On True Religion* [31.57–58] that the first truth allows us to judge truths of lower rungs. Also, he says in the same book [c. 32.60]: when someone "tells material objects 'if you were not bound by some unity, you would be nothing!'" but at the same time [tells them] "'if you were unity itself, you would not be bodies,' one can rightly ask him: 'How do you know this unity, according to which you judge bodies? For if you did not see it, you could not judge that [bodies] do not attain it.'" Therefore, since unity [also] allows us to judge things of lower rungs, the meaning of unity and truth would be identical.

To the contrary:

a. Truth and falsity cannot be predicated of one and the same thing in one and the same respect; however, we do predicate of a body both truth of corporeity and falsity of unity, as in Augustine's *On True Religion* [34.63]: "Every body is a true body but a false unity"; therefore, truth of corporeity is not the same thing as unity of corporeity.

b. Specific differences of truth are different from specific differences of unity: the specific differences of unity are those that we outlined above [in Q1, M1, C3]; and the specific differences of truth are the truth of things and the truth of signs, in many senses; therefore, the meaning of truth is not the same as the meaning of unity.

III. 4. Commenting on Psalm [4:3], "*You seek falsity*," Augustine says [in *Exposition on the Psalms* 4] that "truth alone, which makes all things true, perfects good things"; but if it is [also] goodness that perfects good things, then truth and goodness would have the same meaning.

5. Augustine says in *On True Religion* [34]: truth is intelligible light. And blessed Dionysius [in *On the Divine Names* 4.6] says that "intelligible light is the good that is above all light, as a beaming ray and an emerging effusion of light that enlightens every intellect, both worldly and otherworldly." Therefore, the true and the good mean the same thing, namely, intelligible light.

6. Augustine says in *83 Questions* [6]: "All evil is found [to result] from the privation of form (*species*)." Therefore, all good [is found to result] from the presence of form; however, truth also results from the presence of form in a thing; therefore, both truth and goodness in a thing derive from one and the same [source]; therefore, they mean the same thing.

To the contrary:

a. However, an evil thing can be true, but not good; therefore, "true" and "good" mean different things.

b. No object of one faculty can have the same meaning as an object of a different faculty; but since the true is the object of reason, and the good of the will, the true and the good must mean different things.

Reply:

Although in reality unity, truth, and goodness coincide and are identical, nevertheless, their meanings are different, as was explained previously in the Question on unity (Q1, M1, C2). Indeed, the meaning of "being" (*ens*) and "entity" (*entitas*) is not limited. "Oneness" adds absence of division to "being": hence, "unity" is undividedness of being. However, "trueness" adds absence of existential (*esse*) division to undividedness of being: hence, "truth" is absence of division between that which exists and its existence. "Goodness," however, adds absence of division as far as the well-being of a thing is concerned, over and above undividedness of being and absence of existential division: hence, "goodness" is absence of division between potency and act, where "act" is the completion or perfection of the potential of which a thing is capable. Also, as we touched upon previously in the Question on unity, these meanings differ as far as [the thing's] relation to its cause is concerned: "oneness" reflects its relation to the efficient cause; "truth" reflects its relation to the formal cause; and "goodness" reflects its relation to the final cause.

These causes can also be matched with [the persons of] the Trinity. On this matter Augustine says in *On the City of God* [11.21]: "*God said: let there be light, and there was light; he saw that the light was good.* Hence, we have the speaker, that which is spoken, and that on account of which it is spoken." The meaning of "oneness" refers to the speaker; the meaning of "truth" to the word; and the meaning of "goodness" to the good on account of which the word was spoken. The speaker is the Father, who corresponds to the efficient cause; the word is the Son, who corresponds to the formal cause; and the good is the Holy Spirit, who corresponds to the final cause.

Therefore, the essence of a thing inseparably includes these [three] aspects as vestiges of the first cause, which constitute the "trinity" of one single essence. Augustine says in this respect at the end of *On True Religion* [55.113]: "It is appropriate for us to worship and believe in the Trinity of one substance; one God who created us; his likeness according to which we are shaped to resemble him; and peace, which allows us to partake in unity; God who said *let there be*, and his Word, through whom that which naturally exists was made; and the gift of goodness, whose will was not to allow to perish whatever was made by Him through the Word; one God, whose creative act is responsible for our lives, and whose reforming act allows us to live wisely, and by loving and enjoying whom we live in a blessed way."

Replies to the objections:

I. 1. I reply, then, to the objections that although "that which is" does define the true, nevertheless, the meanings of "true" and "being" are not the same. For when one says "that which is," one implies that which has existence (*esse*), and it is implied further that in that which has existence there is no division between existence (*esse*) and that which is. Therefore, the meaning of Augustine's definition "the true is that which is" is the same as "the true is that in which existence is not divided from that which exists," as was explained previously; but this statement adds to "being."

2. To the second objection, one must reply that when it is said "all things are true to the extent that they are," the limiting expression "to the extent" can [be understood to] refer to the condition of the substrate (*suppositum*) implied in the "true things"; in this sense the expression "all things are true to the extent that they are" is true, because "true" and "being" are never separated in any substrate; in fact it follows: "if it exists, it is true." It can also [be understood to] refer to the condition of the form, or the purport of that which is called "the true"; in this sense [the expression] is false: indeed, it is

not "being" that is the purport of "the true," but the "absence of division between existence (*esse*) and a being (*ens*)," as has been said.

II. 3. To the third objection, about unity, one must reply that "we judge according to unity" in the same way as we judge according to the light of truth, as when we evaluate an artifact by comparing it to the exemplar and plan [in the mind of the artist]. Augustine says about this in *On True Religion* [34]: "This is the true light by means of which you know images in the imagination as false, and thus in a different way [than true things]." One must note that when you say, "we judge according to unity," this means "[according to unity] insofar as unity takes on the function of the formal cause," and thus insofar as it takes on the role of truth, as we demonstrated previously in the Question on unity.

III. 4. Answering the fourth objection, one must understand that "truth perfects good things" as a formal cause, and goodness as a final cause. However, good things have both perfections: truth perfects them as far as their natural existence in relation to their exemplary cause is concerned, and goodness [perfects them] as far as their existence in relation to their final cause is concerned.

5. To the fifth objection, along the same lines, that "both truth and goodness are alike in being intelligible light," one must reply that this is true, but in different senses, because the true is light to the speculative intellect, and the good is light to the practical intellect.

Besides, light has a double effect: to disclose and to set in motion. Indeed, light is the principle of manifesting both itself and other things, as Augustine says in a *Homily on John*, commenting on the following passage from Ephesians 5:13: "*All things that are reproved are made manifest by the light*": for all that is manifested is light. And in this sense "the true *is* intelligible light" because it is the principle of manifesting things. Hence, Hilary [*On the Trinity* 5.3] says: "The true discloses existence."

In addition, light is a principle that sets things in motion. Thus, bodies that are not permeable to light, such as opaque and earthy bodies, are naturally immobile. However, bodies that are permeable to light, such as transparent water and air, are mobile (although not by themselves), air being more mobile than water because it is more penetrable by light. However, those bodies whose substance contains light, such as celestial bodies and fire, are mobile by themselves. And in this sense the good, which is the principle that sets things in motion, is intelligible light. Dionysius [in *On the Divine Names*

4.4] says in this respect: "The good is that to which all things turn and which all things desire."

6. To the last objection, one must reply that just as depriving [an animal] of life, which is the primary perfection of an animal, leads to depriving it of its senses, in the same way depriving something of its form (*species*), which is used to establish the truth [of this thing], leads to depriving this thing of its order [in the hierarchy of things], which is used to evaluate the goodness [of this thing]: this is why it is said that this [i.e., lack of order] is the cause of all evil. Or one can understand "form" in both ways, namely, as a perfection of both being (*esse*) and well-being (*bene esse*), and in that sense all evil results from the privation of form—however, [the appellation] "form" in that sense extends to goodness as well as to truth. . . .

IS THE "GOOD" FULLY IDENTICAL TO "BEING" (*ENS*) IN ITS MEANING?

SH 1, P1, In1, Tr3, Q3, M1, C1, Ar1 (n. 102), 160–61
The first argument is this:

1. That which is desired and wanted for its own sake and for what it stands for, is the good in its substance and meaning, because, as Boethius says in the *Consolation of Philosophy* [3, pr. 10], "The pinnacle and cause of all that is desired is the good. Indeed, one can in no way desire something that contains nothing good substantially nor any likeness of the good." And since whatever is desired is desired for the sake of the good [in it], he left us, as it were, a description of what the good is: "that which is desired by all"; however, "existence" (*esse*) is desired by all in its substance and meaning; therefore, the meaning of "existence" is the same as that of the "good." That "existence" is desired for its own sake is proved by Augustine in *On Free Choice of the Will* [3.7.20]: "Think, to the extent that you can, how great a good 'existence' itself is, which both the happy and the wretched ones desire." Also, if perchance one were to say, "I'd prefer not to exist over being wretched," which would be a case of "existence" not being desired for its own sake, Augustine [ibid., 3.8.22] objects: "Those who say 'I'd prefer this over that' choose something; however, nonexistence is not anything, but nothing"; therefore, "I'd prefer not to exist over being wretched" is not a valid statement. Also, [ibid.] "those who choose not to exist force themselves to choose nothing"; therefore, nonexistence cannot be chosen or desired; therefore, [only] "existence" as such is desired.

2. If one brings forth an objection based on the example of those who kill themselves out of desperation or an inability to endure—for it seems that such people do not wish to exist—Augustine replies in the same text [3.8.23]: "When one kills himself or desires to die in whatever way, they never have a feeling that they will not exist after death, even though they might have this thought at the back of their minds. Indeed, a thought is a trait of someone who thinks rationally or entertains an [intellectual] belief, which can be either true or false; at the same time, feelings dominate our natural or habitual constitution: for it can happen that we think one thing, but feel another—which is easy enough to establish from the fact that very often we believe [intellectually] that something ought to be done, but it would please us to do quite the opposite."

To the contrary:

a. Augustine, *On the Trinity* 8[.3.4]: "As when one says 'a good soul' these are two words, so do they mean two different things: one which makes it a 'soul,' and another which makes it 'good.'"

b. "Existence" is not susceptible to more or less, while "goodness" is; therefore, the meanings of the two are not identical.

c. Boethius in *On Seven Day Cycles* says: "I discern in things that their being good and their existence are two different things."

Reply:

The meanings of "being" and the "good" are not the same, even though the same real things that possess being also always have goodness. Now a being (*ens*) possesses two types of existence (*esse*): first and second. The first is the one that it has naturally; the second is its orderly existence, or well-being. The good in creatures (for God's goodness is not touched by distinction) follows the same pattern. There are two types: natural goodness, which is [really] the same as natural existence, and goodness of order, which is really the same as well-being in a thing. The first type of good is inseparable from existence, and the second type separable. This is why Augustine says in *On the Trinity* 8[.3.5]: "When a soul turns away from the supreme good, it ceases to be a good soul; and yet it does not cease to be a soul, which is already a good that is better than being a body." However, conceptually (*ratione*) the two differ, because "being" signifies the primary intelligible in an absolute sense, without considering its act (i.e., perfection), usefulness, or [place in the] order [of things], while "good" signifies a being with its act (i.e., perfection), utility, or order. Therefore, it adds the aspect of "desirability" or "being sought after" to "being"; and nothing can be desirable except to the extent that it is perfect, useful, or delightful.

Replies to the objections:

1. To the objection that "existence is desired as such" (*per se*) one must reply that if "as such" here is the opposite of "accidentally" (*per accidens*), then the statement is true. However, if "as such" here is the opposite of "under another aspect," then the statement is false, because "being" or "existence" is only desired to the extent that it is considered together with its act, usefulness, or delightfulness.

2. To the other objection, about a person who commits suicide, one must reply, following Augustine in *On Free Choice of the Will* [3.8.23]: "Take a person who is pushed toward suicide by insufferable hardships and believes that there is no existence after death. If such a person desires death, he or she erroneously believes in complete cessation [of existence after death], but emotionally he or she naturally desires quietude. However, a state of quietude is not nothing: in fact, one can attribute existence to it to a greater extent than to lack of quietude. For lack of quietude brings about diverse emotions, and they mutually annihilate each other, while quietude is a stable state, which is most like what we have in mind when we say 'existence.' Therefore, all this desire of death is aimed not at the absence of existence for the one who is to die, but at providing rest for this person. Therefore, while such a person erroneously believes that he or she will cease to exist, nevertheless, by nature he or she desires a state of quietude, that is, of a higher level of existence." Replies to the objections are clear from this.

ARE THE BEAUTIFUL (*PULCHRUM*) AND THE GOOD FULLY IDENTICAL AS FAR AS THEIR MEANING IS CONCERNED?

SH 1, P1, In1, Tr3, Q3, M1, C1, Ar2 (n. 103), 162–63

a. In this regard Dionysius says in *On the Divine Names* [4.7]: "The good," which is God, "is praised by the theologians as the beautiful (*decorum*) and beauty (*decor*), and as love and that which is loved. Now, it is called 'beauty' because it imparts its own individual beauty to each and every being; therefore, it is called 'beautiful' (*pulchrum* or *decorum*) because it spreads beauty." But this is the essence of the good, namely, to spread something around; therefore, the meanings of the beautiful and the good are identical.

b. In the same work: "The beautiful is to be loved as a final cause, for all things are made for the sake of their beauty"; however, the meanings of "final cause" and "something to be loved" denote the essence of the good; therefore, etc.

c. In the same place: "The beautiful is the same as the good, because all things desire the beautiful and the good according to every"—that is, perfect—"cause, and no being is devoid of partaking in the beautiful and the good."

To the contrary:

1. The term "beautiful" is applied when the meaning of the formal cause is intended; hence, God is called beautiful when he is understood as the exemplary cause. Dionysius says in this regard: "The beautiful is the exemplar, because it is responsible for distinction between all things." Indeed, *decorum* and *speciosum*[7] in creatures refer to one and the same thing: namely, a thing is called "shapely" (*speciosa*) based on its shape (*species*), which is the form of the thing. However, the term "good" refers to the final cause; therefore, the meanings of the beautiful and the good are not identical.

2. Augustine says in *On the City of God* 22[.19.21]: "All beauty consists in congruence of parts with some sweetness of color." Therefore, there will be no beauty in simple and spiritual things. However, there is goodness in them: for the most part in God and therefrom in spiritual things; therefore, it remains that the meanings of beauty and goodness, or the beautiful and the good, are not the same.

Reply:

I reply following Augustine in *83 Questions* [30]: the good is referred to in two ways: as something excellent (*honestum*) and something useful (*utile*); "we call 'excellent' that which is sought for its own sake, while we call 'useful' that which is for the sake of something else. 'Excellence' (*honestas*), in my opinion, refers to intelligible beauty, which we [also] appropriately call 'spiritual'; 'usefulness,' however, refers to divine providence. For this reason, although there are many visible things that are beautiful, which are less appropriately called 'excellent' (*honesta*), nevertheless, beauty itself, which makes beautiful all things that are beautiful, is in no way visible. Also, there are many visible things that are useful; however, utility itself, which makes them helpful to us and which we call divine providence, is invisible." It is clear from this statement that insofar as the good is referred to as "excellent,"

---

7. Another Latin term that can mean "beautiful."

it is the same as "the beautiful," while insofar as the good is useful it is not. For these [two aspects of the good] differ: indeed, the term "beautiful" denotes the ability of the good to please our faculty of perception, while the term "good" denotes its ability to delight our affective faculty. This is the difference as far as the consideration of the final cause is concerned.

Also, one can consider [the difference] as far as the efficient cause is concerned: [the term] "good" denotes the flow [of effects] from a cause without considering [their] distinction, while "beautiful" describes this flow with regard to distinction. Hence, Dionysius [ibid.] says: the good first of all "is called 'beauty' because it imparts its own individual beauty to each and every being."

Also, one can consider [the difference] as far as the exemplary cause is concerned, in a similar way: "good" stands for the exemplar upon which something is modeled, insofar as the end is, as it were, a set of regulations—an art—for an artificer who works toward a final goal. Hence, Dionysius says in *On the Divine Names* [4.6]: "The intelligible light is called good"; and continues: "[the light that] gathers together and assembles all intellectual and rational things; and just as ignorance divides those who err, in the same way the presence of intelligible light gathers together and unites the enlightened ones, and even turns [them] to that which truly is." However, "beautiful" refers to the exemplar itself, insofar as it is an art that distinguishes and brings into harmony different elements. Therefore, Dionysius says that [the beautiful] "is the exemplar, because it is responsible for the distinction between all things."

Replies to the objections:

1. To the objection that "the beautiful imparts the meaning of the formal cause, while the good the meaning of the final cause," one must reply that just as at times one uses the term "form" to communicate the meaning of the "end," and the term acquires the meaning of finality, to the extent that [form] is the end or term of being, in the same way the term "end" acquires the meaning of "form," to the extent that it is an art and set of regulations for the artificer: for an artificer adjusts his or her work having in mind its end. In a similar way, the beautiful puts on the garb of the good, and the good the garb of the beautiful, although the primary meaning of "beautiful" seems to be based more on exemplarity, just as the primary meaning of "good" on finality.

2. To the second objection, one must reply that Augustine's statement defines visible or bodily beauty. However, the statement is about the bodily

beauty of the senses insofar as it leads us to intelligible or spiritual beauty. For just as "bodily beauty consists of a fitting arrangement of parts," in the same way the beauty of souls consists of the harmony and ordering of mental faculties, and beauty in the divine consists of the sacred order of divine persons, where one person is not from another, the second person is from the first through generation, and the third person is from both through procession. . . .

ARE THE KNOWLEDGE AND LOVE OF THE HIGHEST GOOD ORIGINALLY IMPLANTED AND IMPRESSED IN OUR MINDS?

SH 1, P1, In1, Tr3, Q3, M2, C1 (n. 108), 169–70

a. Indeed, all wish to be blessed; however, blessedness is the highest good, as Boethius says in *The Consolation of Philosophy* [3, pr. 2]; therefore, all desire the highest good; therefore, the love of the highest good is impressed upon every rational nature.

b. The highest good is that which is desired by all; but that which is appropriate to everyone is impressed upon one's nature; therefore, the desire and love for the highest good is impressed upon one's nature.

c. Augustine says in *On Free Choice of the Will* 2[.9.26]: "Before we become blessed, the notion of blessedness is impressed upon us: it is this notion that allows us to know and proclaim without a shadow of a doubt that we wish to be blessed"; however, no one is blessed except by means of the highest good; therefore, the notion of the highest good and blessedness is impressed upon us.

d. Boethius says in *The Consolation of Philosophy* [4, pr. 2]: "Some indistinct impulse equally drives all humans, both good and evil, toward the good."

To the contrary:

1. Every will that is aimed at its innate goal is right and praiseworthy. Suppose the innate goal of the will and rational intention is the highest good. But then, since the innate goal of every will of both good and evil people is the highest good, every will, or the wills of everybody, would be right; but this is clearly false.

2. One finds ignorance of what is truly good in many people; but then, the knowledge of the [highest] good would coexist with its ignorance.

Reply:

I reply following Boethius in *The Consolation of Philosophy* [ibid.]: "The highest good is offered equally to good and evil people. Now, good people pursue it by means of naturally obligatory virtues, while evil people do so by means of various base desires: the latter is not a naturally obligatory way of reaching the good, but they strive for the same goal." Therefore, the love and idea of the highest good are impressed on us according to our natural disposition and natural sense, although opinion and appetite for perverse choices make one go astray and deviate from the good.

Replies to the objections:

1. To counter the objection, one must draw a distinction, according to Damascene [*On the Orthodox Faith* 2.22], between the natural will, which allows all to seek the highest good rightly, and the selective or deliberating will, which allows one to choose that which is not the highest good and prefer it to the highest good; this type of will is not right. Therefore, in evil people the natural will is right and without error, but the selective will is not right and contains error. Hence, Augustine says in *On Free Choice of the Will* 2[.9.26]: "To the extent that all humans seek the blessed life, they do not err; however, to the extent that each of them fails to stick to the path in life which leads to blessedness, they do err, while they proclaim that all they want to do is reach blessedness. For the error consists in following a path that does not lead where we want to go."

2. To the other objection, one must reply that knowledge resides in our natural sense, while ignorance is in the perversity of erroneous opinion. Therefore, mark Augustine's words in *On Free Choice of the Will* [3.8.23]: "At times our sense is truer than opinion, if the latter comes from error, while the former derives from nature. An example is when an ailing person [who has fever] is often helpfully relieved as well as delighted by frigid water, while he believes that it would be harmful to him if he actually drank it. And at times our opinion is truer than sense: [for example,] if he believes the medical art that [says that] frigid water is harmful (since it will truly harm him), and nevertheless it would be delightful to drink. And at times both are right, as when that which is helpful is not only believed to be so but is also pleasing. And at times both are in error, as when something harmful is both believed to be helpful and continues to be pleasant." . . .

IS EVERY CREATED GOOD SO IN ITS ESSENCE OR BY PARTICIPATION?

SH 1, P1, In1, Tr3, Q3, M3, C2, Ar2 (n. 117), 183–86

I. 1. The preceding arguments seem to suggest that it is good in its essence. However, Boethius presents the following argument on this matter in *On Seven Day Cycles*: "If those things that exist are good by participation, they are not good in any way of themselves: indeed, that which is white by participation is not white of itself, by the mere fact of its existence." Therefore, just as it is possible for that which is white by participation not to be white, in the same way if created things are good by participation, it is possible for them not to be good; but created things can't be not good; therefore, they are good substantially, not by participation.

2. To *participate* means to take *part*; but God or divine goodness does not have parts; therefore, one cannot "take part" in divine goodness; however, creatures are good by virtue of divine goodness; therefore, they do not "take part" in it; therefore, they are not good by participation.

3. Augustine says in *83 Questions* [16]: "Those things that are alike by participation, can be dissimilar"; but creatures, so long as they remain creatures, are good; on this account they possess likeness to the first good, and cannot become dissimilar, that is, opposite to this goodness, so that one could call creatures evil to the extent that they are creatures of this sort; therefore, they are not called good by participation; therefore, they are essentially good.

4. Created goodness is good either by participation or essentially. It is not good by participation: indeed, that which is good by participation can become dissimilar, as has been said; however, goodness cannot be not good; therefore, [created goodness] is not good by participation; therefore, it is good essentially; however, created goodness is the goodness of creatures; therefore, creatures are essentially good.

To the contrary:

a. That which is substantially good is said to be like the First, as Boethius says in *On Seven Day Cycles*; but nothing is like the First except the First [itself]; therefore, nothing is substantially good except the First [itself]; therefore, creatures are not substantially good.

It is clear that nothing is like the First except the First [itself]: indeed, to be like something means to harmonize with it in some quality; but there is nothing common to the Creator and creatures; furthermore, there is nothing in the Creator that is not he himself; therefore, there is no quality in him; therefore, only he himself is like himself.

Also, it is clear from the words of Augustine in *83 Questions* [24] that creatures are not like the First: "Likeness itself can never be dissimilar in any of its aspects; hence, it happens that, since the likeness of the Father—the Son—is called [likeness] because it is by participating in it that things becomes alike—either between themselves or to God—[this likeness] cannot be dissimilar in any of its aspects"; but every creature can be partly unlike the First, and indeed is so; therefore, no creature is similar to him; therefore, neither is created goodness; therefore, creatures are not substantially good.

II. In addition to that, an argument by Boethius [in *On Seven Day Cycles*] is brought up, which he uses to demonstrate that all things are good, which goes as follows: "A common opinion of the Doctors is that all that exists tends to the good; however, all things tend to what is like them; therefore, those things that tend to the good are themselves good." For it is demonstrated that this argument is invalid, because the following line of argument is invalid: "every human being tends to blessedness; all things tend to what is like them; therefore, every human being is blessed." Therefore, either his statement "all that exists tends to what is like it" is false or one must name the reason why tending to the good makes creatures good, given that tending to blessedness does not make one blessed.

Solution:

I. According to Dionysius in *On the Divine Names* [4.1], "just as it is not as a result of some deliberation or judgment, but by its own nature that this sun here illumines all things that can partake in its light by their own nature, in the same way also the good, which is above the sun, emits the rays of its entire goodness—as some faint image [of this goodness]—to all beings."

Replies to the objections:

1. Note that something can be said to be "by participation" in three ways. One way is when that thing has a form that does not accompany it for the entire extent [or duration] of its being. This is the way in which separable forms, such as whiteness or health, are in their supposites by participation (for those forms that are always present [in something] are [in it] essentially). In this regard Augustine says: "Those things that are alike by participation can be dissimilar." Another way is when something has a form that accompanies it for the entire extent [or duration] of its being, except that this form is divided up and multiplied in its supposites, as when a universal form is

multiplied in singular things. For example, multiple men are called "man" in the singular by virtue of participating in the species "man." The third way is when something has a form that is incomplete in comparison to some complete form on which it depends and by which it is caused: for example, a man is called "wise" by participation, because his wisdom is incomplete compared to God's wisdom, which is essentially complete.

According to this, "good by participation" is predicated in three ways. In the first way, humans are called good by participation in the goodness of grace, because grace is a separable form. In the second way, angels are called good by participation in the goodness of glory, because the goodness of glory, even though it is not separable, nevertheless, is multiplied in multiple blessed angels. In the third way, every [created] nature is called good by participation, because goodness is not its being, but some addition to its being; moreover, this is accomplished through a relation to the essentially good, which is God.

Also, note that "substantially good" is predicated in two ways. One way is when the substance [itself] is the good, so that goodness is identical [to substance]. This way of predication is according to the first way of using the term "essential," when we call "essential" that which is of the essence (*esse*) of the thing or that which denotes its essence. In this way, only God is called "the substantial good." The other way is according to the second way of using the term "essential," namely, when "essential" refers to a property that immediately and inseparably follows the essence. In this way creatures are "essentially good" because goodness immediately follows the essence of creatures.

2. To the second objection, that "to participate means to take part," etc., one must reply that divine goodness, indeed, is most simple in itself and does not admit of parts. Also, divine goodness is infinite as far as its effects are concerned. Hence, if one asked about the exact extent of divine goodness, one could not specify it, for its extent is infinite. . . . However, it is not so regarding created goodness. So when it is said that created goodness participates in uncreated goodness, this does not mean that uncreated goodness is divided into parts by individual created goodnesses. The statement that "an [individual] created goodness takes part" refers to the effects [of uncreated goodness], meaning that one [created goodness] receives one effect of the primary goodness, and another [created goodness receives] another.

Therefore, this is the meaning of "participating in goodness itself," namely, this [language] refers to its effects.

3. To the third objection one must say that for as long as a created good remains in existence, it cannot become completely unlike the first good. However, it becomes unlike it to the extent that is loses its being. And it loses its being when it loses its place in the order [of things], which is tantamount to the appearance of evil, according to Boethius's words [in *The Consolation of Philosophy* 4, pr. 2]: "Being (*esse*) is that which retains its order and preserves its nature." Hence, he says that this entails that evil humans lack being (*non sunt*), because they have lost their place in the order [of things].

4. To the fourth one must reply that for as long as created goodness remains, it cannot be not good. However, this goodness does not come from itself, but from being ordered to the highest good. Therefore, it does not follow that it is essentially good.

To the objections to the contrary:

a. To the objection about created goodness, namely, that it is "not essentially good, because it is not like the First," one must reply that there are two types of likeness. One stems from the identity of essence; this is the way the Son in the divine is like the Father, and it is of this likeness that Augustine speaks in 83 *Questions* [23] when he says that "likeness cannot be unlike." Indeed, because this likeness is based on the identity of essence, it cannot in any way be dissimilar. In this way created goodness is not a likeness of the First, or uncreated goodness, and in this way it is only the First that is like the First. However, there is another type of likeness, one that stems from participating in an effect [of some cause]: something is like something else if it participates in its effect. Augustine in 83 *Questions* [ibid.] says that "something that is like [something else] is called that by virtue of a likeness; however, something that is good is called that by virtue of a goodness"; therefore, a created good is called that by virtue of a created goodness, and an uncreated good by virtue of an uncreated goodness. However, a created good is similar to the uncreated good, as has been said; therefore, created goodness is a likeness of divine goodness, as has been said. . . .

II. As for the question why those who tend to blessedness are not all called blessed, while those who tend to goodness are all [supposed to be] called good, one must reply that blessedness denotes the ultimate end itself or the joining with this sort of an end—for it is the "state that is perfect by virtue of gathering together all goods" [Boethius, *Consolation* III, pr. 2]—and therefore no creature is properly called blessed unless it is joined to this end. At the same time, the meaning of "good" is more general, for it denotes either the end itself or that which is ordered to this end, whether it is joined to this end or is still some distance away from it. Therefore, it does follow that if something is ordered to a good, it is good. . . .

DOES GOD PERMIT EVIL TO ARISE IN THE UNIVERSE?

SH 1, P1, In1, Tr3, Q3, M3, C5, Ar1 (n. 120), 188–89

1. "It is in the nature of the Best to bring about the best," as Dionysius says [in *On the Divine Names* 4.19]. However, things would have been better without the admixture of evil; but then why does God allow for evil to be mixed with the good?

2. If someone's activities appropriate to their kind are not the best, such a person is not the best, because someone's goodness manifests itself in their work. . . . But then [the activities of someone who is "best" that are appropriate to their kind] cannot be better in this kind; therefore, they cannot be mixed with evil. . . .

Reply:

The reply is found in Augustine, *Enchiridion* 11: "When evil is well ordered and occupies its proper place, it presents good things in a more flattering fashion, so that they please us more and become more praiseworthy in comparison with evil ones." Therefore, God permitted evil things to exist for the sake of the beauty of good things: for if evil did not exist, the good would only possess absolute beauty, namely, of the good itself; however, when evil exists, the relative beauty of the good grows, so that in comparison with its opposite—evil—the good shines forth more beautifully.

Augustine replies to the objections elsewhere [*Literal Commentary on Genesis* 3.24.37]: "God made individual things good, but as a totality they are '*very good*' (Genesis 1:31)." Therefore, the totality of things is as good as it can be, even though not every individual thing may be the best in its kind. Therefore, as regards singular things, it is said in Genesis 1:10: "*God saw that it was good.*" However, as regards God's completed work, scripture says [in Genesis 1:31]: "*God saw all things that he had made, and they were very good.*" It says, then, that if evil did not exist, things in the universe would have lacked some beauty. . . .

Augustine also adduces another reason, namely, utility. For he says the reason God permits evil things to occur in a political state is in order to derive some good from them. Thus, he says in *City of God* 11[.17–18]: "God makes good use of evil wills, for the temptations of the devil are helpful to holy people. Indeed, God's foreknowledge of some future evil angel or human is always accompanied by the knowledge of how to put them to some good use."

Therefore, one can adduce two reasons why God permits evil things to occur: namely, the greater beauty of good things, and utility.

WOULD THE UNIVERSE HAVE BEEN BETTER WITHOUT EVIL THINGS?

SH 1, P1, In1, Tr3, Q3, M3, C5, Ar2 (n. 121), 189–90

1. Given that evil is lack of order, how can it be "well ordered"?

2. "That thing is whiter which has less black mixed with it" [Aristotle, *Topics* 3.5]; therefore, that thing is better which has less evil mixed with it.

3. A woman with no blemish is more beautiful, and her beauty is more praiseworthy than that of a woman with a blemish. This is why the Song of Songs [4:7] pours the following praise on the Spouse: "*You are all beautiful, my beloved; there is no blemish in you.*" Therefore, the totality of things would be more beautiful and praiseworthy if the blemish of evil were not present.

4. Ecclesiastes 10:[5–6]: "*There is an evil which I have seen under the sun . . . folly is set in great dignity*"; indeed, this is how evil persons are mostly positioned in the hierarchical order;[8] therefore, this sort of "ordering" is [itself] evil, namely, when those who must be at the bottom of the pile end up at the top. Just as Origen says in [*Homilies*] *on Numbers* [14.2]: "Vile human beings are well ordered for vile occupations, for example to clean city streets." Therefore, an evil human being is well suited for a despicable job, and a good one for a more prominent position.

Reply:

Evil in itself is not something ordered. However, it can be ordered in two ways when something else is involved. One way is when a subsistent good is involved, namely, the nature of a sinner when it is positioned to undergo punishment. As Augustine says in *On the Nature of the Good* [7]: "Sinners

---

8. That is, "in dignity." They are appointed as dignitaries.

are ordered through punishments. To the extent that this sort of ordering disagrees with their nature, it can function as punishment, and to the extent that it is appropriate for their crime, it is justice."

The other way is when the good of arrangement is involved. In this regard Augustine says in *City of God* 11 [18]: "He decorated the world as he would a beautiful poem with antithetical statements. Antithetical statements involve an opposition. In this manner contrary statements placed alongside each other enhance the beauty of speech, as in the following example from the Apostle's writings in 2 Corinthians 6:8: '*By honor and dishonor, by evil report and good report.*' [In the same way] the beauty of the world is a result of the 'eloquence' of things (to use a figure of speech), not of words. Hence, in Ecclesiasticus 33:15 we read: '*Good [is placed] against evil, and life against death, [and a righteous person against a sinner], and you see this in all the works of the Most High: one against one, and two against two.*'"

Replies to the objections:

1. As for the first objection, one can make a distinction between three kinds of order: between upper and lower things (top to bottom), between things that are next to each other (juxtaposition), and between things that are opposed to each other. The first of the three kinds of order in the totality of good things works as follows: the bottom to top ordering is of good things to God; the top to bottom ordering is of better things to [merely] good things. Next, the second [of the three kinds], the order of juxtaposition, is when good things are ordered to things that are equally good—if such a relationship can be found. Or things can be ordered to their opposites, such as [good things ordered] in relation to their opposites, bad things. Now, evil has no place in the top-bottom order. At the same time, it does have a place in the order between opposites, as has just been demonstrated. And it is in this sense that evil is said to be "well ordered."

2. To the second objection, one must reply that the two examples are not alike. Indeed, all whiteness is of the same kind, but not all goodness is of the same kind; thus, one can speak of singular good things or of the totality of good things. Therefore, although this analogy works for the case of singular good things—[and in that case indeed] "that thing is better which has less evil mixed with it"—it does not work for the case of the totality of good things. This is clarified by the example that Augustine provides in *On the Nature of the Good* [16]: "Consider how we, halting our voice, fittingly interject pauses into our speech." "Now how much more fittingly does He"—i.e.,

God—"as a perfect artist, make certain omissions in the totality of things!" The example shows that just as the beauty of speech is greater when we interject pauses into it than if it flowed continuously without them, in the same way the beauty of the universe is greater when evil things are well placed within it.

3. To the third objection, one must reply that the first statement is false unless it is qualified. Indeed, a woman can have a blemish in such a place that it would be fittingly placed and result in greater beauty. Another example is a scar on the face of a soldier: if it is in a fitting place, he looks more handsome. Augustine in this regard provides the following example in *City of God* [11.23]: "Just as a painting, when black color in it is placed appropriately, [is beautiful,] in the same way the totality of things is beautiful even [with sinners] when they are placed appropriately, although considered in themselves [sinners] are ugly." . . .

CHAPTER 6

THE TRINITY

IS THERE GENERATION IN GOD?

SH 1, P1, In2, Tr un., Q1, Ti1, C1 (n. 295), 414–18

a. Augustine [says] in the book *83 Questions* [50], "God the Father either was able to generate the Son from eternity and willed [to do so]; or he did not will but was able [to do so]; or he was not able but willed; or he neither willed nor was able. If he willed and was not able, then he was lacking in power. If he was able and did not will, then he was envious. But there is no envy in him. If he was neither able nor willed, then he is both lacking in power and envious. But neither is proper to him." Therefore, it remains that he was able and willed, and it is certain that he knew [this about himself]. But in order for a rational cause to act, willing, being able, and knowing is all that is required. Therefore, he has generated the Son from eternity; therefore, generation is eternal.

b. There is a second argument. The good is naturally and necessarily self-diffusive. Indeed, the glory of the good is to diffuse itself. Because if there were two goods that were equal in all respects, with the exception that one diffused its goodness and the other did not, it is clear that the good that diffuses itself would in doing so be more praiseworthy and better than the other good that did not diffuse itself. Therefore, the full definition of the good entails self-diffusion. Therefore, where there is the highest good, there is the highest diffusion. However, the highest diffusion is that than which a greater cannot be conceived. And a greater diffusion cannot be conceived than one that is according to substance and, even more, according to the whole [substance]. Therefore, the highest good necessarily diffuses itself according to its whole substance, and this [kind of] diffusion is naturally understood [to be] in it. But the power of generating is nothing other than the power of diffusing one's own substance so that something similar in nature is produced. Therefore, the highest being is understood to possess this power in the highest degree from eternity, as that highest good is also eternal. But where there is this power, there is generation. Therefore, there is eternal generation.

If it is said that this conclusion does not follow, because diffusion is understood [to be] in the good only consequently and not naturally or essentially, it is objected to the contrary: it pertains to the perfection and nobility of the good to communicate itself. This therefore is the glory of the good. However, whatever pertains to the perfection and nobility of the good is attributed to the highest good. Therefore, self-communication is necessary in the highest good. And as it is highest, its communication is [of the] highest [order]. While it is a significant communication to communicate one's quality or an accident, a greater communication is to communicate one's substance. Therefore, the greatest and the highest [thing] is to communicate one's whole substance; and this [kind of] communication is necessarily in the highest good. But to communicate one's own substance in order to produce something similar in nature is nothing other than to generate. Therefore, generation is necessarily understood [to be] in the highest good. Therefore, there is eternal generation, because whatever is understood to be in [God] is eternal.

c. There is another argument. A common idea is that whatever pertains to nobility and perfection and power must be attributed to God. Moreover, a power is nobler if it possesses a nobler effect or act. But comparing all acts of power, no act of any agent is nobler than one that produces something similar in nature to the agent itself. But the power that performs such an act, which is to produce one similar in nature to the agent, is the generative power and no other; for the power of the artist produces an artifact, but not one similar in nature. The generative power, however, results in a production of a substance, which is similar in nature [to the one generating], and this is a more powerful production. Therefore, among all powers that produce something, the nobler one is the generative power, which is able to produce a thing that is similar [to itself] in nature. But what pertains to nobility or a nobler power cannot fail to belong to the highest virtue and highest power, which is God. Therefore, the generative power, or generation, is implied in the highest power. Therefore, there is eternal generation.

d. Another argument is this: It is a mark of perfection and excellence in nature if it [the agent] has the ability to produce from itself something that is identical or similar to itself in nature. Thus, if a human being were not able to produce another human being from itself, that would be an imperfection, because nature is a power inserted in things, [which] procreates similar from similar things, as the Philosopher says [*Metaphysics* 4.4]. But whatever concerns nobility and perfection is in the highest nature. Therefore, in this one there is a power to produce from itself something that is similar in nature [to itself]. But this is the generative power. Therefore, in that one [that is, God] there is generative power, and therefore also generation, and likewise the Father and the Son, who [respectively represent] the one generating and what is generated.

e. Another argument. God is incorporeal and inaccessible light; but it is essential to and in the nature of every light to beget of itself a coeval splendor. Therefore, the highest light necessarily contains a light that generates and a splendor that is generated.

f. If it is said that it befits eternal generation to be in God, but this is not [the case] of necessity, then Anselm says to the contrary [in *Why God Became Man* 1.9]: "Whatever is unbefitting of God is logically impossible, and whatever befits God is logically necessary." Therefore, if generation is congruent with or befits God, it is necessarily in God, and especially when we are speaking of the necessity of immutability, because this is in the divine, while the necessity which imposes coercion is not; so of necessity there is eternal generation.

On the opposing side, there are these arguments:

1. First are posited reasons that weaken the first argument, made by Augustine, which demonstrates the necessity of eternal generation. It seems that his argument proceeds poorly, when he says: "If God willed and was not able, therefore he would be lacking in power," because there is no potential in the Son to generate, as there is no potential in him to be the Father. But from this it does not follow that the Son is lacking in power; therefore, neither could it be said that the Father is lacking in power, if he is not able to generate the Son. And so that argument based on the ability [to generate] is not compelling.

2. It seems that this does not logically follow: "he was able and he did not will, therefore he was envious," because he was able to make creatures or the world better than he made them, but nevertheless, he did not will [to do so]. And he was able to create the world before he actually created it, and nevertheless he did not will [to do so]. From these things, however, it does not follow that he was envious; therefore, similarly neither [was he malicious] in that situation [regarding the generation of something similar to himself].

3. There is another argument, which shows that generation does not befit God. Nothing that pertains to imperfection and insufficiency should be

attributed to God. But generation in generable things pertains to imperfection and insufficiency. Therefore, generation is not to be attributed to God. The minor [premise] is clear: because being is threefold; namely, there is temporal being, perpetual being, and eternal being. Where there is temporal being, however, there is corruption [that is, decay and death], and because [temporal] things are not able to preserve the being of their species in themselves, therefore, the generative power is given to them, so that [even though] they are not able to preserve the existence of their species in themselves, they preserve it through the generation [of things] in their likeness; but generation is not found in perpetual substances [e.g., angels], and this is on account of the perfection of their being, which is incorruptible—whence they are able to preserve and continue the being of their species perpetually by themselves. Thus the sun does not generate a sun, nor the soul a soul, as they have the perfect power by which they are able of themselves to be preserved. Therefore, generation always goes hand in hand with imperfection.

4. Another argument: Generation and change differ: because where there is generation, there is a process or movement from nonbeing to being. Where there is change, however, there is not a change according to being; rather, the same being and the same substance remains but takes on a different mode of being. If, therefore, in the divine there is not a process that makes a different being, which is a transition from nonbeing to being, but only one that makes for different modes of being, then the process which is in God cannot be called generation, but more appropriately, change, and so it is not possible to posit generation in God.

5. Another argument. We see that perfect generation has its origin in two, namely, male and female, but an imperfect generation has its beginning in one, as is clear in the generation of plants and even of worms, which is less perfect than the generation of animals and humans, whose generation consists in a twofold principle, namely, agent and patient; therefore, if that which is more perfect in generation should be attributed to God, it should be posited in the divine that the Son himself is born of the Father and even of a mother, which is absurd. Therefore, it remains that generation should not be posited in the divine.

6. Here is another argument which weakens some of the aforementioned arguments: the likening of natural things to the divine involves a comparison of exceedingly remote things, because the distance between creatures and the creator is exceedingly great. For this reason, what is found in created

things does not necessarily have to be posited in the divine, and the foregoing arguments, which proceed by comparing natural things to the divine, are null and void.

7. If on this account, namely, that the created nature is multiplicative of its species, we want to identify something similar in God, therefore similarly, pointing out that creaturely being entails the production of accidents would amount to a demonstration of [accidents] in the divine. From this, therefore, it follows that God has accidents and that he is a quantity and is colored.

8. Another argument is this. If [properties] of creaturely generation are also applicable to God by comparison, since together with transferring the nature of the one generating to the one generated, creaturely generation transfers also the power of generating, by which the generated one is able to generate [as well], then similarly in the divine, the Son himself will have the power of generating another son; but in eternal entities, power is [always] conjoined to act; therefore, the Son will generate another son; and that one will function in the same mode, as will the next one, to infinity. Therefore, there is no eternal generation and neither is a comparison with creatures valid.

Reply:

It must be acknowledged most truly that there is eternal generation. Thus, Richard of St. Victor says in *On the Trinity* [1.9], "In the created nature we read what we ought to think about the uncreated. We see every day in what way subsistence by the operation of its own nature produces existence, and existence proceeds from existence. Surely in that most super-excellent nature, there will be an operation of nature as well? Or does that [divine] nature which gave the fruit of fecundity to this [created] nature remain entirely sterile in itself? And that which contributes generation to others, surely will not be sterile?" As it is said in Isaiah 66:9, "*Surely I who make others give birth, give birth myself? Then will I, who give generation to others, be sterile? Says the Lord.*" Here, reference is made to eternal generation, as it is described in the Gloss. There is therefore eternal generation.

In the same book [Richard] says, "certainly a ray of sun proceeds from the sun, and nevertheless exists coevally with the sun; for as long as [the sun] has existed, it has been producing a ray from itself and was at no time without the ray. If, therefore, this corporeal light has a ray coeternal with itself, why would that spiritual and inaccessible light not have the same?"

And Damascene [*On the Orthodox Faith* 1.6]: "God was not at any time speechless, that is, without a Word; for he always has his own word generated from his own self." Therefore, it is impossible according to Damascene that God does not generate.

Replies to the objections:

We must respond to the opposing arguments. First to those that weaken the argument of Augustine in the book *83 Questions*, it must be said that the argument of Augustine is internally consistent: because he intended through that argument to show that the Father generated the Son who is coequal with himself, and so that argument always presupposes generation rather than proves [it]. Nevertheless, one must reply to the objections.

1. And to the first, that "he could have made a better world and did not will to do so, therefore he was envious": it must be said that there is a difference between generation and creation, because generation always requires that something is produced that is equal in nature and substance [to the generator]. By contrast, creation does not [require this]; instead, it requires that what is created is not equal and differs in substance [to the creator]. "One speaks of envy only where things are done differently than how they should have been done." Therefore, in generation, where there must be equality between the one generating and the one generated, the essential traits of envy are present if what is generated is not equal to the one generating. Therefore, what Augustine says rightly follows: "he was able to generate a Son equal to himself and he did not will [to do so], therefore he is envious," since this is what he should have done, namely, generate one equal to himself. But in creation there is no such obligation, neither is it required that human beings be [made] better than they are, and therefore it does not follow concerning those things which are created [that God was envious].

2. To the other objection, that this does not follow: "the Son wills to generate, but is not able to do so, therefore he is impotent," it must be said that in order for this argument to work, it would be necessary to join willing with inability; whence it surely follows that "someone wills to do this and is not able, therefore he is impotent." But neither the Son nor the Holy Spirit will to generate anything. And therefore "not to be able to generate" does not imply powerlessness in the Son nor in the Holy Spirit, even though it would posit impotence in the Father, because the Father wills to generate; the Son, however, does not, rather [he wills] to be generated. For as it is a perfection

in the Father to generate, so it is a perfection in the Son to be generated, and even in the Holy Spirit to be spirated. Thus, as "to be able to generate" is called a perfection of the power of the Father, so "to be generated" is called a perfection of the power in the Son, and "to be spirated" [is a perfection] in the Holy Spirit. Therefore, on the part of the Father, impotence would follow if he were not able to generate, while on the part of the Son or Holy Spirit, no impotence will follow.

3. To the third argument, it must be said that the following phrase has a twofold meaning: "generation is an imperfection in those who generate," because it can have the sense that [generally] generation is an imperfection in the one that generates and in their power, or that [the ability to generate] is given to the one generating in order to compensate for their imperfection. I say, therefore, that [generally speaking or] in the first sense, generation is not an imperfection; rather generation involves the most perfect mode of acting or producing: for the most perfect mode of acting is the one through which the effect is made coequal and assimilated in nature to the one acting, which is what happens in generation. According to the second mode, however, it can be conceded that generation is an imperfection in corruptible creatures, because it is given [to them] in order to mitigate their imperfection. Thus, it compensates for an imperfection in them. Because a singular entity would not be able to preserve its species in itself, consequently, it receives a power of such great perfection. That, however, which compensates for imperfection is not an imperfection, but is rather more [like] a perfection. Therefore, generation pertains to perfection, and implies the perfection of power in the one generating. Therefore, it should be attributed to God.

To the objection that "it is a sign of perfection in the sun that it does not generate," it must be said that this is not the case; it is rather a sign of imperfection in the substances that they are not able to produce from themselves one similar to themselves in nature. On this basis, if a power were posited in the sun by which it could produce another sun while remaining unchanged, just as it is able [currently] to produce light from itself, this would be the greatest power in the sun—more perfect than the power it has currently, when it is not able to produce a sun from itself. For this reason, it is deficient in power in this respect. However, insofar as it is able in itself to preserve its own species, it has a perfection that corruptible things do not possess, because it is a sign of perfection not to need another for one's preservation. Therefore, it is a sign of perfection in corruptible things that they possess [the power] to produce from themselves similar things, and a sign of imperfection that they are not able to preserve and perpetuate themselves in being [individually]. Similarly, it is a perfection in celestial bodies that they are able to preserve and perpetuate themselves in being, and an imperfection that they are not able to produce out of themselves one similar and coequal in nature [to themselves], as opposed to producing from themselves an unequal, as the sun produces light but not a sun. Therefore, that which implies perfection must be attributed to God, so that he may have the power of producing one similar and coequal [to himself] in nature while remaining [unchanged] in himself.

4. To the fourth argument, we reply that generation is motion or a kind of motion, and it is an act. As far as it implies motion, it [generation] is not proper to God, because no movement or kind of movement can be found in him, because motion is an imperfection in the one moving. But insofar as it [generation] is understood as an act, it means completion that makes the product perfectly adequate to the one producing, and in this sense, generation is not a correlative of change. But to the objection that "where there is a process that makes a difference to a being's mode of being, there is change," it must be said that this does not [necessarily] follow, unless there is a mutation there. For it does not follow that the sun, insofar as it generates light from itself, undergoes a change, because there is no mutation in it. Also, as will become clear later, one mode of being can be replaced by a different one in two ways: in one way when two [individuals] are produced [without a change in the original individual], and this is not a change; and the other way when one different individual is produced [that replaces the original one], and this is [a change].[1]

5. The answer to the fifth argument is that human generation is imperfect because it has its origin in two [persons] and not in one only. For if there were only one power, such that the whole power of generating was either in the man or in the woman, this united [power] would be more perfect than a power that is divided [amongst two]. Therefore, it is that [power] as united and not as divided that should be attributed to God, because [as divided] it

---

1. The first case is production of persons out of divine essence where neither the essence nor the first person is changed, so it is not a change; the second is a case of regular change, for example, when a tadpole changes into a frog and both the individual and its essence change.

pertains to imperfection. But what about the case of plants, whose generation is most imperfect, and yet that generation takes place in a single being? One must reply that although plants are generated from one [plant] intrinsically, nevertheless, there are multiple extrinsic principles of their generation, such as moisture from the earth and heat from the sun, one being the principle of activity and the other of passivity, as if one were male and the other female—the male the active principle, and the female, the passive. From these things, it can be inferred that there is eternal generation, and that in God there is a difference between the one generating and the generated, namely, between the Father and the Son.

6. The reply to the sixth argument is as follows: one can draw a comparison between natural things and the divine being in two ways, because creatures can be considered in two ways, either in themselves or as vestiges of their cause. When they are considered in themselves, we cannot draw a suitable parallel between the creature and the Creator: in fact, in this regard, the difference between the one and the other is the greatest [that there is], nor is there any aspect under which something can be attributed to the Creator in the same sense as to the creature, just as there is no parallel between the finite and the infinite, whether in power, wisdom, or goodness. When, however, creatures are considered as vestiges of their cause, it is possible to find both necessary and fitting parallels between the creature and the Creator; thus, from the power of the creature, we necessarily infer the omnipotence of the Creator, and from wisdom, the highest wisdom, and from goodness, the highest good. Thus, the Apostle says in Romans 1:20: "*the invisible things of God are clearly seen through those things which have been made*"; that would not be the case unless those things which are made are vestiges [of the divine]. Thus, Dionysius says in the *Celestial Hierarchy* [2.3–4], "No existing thing is entirely deprived of participation in the good, as the truth of scriptures proclaims in Genesis 1:31: "*all things are very good.*" Therefore, it is possible to infer valid observations from all things, and on the basis of material beings, to form dissimilar likenesses to invisible and intelligible things." Therefore, insofar as a vestige of the highest Trinity is impressed in creatures, one must say that it is possible to find a suitable parallel based on that vestige of impressed goodness in order to reveal the perfection of the impressing goodness, so that what is more perfect and does not have in itself any sign of imperfection may always be attributed to God. And this is what Richard of

St. Victor says [in *On the Trinity* 1.4]: "regarding whatever exists necessarily, infallible arguments cannot be lacking."

7. To the seventh argument, one can respond that while God is a cause according to a threefold mode of efficient, final, and formal or exemplary causality, he is not in any way a material cause. Therefore, those things in nature which pertain to an efficient, formal, or final cause can be transferred to God, because in these respects, creatures are vestiges [of God]. But those things which pertain to the material cause, such as accidents like "colored," which can be found in the material body, or "oblivious" in the soul, more specifically in the material intellect, cannot in any way be transferred to God, except figuratively or improperly, and in this way the creature is not like the Creator. However, the ability to generate something similar from oneself pertains to an efficient cause and, moreover, is a sign of the nobility of a power. Therefore, this must be attributed to the power of God.

8. To the final argument, one can respond that if perfection consists in oneness or singularity, while imperfection is in multiplicity, when there are multiple individuals, and each one of them in all respects and in every way has the same traits, all but one are superfluous. Consequently, it must be said that as the Son is perfect in every mode of perfection, just one of him will suffice. Therefore, this is an indication of imperfection in the process of human generation, namely, that the one generated is able to generate: for this indicates that the one generated is not a perfect son.

WHAT DOES IT MEAN TO GENERATE IN THE DIVINE ESSENCE?

SH 1, P1, In2, Tr un., Q1, Ti1, C2 (n. 296), 419–21

The second chapter inquires into the definition of generation in the divine essence.

I. And regarding this we will consider whether generation in God is the same as understanding in God.

In support of the claim that it is, some have tried to argue:

1. God lives the most noble life, which is a life of understanding; but God's life and his action are one and the same. Therefore, if generation is understood as a sort of action, then generation and understanding are the same in God.

2. The primary intelligence understands itself without departing from itself; hence, its act of understanding does not depart from it; but to understand is nothing other than to generate a species in oneself. Therefore, to understand oneself is nothing other than to generate one's own species in oneself. Therefore, God's understanding involves generating his own species in himself. But this is what it means to generate the Son. Therefore, in God, to understand is nothing other than to generate the Son. And since the fact that he always understands himself is a sign of the excellence of his essence, it is necessary always to posit in him both the one generating and the one begotten. But those names imply two things, namely, something like action and relation; for when I speak of that which generates, I speak of an action, and also of a relation [to a recipient of the action]: for a relation always accompanies action in an agent. Because therefore God's substance and his action are the same on the part of the action and that which is predicated under the aspect of passion, as in the case of understanding and being understood, no diversity can be found in him or in his essence. Therefore, any plurality that is implied in the case of the agent of understanding and its object—namely, when [God] is multiplied into the one who understands and the one who is understood—must necessarily be only relational. If, therefore, we were to decouple relation from the aforementioned action by using their proper names, we would arrive at a plurality, which is signified by the names "Father" and "Son." For this name "Father" properly signifies that relation which accompanies the act of him who generates. From this, therefore, we can infer that "for God to understand himself" amounts to nothing other than the generation of his image and species in himself, since understanding involves the generation of the species of the thing understood.

On the other hand:

a. Unlike understanding, generation never involves one and the same thing producing itself; therefore, generation is not the same as understanding in the divine essence.

b. Where generation is posited, there is multiplicity and a difference between the one generating and what is generated; but saying that God understands himself does not imply difference or any multiplicity, because God's understanding of himself is nothing other than his, as it were, turning on to his own self. Therefore, generation is not the same as understanding [in God].

II. Second, we must consider whether generation is the same as speaking in the divine essence.

That it is: 1. Anselm [in *Monologion* 33] says that "insofar as the highest essence speaks itself, the Father generates and the Son is generated." Therefore, his internal speech is the same as the generation of the Word. Thus, speaking his Word and generating are the same in God.

2. Augustine [in *The Literal Commentary on Genesis* 1.2.6] says of Genesis 1:3 ("*God said, let there be light*") that "'*God said*' implies the generation of the Word, in whom light was made." Therefore, speaking and generating are the same for him.

On the other hand:

a. Anselm says [in *Monologion* 63]: "every person speaks of themselves and of others"; therefore, if generation means speaking in God, any person can generate itself and others, which is false.

Solution:

Human beings do not have the power to determine the "what it is" of eternal generation, let alone of the eternal [divine] substance. Recognizing this, the prophet Isaiah says in 53:8, "*who will be able to describe his generation?*" This implies that no one can do so and that this ability is instead a reward of faith. According to the common definition, however, generation results in the production of a substance. However, there are several types of this production, because the substance produced is either similar or dissimilar in nature to the being that produces it. In the latter case, production entails an equivocal generation, as when a maggot is produced from carrion. The former is the case of univocal generation. But univocal generation can occur in a number of ways. Sometimes that "substantial product similar in nature" is produced out of a part, and not the whole of the original substance. When one human being begets another, for example, the production is partial. Sometimes, however, the whole substance is reproduced. This is the nature of production in the divine persons, who derive one from another. After all, the divine essence is supremely simple, and wherever it is present, it is present in its entirety, and not merely a part of it. Therefore, substantial production in the divine persons involves the entire substance, not a part. Yet this production can occur in either a principal or a nonprincipal mode. In the principal mode, the product that is produced has the power and property of producing another from itself. This is the way in which the Son is generated by the Father, whose property he retains, insofar as he has the power of producing another from himself, namely, the Holy Spirit. By contrast, the Holy Spirit is produced in the nonprincipal mode, because he does not retain the property of producing another from himself even though he is produced substantially. Therefore, the first product, namely, the Son, is generated; the other, which is the Spirit, comes forth by way of procession. Nevertheless, when we speak of the generation of the Son as principal, and the procession of the Spirit as nonprincipal, no inequality is implied, but only a difference in properties. In the same way, when we call something "primary" or "nonprimary" [in God], we do not designate a priority or posteriority in time but an order of nature. From this, it is clear that generation in the divine involves the univocal production of something similar in nature in its entire substance according to the principal mode. The reason this production is called generation is that, among all kinds of production, generation is the principal and highest type in which what is produced possesses the power of producing another from itself.

I. What it means to generate, then, differs from what it means to understand, just as what it means to exist differs from what it means to generate. In God, what it means to exist is understood in an absolute sense; similarly, what it means to understand in God is predicated absolutely. But generation by definition implies a relation. Therefore, generation by definition is not the same as understanding; rather, generation accompanies understanding. As we see in the soul, when "the mind understands itself," it follows that it generates knowledge of itself. Nevertheless, it is not the same thing for the mind to know itself and to generate knowledge of itself: these are two different things; however, it is said that "one accompanies the other." Thus, in the divine essence, it is not the same thing for God to generate his species and to understand; however, God's generation of his species or image within himself accompanies understanding. Thus, it is not true when it is said that "God understands himself" means that "God generates his species in himself." For it is not possible to understand through a species, where an act and an essence are the same, nor where a species is the same as the essence. Therefore, when it is said that "in understanding, he generates" or "to understand is to generate his species," this is taken in the sense of accompaniment. However, in the mind there is a greater difference than in the divine being [between understanding and generation]. Nevertheless, the generation of one's own species necessarily entails the one generating and the one that is generated.

Replies to the objections:

1. To the first objection, one can reply that even if the one understanding, what is understood, and the divine act are the same in God, nevertheless, there is a conceptual difference between generation and understanding on account of the accompanying relations.[2] For generation implies a relation that is engendered by an act; to understand, however, refers to the divine being and substance itself. To generate, however, does not add to understanding, as neither does relation to essence; rather [generation] accompanies the understanding, or follows it, because the generation of one's own species in oneself follows or accompanies [an act of] understanding. It is also for this reason that one can say that in the divine, one and the same [thing or agent] understands itself, whether one takes "the same" as a masculine or as a neuter. However, one cannot apply the same [indiscriminate] "masculine or neutral" language to [the expression] "generates himself," for it is by reason of this relation that plurality or distinction is posited [in the divine], which is signified by the names "Father, Son, one generating and one generated," as was said previously.

2. And through the preceding, the reply to the second objection is clear.

II. In response to the question whether speaking is the same as generating in God, one can say that "to speak" in God means, in one way, "to manifest" and thus refers to the essence [of God]. And in this sense every person "speaks" or "says" another, because every person manifests another [person]. Thus, the gospel of John 14:11 says: *"I am in the Father and the Father is in me"*; likewise, Matthew 11:27: *"no one knows the Son but the Father, nor the Father but the Son and the one to whom the Son wills to reveal him."* Notice here how one person is manifested in another. In another way, "to speak" means to bring forth a word: and so "to speak" implies a proportionality between the origin or source and that which comes from the source, because the one bringing forth is the principle of the word that is proffered. In this sense, "to speak" is taken notionally and befits only the Father. Here, to speak is the same as to generate, albeit not in the first mode, because this would imply that every person generates himself and other persons, whereas the second mode implies a relation between a beginning and that which comes from this beginning. For the Son "speaks" the essence and the property of the Father, and this is why he is the Word [of God]. As for the Holy Spirit,

2. In the case of generation.

even though he might "speak" the whole essence of the Father, namely, power, wisdom, and goodness, nevertheless, he does not in himself speak the property of the Father by which the Father produces another from himself; therefore, he is not called the Word as the Son, nor is his production called generation, which is the sort of production proper to the Son, as has been stated. For the word fully manifests properties based on the meaning and intention of the one speaking; therefore, the Holy Spirit is not the Word nor is he brought forth from the Father like the Word, but he "is spoken" in the sense of "manifested." And this is the solution to this question. . . .

IS THERE A PROCESSION OF THE HOLY SPIRIT?

SH 1, P1, In2, Tr. un., Q1, T2, C1 (n. 304), 438–40

a. There are two principles of diffusion in things: nature and will. The most perfect diffusion by nature is generation, whereas the most perfect diffusion of the will is through love. And [these two comprise] the glory of the good in things: for that good, which diffuses itself in both ways, is more praiseworthy than the one that diffuses itself in only one or the other. If, therefore, what is praiseworthy and perfect cannot be lacking in the highest good, there is in the highest good, namely, God, a diffusion of generation, which results in a difference between the one generating and the one generated, namely, Father and Son; and there is a diffusion through the mode of love there, which we call the procession of the Holy Spirit.

b. Just as the highest good does not lack the highest power of nature, so it does not lack the highest power of the will; but the highest power of nature necessarily involves a diffusion by generation. Therefore, the highest power of the will entails a diffusion of love. For as generation is highest among natural diffusions, so among diffusions of the will, that one is highest which is love.

c. It is essential for the highest good to be diffusive or communicative. Since there are two types of diffusion or communication, namely, of nature, as in generation, or gratuitous, as in a gift, two modes of diffusion or communication are germane to the highest good: generation, as the Son from the Father, and donation, as the gift from the one giving. Therefore, beyond eternal generation, there will be a diffusion which is through the mode of donation. However, a diffusion through the mode of donation is the procession of love. For "love is the first and perfect gift by which all other things are properly given: for the one who gives his love to another holds all things in common with that one. However, that which is given not from love is not strictly speaking given. For what is given from fear is more like extortion than a gift; and what is given from greed to obtain a certain thing, is more like commerce."

d. "Love is an internal gift in the one giving, by virtue of which an external gift is given; therefore, the gift of love is prior to a certain external gift." Therefore, in the highest giver, the gift of love is prior to any external gift conferred on creatures, namely, being, and thus it is prior to his distribution of goodness to creatures. Thus, the gift of love in God is eternal. But this gift is defined relatively to the giver. Therefore, it is necessary that the giver and the gift, which is the Holy Spirit, are eternal.

e. The highest goodness must contain the highest and most preeminent love; it is highest, insofar as one loves another as himself; and preeminent, since he wills that other person to be loved by a [third person] as that [third person] loves himself. The first point is proved insofar as we posit that Socrates loves Socrates as himself, but Pylades loves Orestes as himself and also wills him to be loved by a [third person] as that [third person] loves himself. Which of these loves is preeminent and most praiseworthy? The love of Pylades and Orestes. But there is a common idea according to which what is praiseworthy is attributed to the highest good. Therefore, it is necessary to posit that the highest good loves another as himself and wills that this other be loved by [yet] another as that other loves himself; but this [love] is not able to occur in fewer than three persons; therefore, there are three persons; therefore, there is a Holy Spirit; but he does not have being unless by "proceeding"; therefore, his procession exists.[3]

3. The position expressed in "e" seems to be somewhat different from the position of Richard of St. Victor expressed in "g," even though one would expect them to be entirely consistent. However, the parallelism of Latin constructions in "e" suggests that, among three lovers that are involved (A, B, and C), at the initial level A loves B as A loves "himself," that is, A, and at the higher level A also wants B to be loved by C as C loves "himself," that is, C. In "e" it would be a stretch to interpret the grammar in the sense that A wants B to be loved by C as C loves A, because, first, no love of C for A has been mentioned, and second, one does not know if C loves A as strongly as C loves "himself," that is, C. The situation is different with Richard's opinion in "g" because he expressly mentions that A loves B and is loved back by B and makes it explicit that A must want C to be loved by B as B loves A, not as B loves "himself," that is, B. However, the two passages are not in

f. If there were two goods, and one diffused itself by nature and by will, and the other by will only, clearly the more praiseworthy would be the good that diffuses itself by both modes than the one [that diffuses itself] by one only. But what is most praiseworthy must be present in the highest good. Therefore, it is necessary to posit both modes of diffusion in the highest good, where the natural diffusion is generation and the voluntary diffusion of the highest good is procession. Therefore, there is procession.

g. Richard of St. Victor says in *On the Trinity* [3.11]: "as the highest love cannot be lacking what is greatest, so neither will it be able to lack what is preeminent. What is preeminent in true love, however, seems to consist in willing that another be loved as one is [loved] oneself; accordingly, nothing is more glorious in mutual, fervent love than that you will for another to be loved in the same way [as you are loved] by the one you love supremely and by whom you are loved supremely. Therefore, it is proved that the consummation of love is in desiring to share in common with someone else that love exhibited toward oneself." From this it is established that while the highest or maximal love proves the duality of persons, the preeminence of love proves the Trinity.

h. Richard of St. Victor says in the same place: "it is a sign of great weakness not to be able to accept this sharing of love, while to be able to accept it is a sign of great perfection. Even better is to accept this [love] joyfully, while the best thing is to seek it out desirously." For if it is a good thing to be able to accept it, it is better to accept it joyfully, and it is the best thing to seek it out desirously, then "from this, we can clearly deduce that the preeminent degree of love and, by the same token, the fullness of goodness, cannot exist where a defect of the will or faculty prevents the sharing of love and the communion of preeminent joy. Therefore, those who are and should be supremely loved," namely, the Father and the Son, "must both with the same desire seek this shared object of love and possess the desire for him in perfect concord."

i. Richard says [in *On the Trinity* 3.14]: "nothing more pleasant can be found than the sweetness of love, nothing in which the soul could take more

---

conflict as far as the main doctrinal point is concerned, that is, that in order to have a trinity of persons, A must desire for there to be a third person, C, to love the second person, B. In the first scenario C will love B as C loves C, i.e., as strongly as A, because A loves B as A loves A. In the second scenario C will be loved by B as strongly as B loves A.

delight. However, this delight is only possessed by the one who in receiving love has a companion and co-beloved. Thus, the communication of love cannot happen at all with fewer than three persons. For there is nothing more glorious, nothing more magnificent, than to have in common every useful and sweet thing."

k. [Richard, *On the Trinity* 3.15]: "Note that in the divine persons, the perfection of one requires the addition of another and consequently the perfection of either of the pair requires association with a third." Now, as "in both of the persons an equal [degree of] benevolence exists, it is necessary that with similar devotion, and for a similar reason, they require one to share their preeminent joy," namely, the Holy Spirit.

l. [Richard, *On the Trinity* 3.15]: "For as long as this one alone is loved by another, he seems to possess alone the pleasures of his preeminent sweetness; similarly also the other, for as long as he does not have a shared beloved, lacks communion in his preeminent joy. So in order that both could communicate this kind of sweetness, it is necessary that they have a shared [object of] love," namely, the Holy Spirit.

On the other hand:

1. That which is predicated by superabundance befits only one [person]; but the highest or supreme good is predicated by superabundance; therefore, this can only befit one [person]. Therefore, in God, there is only one person, otherwise supreme goodness would befit many, which is contrary to the nature of the superlative.

2. The good is diffusive of its being; but the Holy Spirit is supremely good; therefore, he diffuses his being in the highest way. Now if the good is diffusive and the supreme good is supremely diffusive, the Holy Spirit supremely diffuses his being. But the highest diffusion entails a diffusion of one's whole substance. Therefore, the Holy Spirit gives to another the whole of his substance. Therefore, another person derives from him and there is a fourth person in the Trinity. But for the same reason, that one would diffuse his substance to another and another to another, and so on, ad infinitum. Therefore, an infinity of persons would be produced, which is unbefitting. Thus, the highest goodness must remain in one person. If it is said that the Holy Spirit does not diffuse himself to another person, but to creatures, and thus does not diffuse his substance to produce something like himself, then one objects that it follows that the Holy Spirit is not an eternal good, because he does not diffuse himself in creatures from eternity, since creatures have not existed from eternity.

3. The same kind of supreme goodness is in each of the three persons. Therefore, as the Father diffuses his substance because he is supremely good, similarly the Holy Spirit will diffuse his substance, as the supreme goodness is in him of the same kind and in the same mode as in the Father.

4. It seems that the highest love does not by necessity entail a plurality of persons. For love or charitable love can be in one alone, as Augustine says [in *On Christian Teaching* 1.23] that "through charity we should love first of all those things which are above us and second those things which we are." Therefore, someone could love himself in charity.

5. The divine essence loves himself, and does so, clearly, by a more excellent mode of desiring; therefore, he loves himself by charity; for this reason, the highest charity does not necessarily require a plurality of persons.

Reply:

It must be acknowledged, as scripture says, that there is a procession of the Holy Spirit.

Replies to the objections:

1. In response to the first objection, it must be said that what is best befits one alone, namely, the goodness of God or the good generally, that is, taken in the neuter;[4] nevertheless, it befits a plurality of persons insofar as they comprise one highest good.

2. To the second objection, we can say that the highest good is understood as the highest and most orderly diffusion; thus, the supreme goodness precludes confusion and infinitude. If, therefore, we posit a highest diffusion, it should be posited in only three persons, one of whom is the beginning, namely, the Father, one who is the middle, namely, the Son, and another who is the terminus or end, namely, the Holy Spirit.

3. To the third objection, which objects that "the goodness in the three persons is the same and it exists in them in the same way," we can say that this is true; nevertheless, it is in persons that exist in diverse ways. For it is in the Father who exists in the mode of a first principle or beginning, in the Son who is in the mode of a medium, and in the Holy Spirit who is in the mode of an end. Thus, there cannot be a diffusion from the person of the Holy Spirit, because this is contrary to the mode or nature of his person, which is that of an end or terminus.

---

4. The abstract term for "the good" (*bonum*) in Latin is neuter.

4. To this objection, we can say that by charity, one is able to love themselves, but not in the full sense of charity, because "in order for love to be charity," namely, in the full sense of charity, "it must be directed at another," as Gregory says [in *On the Gospel* 17:1].

5. To this, we must reply that if the divine essence is understood to love himself without persons, he does not love himself in the most noble mode, namely, through the sharing of love, but in a private way. If, however, he is understood to [love] through persons, then he loves supremely, and such love cannot exist without a plurality of persons, as has been shown. That the persons are three in number, however, can be shown in this way: if we posit a fourth person, and there are only two modes of production, namely, the mode of nature or the mode of the will, then this fourth person is produced either through the mode of nature or through the mode of the will. If, however, it is produced through the mode of nature, since this mode is the same as generation, then the person produced will be the Son, and there will be two sons in the Trinity, which is unfitting. If he is produced through the mode of the will, which is the mode of procession by way of gift or love, by which the Holy Spirit proceeds, then this fourth one will proceed in the same mode as the Holy Spirit and will not differ from the Holy Spirit, whether by essence or relation.

TO WHOM DOES IT BELONG TO PROCEED?

SH 1, P1, In2, Tr. un., Q1, T2, C2 (n. 305), 441–42

Next we will consider to whom it belongs to proceed. And assuming, as is proved in the following, that in the divine persons there is a person who is not from another, that is, the Father, and persons who are from another—one that is from another and from whom another is derived, namely, the Son; and another, who is from another and from whom no one else derives, that is, the Holy Spirit—it is clear that procession pertains only to those persons who come from another.

I. We will first consider whether procession is proper to the Holy Spirit in the same way as generation is proper to the Son.

That it is:

a. Hilary of Poitiers, *On the Trinity* 5.[37], "By virtue of the power of [the divine] nature [acting] on the same nature, the Son subsists by generation."

And from the power of [the divine] nature [acting] on the same nature, the Holy Spirit subsists by procession. Therefore, as being born is proper to the Son, so procession is proper to the Holy Spirit.

On the other hand:

a. Wherever we can say that one is produced by another, there is procession; but the Son is produced by another; therefore, he proceeds. Therefore, procession is proper to him and not only to the Holy Spirit.

b. Both the Son and the Holy Spirit are said to proceed, either univocally or equivocally or analogically. If univocally, then they proceed in the same way; but the way in which the Son proceeds involves generation, and thus, generation would also pertain to the Holy Spirit, which is false. Nor do the Son and Spirit proceed in an equivocal or completely different sense, because both involve derivation from another. If they proceed analogically, then procession is predicated in the sense of priority (*per prius*) of the Son, because he proceeds in a more primary mode, and in the sense of posteriority (*per posterius*) of the Holy Spirit; in this case, procession would be more properly appropriated to the Son than the Holy Spirit.

Reply:

Procession can be understood in two ways: either absolutely and precisely or with the superaddition of a certain dignity or distinction. According to the first mode procession is the property of the Holy Spirit, because the Son's procession is not understood without the addition of a certain dignity, which involves proceeding according to a more primary mode, or proceeding from another in such a way as to receive [from the Father] also the power of generating another while proceeding. This mode of procession should be called generation, as procession through generation is more primary among all modes of proceeding and so receives its name from what is more dignified in it, or through a superadded distinction, as humans are not properly defined as sensory but as rational [animals]. However, "procession" precisely and absolutely understood is only proper to the Holy Spirit.

Replies to the objections:

1. To the first objection, we may respond that although procession is common [to multiple persons], nevertheless, procession, when it is not understood according to its primary mode, is proper to the Holy Spirit. In his case, procession is understood precisely as involving procession only. The other

form of procession, according to the primary mode, is proper to the Son and is [called] generation.

2. To the second objection, we can say that procession is not predicated univocally or equivocally but by analogy in the sense of priority or posteriority, nevertheless, with a [further] distinction [between them], because procession is either understood in an unqualified sense (or absolutely) or under a certain mode [in a qualified sense]. When procession is understood in a qualified sense, if this is a procession by way of intelligence, it is the procession of the Son; otherwise it happens through the mode of love, as in the case of the Holy Spirit. As for procession defined absolutely, it is any production of one from another. One must say, then, that procession understood under a certain mode is attributed to the Son in the sense of priority and to the Holy Spirit in the sense of posteriority, because the procession of the understanding from the mind is prior to the procession that occurs through the mode of love from both [the mind and its understanding]. However, to proceed, understood absolutely, principally befits the Holy Spirit, because it befits his essence only to exist from another, and not to be one from which another derives, and therefore it befits him to proceed only and not to produce another from himself. [And in this absolute sense], the Son proceeds in a posterior sense, because it does not befit the Son only to be from another but also to produce another from himself. Thus, it befits him not only to proceed but also to produce another. Therefore, common procession, if it is considered as common, first befits the Holy Spirit, because this level of precision does not add anything to what is common. But if we consider procession in terms of a certain mode, it first befits the Son, because he proceeds in a more primary way.

II. Here, we will consider whether procession through the mode of love is proper to the Holy Spirit.

It seems it is not 1. Because the whole Trinity loves, as will be shown in the following.

On the other hand:

a. Augustine says [*On the Trinity* 6.5.7:] "the one by whom the two are conjoined is not either of them," for the Father is the one who loves, the Son is the one who is loved, and what conjoins them both is love. Therefore, the Holy Spirit alone is love and neither [the Father nor the Son] is the love by which they both are conjoined. Therefore, to proceed through the mode of love properly belongs to the Holy Spirit alone, which is what we concede.

Reply to the objection:

1. To the objection that "the whole Trinity loves itself," it must be said that this is true, when we understand love essentially, not notionally, as will be shown more fully in what follows.

WHO PROCEEDS THROUGH THE MODE OF LOVE OR A GIFT?

SH 1, P1, In2, Tr. un., Q1, T2, C3, A2 (n. 307), 443–46

1. Since any type of loving implies love, and loving is proper to the whole Trinity, because we must say that the Father, Son, and Spirit all love, therefore both loving and love are common to the whole Trinity. But love comes from and proceeds from the one loving. Therefore, procession through the mode of love will be common to the whole Trinity.

2. Augustine says in *On the Trinity* [15.17.28], "If the Father, Son and Holy Spirit are simultaneously all called one but not three wisdoms, why would Father, Son, and Spirit not likewise be called one and not three loves?" Love, then, is common to the whole Trinity; if, therefore, to be love is to be a gift, it befits the whole Trinity to be a gift. Similarly, as it is the same to be charity as it is to be love, and all love proceeds from the one loving, it befits the whole Trinity to proceed.

3. In an antiphon it is said about the Trinity: "the Father is love; Christ, grace; their communication, the Holy Spirit." Therefore, "being love" is appropriated to the Father, and procession will also be appropriated to him.

4. Where there is a gratuitous love and an indebted love, the designation "love" will be more appropriate to gratuitous love than to indebted love. As therefore gratuitous love befits the Father, and indebted love befits the Holy Spirit, then a love that involves a combination of both will pertain to the Son. Thus, love befits the Father more and the Son less and the Holy Spirit the least. Richard of St. Victor proves that this is true in *On the Trinity* [5.16]: love, he says, "is gratuitous, when one freely gives it to someone from whom [the giver] receives no gift; love is indebted when one repays someone from whom he receives something gratuitously with nothing but love; love is of a mixed variety when in loving, one in turns both freely receives and freely gives it." "But that person, to whom it belongs to proceed, but nevertheless

not to have one proceeding from himself, because he accepts the whole of what he has from another source, necessarily has the fullness of indebted love." "However, that person who is not considered to have accepted anything from anyone else, as a result of which he would incur an obligation or acquire a debtor in any respect, in no way seems to be able to have indebted love, but only gratuitous." However, that person who accepts and offers [love], like the Son, has a love combined of both [gratuitous and indebted love]. "It is clear therefore that in [only] one of the three is there highest love that is exclusively gratuitous," namely, in the Father. "In the other there is highest love that is exclusively indebted," namely, the Holy Spirit; "and in the third," namely, the Son, "there is highest love that is on the one hand indebted," insofar as he receives from the Father, "and on the other hand, gratuitous," insofar as he gives to the Holy Spirit. Therefore, love is common to the three persons and is not most appropriate to the Holy Spirit [only].

5. The one whom it best befits to be called wisdom, is also best described as a gift. This is true, because among the seven gifts, of which Isaiah 11:2–3 speaks, the highest and most preeminent gift is wisdom. As it properly befits the Son to be called wisdom, he will also rightly be called a gift, as is clear from Augustine's *On the Trinity* [15.17.31], "the only Word of God is the one we properly call by the name of wisdom, although generally speaking both the Holy Spirit and the Father are wisdom." Therefore, as the same Son comes from the Father as wisdom from the mind, so he proceeds through the mode of donation; therefore, he is properly the gift.

6. The Spirit receives its proper name because it is spirated. As therefore wisdom or intelligence is spirated, it befits wisdom to be the Spirit. That [wisdom] is [in fact] spirated is clear because it [wisdom] is inspired, as Job 32:8 says: *the inspiration of the omnipotent gives understanding*. Therefore, it is also spirated. If, therefore, the Son proceeds from the Father as wisdom from the mind, it befits him to be the Spirit. Therefore, the procession of the Son is through the mode of spiration.

7. The principle of knowing or understanding is properly called wisdom. If, therefore, the Holy Spirit is properly the principle of knowing or understanding, as such, he is properly [called] wisdom. The proof of the middle term[5] is taken from 1 Corinthians 2:10: "*God has revealed himself to us through*

---

5. The edition here gives "middle term" or "middle proposition" (*media*), while it is more common here to refer to the "minor premise" (*minor*).

the Spirit, and the Spirit searches all things." And likewise, [in 1 Corinthians 2:12,] *"we accepted the Spirit, who is from God, in order to know."*

8. Intelligence or understanding is properly generated by the mind. Therefore, because the Holy Spirit is the spirit of understanding, he will be generated. The middle term is proved through Wisdom 7:22: *"in her [wisdom] is the spirit of understanding, holiness, etc."*

9. The spirit is called the beginning of knowledge and understanding, while love is the beginning of desire and wisdom is the beginning of knowledge. Therefore, just as the Holy Spirit is properly called love, he should be properly called wisdom.

10. What interprets the meaning of truth is the [human] word. But the Holy Spirit is what interprets the meaning of truth. Therefore, he is the word. The proof of the middle term is from John 16:13: *"when the Spirit of truth comes, he will teach us all truth."* And 14:26, *"he will teach you all things, and he will instruct you in all things, whatever I will have told you."*

On the other hand:

1. Augustine in *On the Trinity* [15.17.29], "In this Trinity, only the Son is the Word, only the Holy Spirit the Gift, and the only one from whom the Word is born and the Holy Spirit proceeds is the Father."

2. Augustine says in the same place: "as we call the only word of God properly by the name of wisdom, while generally saying both the Holy Spirit and the Father are wisdom, so the Holy Spirit is described properly with the term 'charity,' while generally speaking both the Father and the Son are charity."

Reply:

Love is understood in a number of ways. In one way it is called the unqualified (*simpliciter*) attraction to the good, and in this way, it befits all three persons. In another way, it is called the free or independent movement of the will—namely, of that faculty which is called the will—towards the good,[which can also be] in response to someone else. Insofar as it is considered as the free or independent movement of the will, it is appropriated to the Father according to the argument given by Richard [*On the Trinity* 5.16–17, 19–20], namely, that gratuitous love is appropriated to the Father. Insofar as it is considered as the free movement in response to someone else, it is appropriated to the Son according to the argument given by Richard, namely, that a mixed love is appropriated to the Son. Insofar as it is considered strictly as a response to someone else, it is appropriated to the Holy Spirit according to the argument given by Richard, that indebted love is appropriated to the Holy Spirit. In charity, therefore, we must consider a condition that properly befits the Father, another that properly befits the Son, and another that properly pertains to the Holy Spirit. And by reason of these appropriations, it [love] is sometimes said to befit one [person], sometimes another.

On another note, charity or love can be understood in multiple ways: commonly, through appropriation, or properly. Since love or charity is a will for the good, and the will is understood in multiple ways, so therefore is love. The will is called the power of willing, or the movement of this power, or even that which is willed—and this diversity can be attributed to the divine. Insofar as the will is understood as that which is willed, it is the same as the preference for the good, and so it is understood commonly and befits the whole Trinity. When the will is described as a power, one can take it as moving itself. Two notions are at stake here: a [moving] power and an instrument, as Anselm says [in *On Divine Foreknowledge and Free Will* 11] that "the will is an instrument that moves itself." Insofar as it is moving, it comprises a principle of origin and thus befits the Father. When considered both as what is moved and as that from which an act or movement comes, it belongs to the Son; when the will is described as the motion elicited by the will insofar as it is moving and moved, it befits the Holy Spirit. And according to this typology, love is regarded as the gift or free emanation of shared love (*a condilectis*) and thus pertains to the Holy Spirit properly. Thus, when the will is described as what is willed, that is, as the preference for the good, it is understood commonly and befits the whole Trinity; insofar as it is the moving principle, it is appropriated to the Father; insofar as it is something moved, that is the principle of the will which is movement, it is appropriated to the Son; and insofar as it is considered as the motion coming from the will in the two [aforementioned] ways, it befits the Holy Spirit properly, because according to this typology, he is the gift or free emanation of their shared love. Therefore, although love in a certain sense befits the whole Trinity and through a certain appropriation [it befits] the Father and the Son, nevertheless, insofar as it is taken in its proper sense, it befits the Holy Spirit, as Augustine says in *On the Trinity* 6.[5]: "there are three [persons] and not more: one loving the one who comes from him, and another loving the one from whom he comes, and that love [between them]."

Replies to the objections:

1–3: The solution is already clear to the first three objections.

4. To the fourth objection, we must say that, formally speaking, all love is gratuitous because what is given out of love is given freely, and not out of obligation. Referring to the motive cause of love, we accept the distinction of Richard between indebted love, gratuitous love, and a love comprised of both [kinds of love]. For what moves gratuitous love is not anything received [as a gift] but the pure liberality of the one loving. Indebted love is set in motion only by a received good. A love comprising both involves both [giving and receiving]. Gratuitous love does not have its origin in another; however, indebted love has an origin only from another but is not the origin of another, and a love of a mixed type has its origin from another and is the origin of another. Thus, gratuitous love befits the Father, indebted love the Holy Spirit, and a "mixed" love, the Son. Because love as such, however, is properly predicated as proceeding and having its origin from another, namely, from the one loving or from those loving [i.e., the ones who love] each other and does not imply origin toward another but from another, therefore, love is properly attributed to the Holy Spirit, who has his origin from the Father and the Son and is not the origin of another person.[6]

5. To the fifth objection, we must say that a gift can be understood in two ways: for a gift can be described as given, and it can be described as given as a gift. In other words, there is a gift given as a gift and a gift that is not given as a gift. A gift given as a gift is love, because this is the means by which all gifts are given, and even love itself is given. However, gifts that are not given as such are those which are given out of love, but nevertheless are not love itself. Therefore, among gifts, the best kind that is given from love is wisdom. Nevertheless, the highest gift given as a gift is love, and therefore love is properly called a gift, not wisdom.

6. The answer to the sixth objection is clear from the previous.

7. To the seventh, we respond according to pseudo-Augustine in *On the Spirit and the Soul* [6], that "every interaction with the divine is a gift to us," that is, the Holy Spirit. Thus, "in some way," as he says, "the Holy Spirit seems to be closer to us." And this is because he [the Holy Spirit] is love according to his [personal] property, which is what is first given to us, and through him

---

6. Origin "toward another" may mean "spontaneous motion to please another" as opposed to "motion triggered by another's act."

is given to us the Son and the Father and even their proper qualities, namely, wisdom which is appropriated to the Son and power which is appropriated to the Father. As such, [the Spirit] is the inspirer of wisdom, as the Apostle says in 1 Corinthians 2:10, and even the giver of power, as described in Luke 24:49: *"remain in this city, until you have been filled with power from above."* Although the whole Trinity is therefore the principle of wisdom, power, and even goodness in us, nevertheless every gift of God is appropriated to the Holy Spirit, because he himself is love. Thus, although he is the principle of wisdom and understanding in us, nevertheless, it is not wisdom that is appropriated to him, but the gift, as stated earlier.

8. To the eighth objection, we respond that the "spirit of understanding" can be defined in two ways: appositively or possessively. When it is defined appositively, the "spirit of understanding" means the "spirit who is understanding," and this is how it is used here. When it is used possessively, its referent is either the person of the Son (the Holy Spirit is "his" as it proceeds from him), or the Holy Spirit's effect in creatures, which is the understanding we receive from him. In addition, "of understanding," understood appositively, can be accepted either essentially or personally: when it is understood essentially, it befits the whole Trinity, and thus it is even possible to say "the Holy Spirit is understanding"; when it is conceived personally, it is appropriated to the Son.

9. To the ninth objection, the solution is clear from the preceding.

10. To the tenth objection, we answer according to Richard of St. Victor [*On the Trinity* 6.12], "because a word proceeds from the mind and it is through the word that keenness of mind becomes known, the Son is rightly called the Word of the Father, through which or through whom paternal love is manifested. For in the Father, every truth is conceived, and in his Word, every truth is proved, in the Holy Spirit, every truth is heard, as it is said in the Gospel of John 16:13: *"for he will not speak on his own but he will speak whatever he hears."* Therefore, the Father cannot be called the Word, since he is not from another, neither the Holy Spirit, who is not from one only, but only the Son, who is from one only, and from whom emanates the manifestation of every truth." Therefore, to interpret the truth is not sufficient for being the Word, but in addition to this, it is required that he be from one other person, only, as Richard says.

CHAPTER 7

CHRISTOLOGY

ON THE FITTINGNESS OF THE INCARNATION SHOULD NATURE NOT HAVE FALLEN DUE TO SIN: WOULD THERE BE ANY REASON FOR THE INCARNATION?

SH 3, In un., Tr1, Q2, T2 (n. 23), 41–42
It is shown that there would be:

a. Dionysius says [in *On the Divine Names* 4.1 and 7; *The Celestial Hierarchy* 4.1]: "The good is diffusive of its being (*esse*)"—for we say that in the divine the Father spreads his goodness to the Son through generation, and both spread [their goodness] to the Holy Spirit through procession, and this diffusion is within the Trinity, and this is the highest [form of] diffusion before creatures come into existence. Therefore, if the greatest good does not spread itself to creatures when they do come into existence, one can still think of a greater diffusion than the diffusion [that happens within the Trinity]. Therefore, if the diffusion of the greatest good is to be greatest, it is more fitting that it should spread itself to creatures [as well]. However, one cannot think of this diffusion [that extends to creatures] as the greatest unless [God] himself unites himself to a creature; therefore, it is fitting that God should unite himself to a creature, and most [fitting that he should unite himself] to a human creature, as has been shown; therefore, even if one were to assume that [human] creatures did not fall, still the greatest good should have been united with them.

b. Blessedness is only in God; a rational creature can be beatified in its entirety, but the rational creature that is the human being has two types of cognition, namely, sensory and intellective, and takes pleasure in both; therefore, if the human being can be beatified in its entirety, therefore, [it must happen] according to both the senses and the intellect; therefore, the human being must be beatified in God in respect to both faculties. However, if one takes God in himself and in his own nature, the senses cannot be beatified in him, but the intellect alone. Indeed, the senses are only delighted and beatified in something sensory or bodily; therefore, if the human being in its entirety is to be beatified in God, God must be in a body accessible to the senses; however, it is not fitting for God to assume just any corporeal nature, but only the human, as was said.

c. Three scenarios are logically possible: three persons in a single substance; the opposite of this, that is, three substances in a single person; and in between these two scenarios, three persons in three substances. Now, one of the opposite scenarios—three persons in one substance—does really obtain, namely, in the Trinity. So does the intermediate scenario—three persons in three substances—when three human beings or three angels are present (alternatively, if one takes one person of the Trinity, one angel, and one human being). Therefore, the third scenario should also obtain, namely, one person in three substances. But this can only happen through a union of the divine and human natures. Indeed, no other creature, except the human being, contains two substances, namely, spiritual and corporeal, or soul and body. Also, no creature can perfect the human being by uniting with it: indeed, no angel can accomplish this, because the human being is equal to an angel as far as his or her superior part is concerned. Therefore, in order to achieve perfection in the order of things, it is fitting that the divine nature be united to the human nature in a single person, so that just as there are three persons in one nature and three persons in three natures, so there would be three natures—namely, divine nature, body, and soul—in one person.

d. We find the unity of nature in three persons, namely, in God, and this is a sign of perfection in [that] nature. Also, we find the unity of person in multiple natures, namely, in the human being. But if existing in multiple persons is a sign of perfection in a nature, then being able to exist in multiple natures should be a sign of perfection in a person. Now, what is greater in perfection must always be attributed to God, as far as both nature and person are concerned. But then, just as the divine nature exists in multiple persons, so the divine person should be able to exist in multiple natures. However, this situation cannot obtain from all eternity, because no plurality of natures could exist from all eternity. Therefore, some divine person must have begun to exist in multiple natures in the course of time. But the only way this is possible is if a divine person is united to a creature. Therefore, it is fitting, in order to manifest the perfection of divine personhood, that the divine nature be united to a created nature through a divine person. However, as has been said, it is not fitting [that it be united] to any nature, but only to the human nature. Equally, as has also been said, [it is] not [fitting that] any person of the Trinity [be united to the human nature], but only the Son. It remains, then, that even in the absence of the fall of the human nature, a union [of two natures] in the person of the Son would still be fitting.

An authoritative statement to the contrary:

1. "There was no point for us to be born except to be redeemed." Therefore, the incarnation is useless unless redemption is to follow. However, if there were no fall, there would be no redemption. Therefore, if we hypothesize that [the human] nature did not fall, the incarnation would be absolutely fruitless. But then it would not befit God to become incarnate, because it does not befit God to do anything in vain.

Reply:

One must concede, without prejudice, that even in the absence of the fall of the human nature, still the incarnation would be fitting, according to what St. Bernard says commenting on Jonah 1:12, *"For my sake this great tempest is upon you."* He expounds this statement about the Son of God, saying that Lucifer foresaw that the Son of God would assume a rational creature and be united to it, [that is, he] "saw and envied it." It was this envy that precipitated the fall of the devil and moved him to tempt man, whose fortune he envied, in order to ensure that the human nature through sin would no longer be worthy of being assumed by and united to God. It is clear from this that Lucifer thought that the union of the human and divine natures would occur in the absence of the fall of the human nature, and even that he thought of the fall as an impediment to such a union, which is the reason he arranged for the fall to happen. Based on this, it remains that even in the absence of the fall, the incarnation would still be fitting. In addition, what Augustine says in *The Soul and the Spirit* [9] suggests the same thing: "God became man in order to beatify in himself the entire human being, so that whether one would enter internally through the intellect or exit externally through the senses, he or she could 'find pastures' in their Creator: internal pastures in the knowledge of the deity, and external pastures in the flesh of the Savior." But this reason remains even in the absence of the fall of the human nature.

Replies to the objections:

1. To the objection, one must reply that that authoritative statement should be understood as presupposing the guilt of the fallen nature. Hence, the meaning is that if the Son of God were to be incarnated but did not redeem the guilt, it would be of no use to the human nature because it would neither

be beatified nor redeemed. But the situation is different if one assumes the absence of the fall of the human nature, as was just discussed. . . .

ABOUT THREE OPINIONS (AND DOUBTS THAT ACCOMPANY THEM) ON THE ONE WHO IS CONSTITUTED AS A RESULT OF THE ASSUMPTION [OF HUMAN NATURE]

SH 3, In un., Tr1, Q4, Ti1, D3, M4, C1 (n. 46), 68–70

I. The first of these opinions, first, says that as a result of the incarnation of the divine Word, some man was constituted out of a rational soul and human flesh, who subsisted prior to the union by a natural, not temporal priority. Second, it says that that man began to be God and that God began to be that man, so that God was made man, and conversely, that man was made God. Third, because there are two complete substances in Christ, each of which constitutes a "what" or quiddity (*quid*) in the unity of the person, it says that Christ is two, according to the statement [of Augustine in *Against an Arian Sermon* 8] "a giant of double substance." Fourth, it says that the one who assumes is that which is assumed—that is, the Son of God is man, or the son of man—but neither plays the role of a substrate or supposit to one another. Fifth and last, it says that that man's nature is not divine and human, but only human.

The second opinion says, first, that that man is not merely constituted out of these two, namely, out of a rational soul and human flesh, but out of three substances—namely, deity, soul, and flesh—in the unity of the person—however, this does not imply that the deity there is like a part. Second, it says that the person of the Word was simple before the incarnation, but as a result of the incarnation, it became composite by reason of the assumed nature. Third, it says that the divine person assumed a "what" or quiddity: namely, not "this" or "that" man, but the human nature (which is contrary to the first opinion)—and on these grounds it says that Christ is only one, not two. Fourth, it says that it is not that that man began to be God, but vice versa, because that human supposit had no existence prior to becoming God, neither by temporal nor by natural priority—which is [also] contrary to the first opinion.

The third opinion says that those two—namely, soul and flesh—are united to the person of the Word, or to the divine nature in the Word, in such a fashion that these two or three do not constitute any one substance or person; rather, the Word of God, as it were, is clothed in these two as in a garment of sorts. Hence, it says that Christ insofar as he is man is not a "what" or a quiddity, nor did the Word begin to be a "what" as a result of the incarnation, but [rather acquired] a certain state (*qualiter ens, quodam modo se habens*).[1] Consequently, it seems to say that that union was not of a substantial kind, but, as it were, like that of an accident with its subject, drawing on the texts from Philippians 2:8: "*And being found in fashion (habitu) as a man.*"

II. These are the three opinions by themselves. Next, we must see how they are different. There are three pronouncements [on the matter]. The first of them draws a distinction between these three opinions. Since there are two natures in Christ's hypostasis, one must (1) view each nature as constituting a "what" or quiddity in one person, or (2, 3) one [nature] as constituting a "what" and the other as [functioning] in the way of a habit (*habitus*). This can happen in two ways: either (2) the human nature will function as a habit, and the divine nature will constitute a "what," or, vice versa, (3) the human nature will constitute a "what" and the divine nature would function as a habit: just like it is said about the saints that they have God through an indwelling (*inhabitantem*) grace, so Jesus Christ, as the holiest of holies, [has God] in the highest way, through the grace of union. The second opinion is said to assume the first position; the third opinion is said to assume the second position; and the first opinion is said to assume the third position—perhaps, because it is mostly that opinion that refers to that man as deified.

However, there are objections against that:

1. Indeed, according to the first opinion, Christ is two according to his two natures: but this would not have been the case if the divine nature were there as a habit.

2. The first opinion should be reproached more than the third, because it is simply more in accord with the faith for God to be "*found in fashion (habitu) as a man*" than for a man to be "found in fashion as God," because the former is stated in scriptures, while the latter is not. Therefore, those opinions do not seem to be distinguished for the aforesaid reasons.

---

1. *Quodammodo se habens* and *qualiter ens* usually translate Aristotle's πως ἔχων from *Nicomachean Ethics* 2.4.3, which is usually rendered into English as "in a certain state."

For this reason, others say that the difference between these opinions is as follows: the first two assert that the Word assumed a "what," but the third asserts that he did not assume a "what" but a "state" (*quomodo se habens*). Also, the first opinion states that he assumed a "what" in the sense of "man," or, more precisely, some substance that is a body-soul compound. The other opinion, however, states that he assumed a "what" in the sense of human nature, not "man." This is why the first opinion claims that Christ is two; the second claims that he is one; the third opinion claims that Christ is not a "what" insofar as he is human, because that union is more like the union between an accident and its subject. Therefore, the first opinion concedes that God began to be man and man began to be God; the second, however, denies that the man began to be God, but claims the converse; and the third claims that he did not begin to be a "what" but in a state (*quodam modo se habens*).

Others distinguish [between these three opinions] in a different way, claiming that they look at the three types of existence (*esse*) in Christ: moral existence, natural existence, and rational existence. Thus, the first opinion considers [Christ's] natural existence and, because there are two natures in Christ, claims that Christ is two; further, because each nature is a complete substance (which is why [Christ] is called "a giant of double substance"), it claims that God began to be man and man began to be God. The next opinion, however, considers [Christ's] moral existence. Indeed, the name "person" denotes dignity, and dignity pertains to moral existence: this is why moral properties pertain to persons. This opinion says: because the person [here] is one, Christ is one. Further, because [two] natures are united in a person [here], in such a way that God is man and vice versa, [this opinion] claims that Christ is one. And because [in this case] one does not deal with a union of two complete substances, that is, this is not a union of two persons but of two natures (by "human nature" I understand a body-soul compound)—that is, [here we deal with] "this man" consisting of the divine and human natures—therefore, [this opinion] does not concede that a man [here] began to be God, but the opposite, and it is not man who is deified here but God who is humanized. However, the third opinion considers [Christ's] rational existence. For this reason it claims that Christ is a "what" insofar as he is God and in a state (*aliquo modo se habens*) insofar as he is a man. This is on account of the existence of the human nature, which comes after the hypostasis [here] is complete. Indeed, although two natures are united in this person, one of them comes after this person is [already] in existence, and that which comes after the hypostasis is [already] in existence, does not qualify as the "what" or quiddity of that hypostasis, but as its state (*qualiter ens, quomodo se habens*). For this reason this [last] opinion claims that Christ is not a "what" insofar as he is a man.

This is the difference between these opinions. The third was condemned by a Decretal of Pope Alexander [III], because it verges on error, as will be made abundantly clear later. . . .

DOUBTS ABOUT THE THIRD OPINION

SH 3, *In un., Tr1, Q4, Ti1, D3, M4, C4 (n. 56), 80–82*

As far as the third opinion is concerned, there is a doubt whether Christ, insofar as he is a man, is a quiddity: the third opinion denies this and the first two opinions concede it.

The objections go as follows:

1. Christ is both God and man; however, being God amounts to being a "what" (*quid*), and so does being a man; but if Christ is a quiddity insofar as he is a man, then Christ is two "whats," and therefore two [things]—which is incongruous.

2. Suppose that Christ is one "what" by virtue of a unity [he has as] created; it is also clear that he is essentially one "what" by virtue of a unity [he has as] uncreated; but these are essentially different unities; therefore, Christ will be essentially two [things]; therefore, Christ is not [something] one.

3. Substantial forms make [things] substantially different. Suppose that there are two substantial forms in Christ that are essentially different: this would be logical if Christ were a quiddity insofar as he is a man. But then these [two forms] would create a substantial difference within Christ. Therefore, if one were to posit "humanity" as a substantial form in Christ (which would happen if he were a quiddity insofar as he is a man), in addition to "divinity," one would have to admit that there is a substantial difference within Christ; but then he is two [things].

4. Also, "one quiddity of nature in three persons makes three persons—namely, Father, Son, and Holy Spirit—into something one"; therefore, "multiple quiddities of natures [in one person] would make one person into something multiple." Therefore, if it is inappropriate to say that Christ is multiple [things] and not one, it remains that Christ, insofar as he is a man,

is not a "what," because he is a "what" insofar as he is God. Therefore, the opinion must be true that claims that when we state that "Christ is a man," what is meant is not that Christ is a quiddity but that he is "in a state" (*aliquo modo se habens*).

5. Christ, insofar as he is God, by virtue of his divine nature and by virtue of being a divine person from all eternity, has complete being—nor does his humanity add anything to that person or that nature by coming in. Therefore, since that which follows the complete being of that person and nature has the status of something added, and is not quidditative in respect to that [person and nature], it remains that Christ, insofar as he is a man, is not a quiddity.

To the contrary:

a. The Decretal of Pope Alexander: "Since Christ is perfect God and a perfect man, how would anyone dare say that Christ, insofar as he is a man, is not a quiddity? However, in order to avoid such an abuse in the Church of God, let [this position] be condemned at a gathering of Masters." On the basis of this Decretal, it is clear that the third opinion has been condemned.

Solution:

One must reply that when we hear the expression "Christ is a man," we need to consider either the nature of the thing or the way of speaking. If, considering the nature of the thing, one were to say that Christ, insofar as he a man, is not a "what" or "something," this person would err without a doubt and would hold that opinion that has been condemned. However, if, considering the way of speaking, one were to say that in the expression "Christ is a man" (or "was made man") the term "man" is not predicated of Christ as a "what" (even though he is a "what" [insofar as he is a man]) but as "being in a state" (*quomodo se habens*), he would not seem to be completely in error, taking into consideration the statement of the Apostle from Philippians 2:8: "*being found in fashion (habitu) as a man.*" Augustine, discussing this statement in *83 Questions* [73], distinguishes between four different ways of "having" something (*habitus*).[2] One of these ways is when "the nature of what is had is not changed, but it receives a different shape and form" when it begins to be had. "A garment serves as an example: when it is taken off and put

---

2. *Habitus* as a noun means "state" or "way of being," but technically it is the past participle from the verb "to have," so the linguistic aspect of the discussion is difficult to capture in English.

down, it does not have the same shape as when it is worn; this type [of having something] suits the comparison" "*being found in fashion as a man.*" Accordingly, we would reply to the aforesaid question that Christ, insofar as he is a man, is a "what" and "something," but ["man"] is not predicated [of him] as a "what." However, in order to avoid perpetuating opinions that verge on error, one should state with no further distinctions that Christ, insofar as he is a man, is a "what" and "something."

Reply to the objections:

1–4. First, if one considers the first opinion, that Christ is "two" in the neuter,[3] but not in the masculine[4] [it must be affirmed]: indeed, he is someone (*unus*), that is, one person, but not something one (*unum*), that is, not one nature. For this reason, it is not unfitting, in one sense, to grant the reasons that demonstrate that Christ is two.

5. As for the last argument, when it is objected that "humanity comes in after the complete being [of Christ has been in place], and therefore is not a 'what,'" one must reply that it is not logical. Indeed, even if it does come in subsequently, nevertheless, it is assumed into the unity of the person. In the same way, if one assumes that the soul is created before the body and it is only subsequently that the body is united to it, it would not follow on this account that the body would not be a "what" of the [complete] human being, despite the fact that it postdates the complete rational being of the soul.

However, if one considers the second opinion, it is unfitting to admit that Christ is two, for he is strictly something one.

Replies to the objections:

1. To the first objection: when it is said that "Christ is God and man," "if the meaning is that the coordinating conjunction joins two supposits, then it is false; however, if the meaning is that the coordinating conjunction joins two natures, then it is true"—because there is only one supposit there but different natures. As for the objection that "he is a 'what' insofar as he is God, and he is another 'what' insofar as he is a man, therefore he is two," it is not logical, because the "'what' insofar as he is a man" is not numbered together with the "what" that is God, because these "whats" do not belong to the same genus.

---

3. That is, two things.
4. That is, not two persons.

2. To the other objection, one must reply that it is permissible to follow the Doctors in this case: although "the binary number in Christ [consists of] essential [unities], nevertheless, one of the unities of this binary number, as it were, degenerates into an accident," namely, that unity that represents the human nature. And "therefore that binary number does not number subjects or substrates, but natures, in the same way that the number of accidents does not number subjects, but their forms."

3. And this makes clear the solution to the other [objection], because these substantial forms essentially make natures differ, but not the supposit, because "one of them," as has been said, "as it were, degenerates into an accident," for the reason that it comes in later.[5]

4–5. And this makes clear solutions to the other objections. . . .

IS A PERSON ASSUMED?

SH 3, In un., Tr1, Q4, Ti1, D2, C4 (n. 35), 54–56
Arguments in favor:
1. First, following a statement by John Damascene, Book III, c. 7:[6] "God the Word, when he became incarnate, did not assume that [type of] nature that is observed by mere contemplation[7]—for this would not be an incarnation but a pretense thereof—nor [the type] that is observed in a species . . . but [the type] that is in an individual . . . for he assumed the foundations of our materiality: not as already subsisting on their own and presenting an individual with a prior existence, but as subsisting in his own hypostasis" [i.e., the person of the Son]. Therefore, he assumed the [type of] "nature that is in an individual"; but the nature that exists in an individual is the person; therefore, he assumed a person—for "person" is an "individual substance of a rational nature,"[8] which [definition] matches the [type of] "nature that is in an individual."

---

5. A linguistic point lost in translation: both the term *ac-cidens* (from *ad-cidens*) and the term *ad-veniens* (translated as "that which comes in later") contain the prefix *ad-*, which signifies addition.
6. Correctly, *On the Orthodox Faith* c. 55 (III, c. 11), ed. Buytaert, 203–4; ed. Migne, PG 94, 1024.
7. Which is to say, that is purely intellectual.
8. Boethius, *On the Two Natures and One Person of Christ*, c. 3.

2. Richard of St. Victor says in *On the Trinity* [4.15] that "the divine person is defined by origin, the angelic person by quality, and the human person in both ways." However, in the assumed human nature there is a separate property of origin compared to [the one] in the Son of God, because [Jesus Christ] descends from his [human] mother according to the flesh and from the [divine] Father according to his divine nature. Also, there is another property of quality or form [in the human nature].[9] Therefore, there would be two different personhoods.[10]

3. Anselm says in *On the Incarnation of the Word* [6] that the Son of God did not assume humanity in an unqualified sense, but *this man*, namely, Jesus. Therefore, since *this man Jesus* is an "individual substance of a rational nature," [the Son of God] assumed a person.

4. According to another definition, "person" is a thing that is distinguished by a property that is a mark of dignity. Hence, Boethius says in *On the Two Natures and One Person of Christ* [2] that "this name suits substances of greater dignity." But then, if when a man is assumed, his nature is exalted but his property or dignity is not diminished in any way, it remains that the person is assumed.

5. Three acts here concur simultaneously: to create, to assume, and to unite. It is clear that to create is prior than to assume; thus, the termination of [the act of] creation is the beginning of [the act of] assuming; but then, since [the act of] creation terminates at an actual being, an actual being will be assumed, and thereby a person, because in this case the "actual being" is a person.

To the contrary:

a. Augustine, in *To Peter on Faith* [17.60]: "God assumed the human nature, not a human person." Therefore, he has not taken on a person.

b. Boethius, *Against Nestorius*:[11] if in Christ "a union of natures took place while two persons remained, no one thing could have come out of these two. ... Therefore, according to Nestorius, Christ is no one thing, and thereby completely nothing, for something that is not one thereby has no existence whatsoever. However, we clearly and truly profess that Christ does exist;

---

9. And according to Richard of St. Victor those two extra properties would constitute a human person.
10. And therefore the extra person would need to be assumed.
11. Correctly, *On the Two Natures and One Person of Christ*, c. 4.

therefore, we imply that he is some one thing. But if it is so, there is no doubt that Christ must be one person."

c. If a person is assumed, there must be two persons in Christ. Indeed, one cannot say that "a human person is assumed" if [what was assumed] was not a person prior to its assumption; in this case, Christ would contain different natures and diverse persons; therefore, he would be one neither in nature nor in person. But then [Christ] would be no different from other humans as far as the union of God and man in him is concerned—which is most absurd. It remains, therefore, that no person was assumed.

Solution:

One must concede the latter and reply to the objections by saying that three distinctive features are required for something to be a person: singularity, incommunicability, and dignity. The distinctive feature of singularity is present in every soul that is in a body, for it is separated from every other soul by some singular property. The distinctive feature of incommunicability is present in everything singular, such as *this donkey*, an animal; however, no soul existing in a body has this, because the soul and the body come together (*communicent*) to constitute one being. The distinctive feature of dignity, however, is that which distinguishes one human being[12] from another by means of individual rationality, which is the property that has the most dignity, because, as Boethius says, "this name 'person' suits substances of greater dignity." Therefore, for something to be a person, these three distinctive features are required: singularity, incommunicability, and dignity (i.e., the property with most dignity). One must say, then, that the first distinctive feature, namely, singularity, is in Christ's soul, as well as in his body; the first and second distinctive features are in the soul-body composite (it is this [pair of distinctive features] that is meant when I say "this man" pointing at a soul-body composite, i.e., something singular). However, the first, second, and third [distinctive features] are in the God-man Christ. And although [Christ] could have the first and second [distinctive features] by virtue of his human nature, nevertheless, he could have the third only by virtue of the divine person; therefore, [the trait of] being a person [is] not [present] in Christ by virtue of his human nature. Indeed, "person" is defined by the most

---

12. Most of the MSS add *purus* ("pure") to "one human being," which is an unusual addition that is, perhaps, intended to function as an adverb and to mean "absolutely" distinguished.

excellent property with most dignity; however, the property with the most dignity in Christ does not come from his human nature but from the divine person; it remains, then, that no [human] person is assumed. Indeed, one must distinguish persons based on what is nobler in them. Therefore, since the noblest feature in an assumed man is to be the Son of God, it is this [i.e., being the Son of God] that gives him personal distinction: to be one and the same person with the Son of God.

Replies to the objections:

1. To the objection based on John Damascene's statement about "assuming the [type of] nature that is in an individual," it is true; however, it does not follow from this that he assumed a person, because the term "individual" denotes merely the distinctive feature of singularity or incommunicability, but not dignity, which defines "person."

2. To the second objection, based on Richard, one must reply that although in the assumed man there *is* a separate property of origin compared to [the one] in the Son of God, nevertheless, it does not follow that there is another person, because "person" implies the degree of completion and finality that does not allow for a closer union, as well as the sort of distinction that is accomplished by means of a property of greater dignity, which do not suit Christ as man.

3. To the third objection, based on Anselm, one must reply that when he says, "he assumed this man," this does not denote the person—because both the Son of God and the son of man share the same one person—but it denotes the individual, namely, this singular [compound] that is constituted out of body and soul. And when one objects that "this is an individual substance of a rational nature, and therefore a person," one must reply that the sense here is the same as in the term "individual," with the [aforesaid] triple distinction implied. Hence, one must reject [the conclusion that he assumes a person], because [this substance] is not individual [to the extent of the person], because it is still capable of a union with a substance of greater dignity.

4. To the fourth objection, the reply is already evident, because neither is a person assumed nor is there a diminution of dignity, but [it is simply that] personhood stems from a property of greater dignity.

5. To the fifth objection, one must say that sometimes something is created separately, and sometimes [it is created] in something else. If it has been created separately, not in something else, and it is an individual of rational

nature, it will be a person. However, if it is created in something else, it will not be a person even though it may be an individual of rational nature, because it is not a substance that is distinct from everything else. And in this sense, not even the rational soul, which is created by means of its infusion into a body, is a person. In a similar way, this composite of body and soul that is assumed by means of creation and created by means of assumption, thereby cannot be called a person. And if Anselm's statement from *On the Incarnation of the Word* is used as an objection, to the effect that "God is a person, the assumed man is a person, therefore there are two persons in Christ," I reply [Anselm, ibid., 6] that "just as the Father is God and the Son is God, but this does not imply that there are multiple gods, but only one God, in the same way, in Christ, God is a person, and man is a person, but this does not imply that there are two persons, but only one. And the Son of God cannot be referred to without referring to the son of man, and vice versa, because the two are identical, and the Word and the assumed man share the same group of properties. At the same time, different persons cannot share the same group of properties or be predicated one of another." . . .

IS CHRIST AN INDIVIDUAL INSOFAR AS HE IS A MAN?

SH 3, Tr1, Q4, T1, M4, C3, Ar3 (n. 52), 75–77
One speaks of two types of individuation: first and second. The first type is rooted in the hypostasis itself; one hypostasis of itself is distinguished from any other by virtue of its singular property; in this sense we say that Peter is different from Paul. The second type is based on the properties that subsequently come to be in this hypostasis. In this sense, individuation stands for a combination of properties, which are never the same in another [individual]. Thus, "individual" can mean one of these two things. The first meaning is that of "hypostasis," which is the singular substance[13] itself by reason of the singularity of substance: indeed, even if one took away all the properties that exist in Peter and Paul, still they would remain two distinct substances. The second meaning of "individual" is that of a combination of properties, which are never the same in another [individual].

---

13. The Latin *sub-stantia* is a calque from the Greek ὑπό-στασις (hypo-stasis).

It is demonstrated that Jesus Christ,[14] insofar as he is a man, is an individual in both senses:

a. Indeed, it is clear that he is an individual in the first sense. For insofar as he is a man, he is an individual in substance,[15] which of itself is separate from other humans. Also in the second sense, because insofar as he is Jesus or a man, he possesses a combination of properties, which cannot be found in anyone else. Therefore, he is an individual in both senses of "individuation."

b. Just as it is clear that Socrates is distinguished from other [humans] by means of his singular substance, in the same way Christ, insofar as he is a man, is [distinguished] from other humans. And just as Socrates is distinguished from others by means of his qualitative characteristics and size, in the same way Jesus Christ, insofar as he is a man, is [distinguished] from other humans. However, this is what makes Socrates an individual. Therefore, it remains that Jesus also should be considered an individual.

To the contrary:

1. John Damascene says [in *On the Orthodox Faith* 3.3]: "No common species must be posited or assumed in the Lord Jesus Christ." Therefore, Christ is not an individual belonging to the species "man," nor to any other; therefore, he is not an individual insofar as he is a man.

2. If Christ, insofar as he is a man, is an individual, then he is a certain "who" (*quis*) insofar as he is a man, as well as, similarly, a certain "who" insofar as he is God, because he is a person [that way]; therefore, he is two "whos"; but the position that God and man do not constitute one Christ contradicts the Creed ["Quicumque"].

Solution:

In order to clarify the question, one must note that there is a difference between hypostasis, person, individual, and supposit (i.e., a substrate or underlying nature). A hypostasis is some incommunicable existence or substance [that consists] of any distinguishing [factors] whatsoever. This is according to Richard of St. Victor [*On the Trinity* 4.3], who sometimes uses "hypostasis" in the sense of "person." A person, however, both in name and in essence, is a rational incommunicable substance that is distinguished by

---

14. See Richard of St. Victor, *On the Trinity* 4.3. A significant number of manuscripts diverge on the exact wording in this line, so it has been rendered for clarity to reflect the general thrust of the discussion.

15. A number of manuscripts have "he is a substance."

its property of dignity. It is clear from this that every person is a hypostasis, but not vice versa. Indeed, the hypostases of rational natures, which imply dignity, are their persons. However, the hypostases of other natures do not constitute persons, except grammatically speaking—and even this is in relation to acts of rational natures, namely, acts of speaking: the first person is the one who speaks, the second is the one to whom speech is directed, and the third is the one about which speech is. Now, "individual" has two meanings, as was said previously: in one sense, it is an individual substance, which is of itself different from any other; in another sense, it is [something] that possesses a combination of properties that is not matched [by a combination of properties] in anything else. Further, an underlying nature, or a supposit, signifies a compound of form and matter, for example, a soul united with a body, as far as composite things go. In simple things, however, it is the thing (*res*) itself that is referred to as the underlying nature. However, in the proper sense, "essence" is "that which gives a thing existence"; "nature" is that, by which [a thing] functions, acts, or undergoes [something]; "what is" (*quid est*) is the underlying nature [or supposit]. For example, if one refers to "God and deity," "God" refers to that which exists (*quod est*), and "deity" refers to that, by which it exists (*quo est*). "Who is" (*qui est*), then, refers to the supposit, which is a "thing of nature," such as one of the persons in God or one of the humans among human beings. These observations suggest that "hypostasis" is common to "person" and "individual." Hence, Christ, insofar as he is the Son of God, is a "hypostasis" in the sense of a "person." However, insofar as he is a man, he is a "hypostasis" in the sense of an "individual." It remains, then, that he has been a person from all eternity, but not an individual.

Replies to the objections:

1. A reply to the statement by John Damascene is clear from what has been said. It must be understood in the following sense: "No common species must be posited in Christ," that is, it is not appropriate to predicate of Christ a common species, which would contain both divine and human natures and, as it were, conflate both, namely, divinity and humanity. However, one can admit [predicating of Christ] a common species insofar as his human nature is concerned, [that is, the one he shares in common] with other humans.

2. To the second and last argument, one must reply that "individual" or individual substance constitutes the middle between "person" and "underlying

nature" (or supposit); however, a middle must harmonize with its extremes; therefore, individual substance must have something in common with the extremes. Therefore, since there are multiple underlying natures in Christ, but only one person, one must say of the "human individual" [in him] that it is both something different from that, according to which he is God, and not different. [They say] the latter [i.e., that it is not different] when they refer to the person, and [they say] the former [i.e., that it is different, when they refer] to his underlying nature. And this is the way to make sense of a number of authoritative statements.

To the objection that "he is a certain 'who' [insofar as he is a man] and another 'who' [insofar as he is God], therefore, he is two 'whos,'" one must reply that this is not logical. Indeed, "two" refers to "numerically one and numerically one," but this mode of speaking is valid [only] of things whose positions are distinct. However, no such situation obtains as regards the individual substance of the son of man and the person of the Son of God, which are united without any distance between them, in such a way that the son of man is the Son of God and vice versa. . . .

IS CHRIST ONE OR TWO [THINGS]?

SH 3, In un., Tr1, Q4, Ti1, D3, M4, C3, Ar1 (n. 50), 73–74
That he is [two]:

1. First, there is an authoritative statement of Augustine in *Enchiridion* [35], which is quoted in Book III of [Lombard's] *Sentences* [6.2]: "Both substances, divine and human, are one single Son of God the Father, but [he is] one thing on account of the Word, and another on account of his humanity." Therefore, Christ is one thing and another thing; therefore, he is two.

2. Isidore in *On the Trinity* [i.e., *Sent.* 1.14.5]: "[One] '*mediator between God and men, the man Christ Jesus*' [1 Timothy 2:5]; although he is one thing on the Father's side, and another on the Virgin's, he is nevertheless not [one and] another one."[16] Therefore, Christ is one thing and another thing; therefore, he is multiple things (in the neuter).[17]

---

16. That is, not two persons. The terminological difference in this section is between the neuter form *aliud* ("something," "another thing") and the masculine form *alius* ("someone," "another person").

17. See previous note.

3. Anselm in *On the Incarnation of the Word* [6]: "God and man in Christ are not two different ones (*alius*), although God is one thing (*aliud*) and man is another." Therefore, [he is two].

4. Those things are different whose definitions or substantial natures (*rationes*) are different; but the natures of God and man are different; therefore, because Christ is both God and man, he is different things.

5. Something of Christ is the same as what the Father is (for he is God), and something of him is not the same (for he is a man); therefore, he is two, and not something that is one.

To the contrary:

a. Bernard, in *To Pope Eugene*, distinguishes between different degrees of unity. Among them, according to him, is the highest degree of unity, by which the three persons are one by the unity of substance. Second, he says, there is that [type of] unity, by which, conversely, three substances are [united] in one person. Therefore, the unity of three natures in Christ is greater than the unity of two natures in the human being. But then, since the human being is not considered to be multiple on account of its two natures, but is seen as something one, neither should Christ be considered to be multiple but should be seen as something one.

b. Boethius says in *On the Two Natures and One Person of Christ* [4]: "Every thing that exists, insofar as it exists, is something one." But we profess that Christ truly exists; therefore, we acknowledge that he is something one.

Solution:

One must reply that there is a difference[18] between saying "this is that" and saying "this is of that." Also, it is appropriate to refer to the difference between "nature" and a "thing of a nature"[19] in all things apart from the First, that is, God. One must say, then, that although there are multiple natures in Christ, they are not predicated of Christ in the subject [case, i.e., in the nominative], that is, we do not say that "Christ himself is [multiple] natures." Now [we do not predicate in the nominative] insofar as his human nature is concerned, because as far as his divine nature is concerned, "nature" and a "thing of a nature" are not different, because [in the divine] the person is the

---

18. Taking the reading *differt* from the apparatus instead of *refert* in the main text.

19. That is, a "thing that has a certain nature" or "an instantiation of a certain nature."

essence, and there is no difference between saying "this is that" and "this is of that," because [in the divine] the person is the divine essence and the person is of the divine essence. However, as far as his human nature is concerned, there is a difference. Indeed, it is false to say, "Christ is the human nature," but it is true to say that "Christ is of the human nature" or "one who has the human nature." Therefore, since the human nature is not predicated of the person, namely, of Christ, essentially, but only obliquely,[20] Christ is not said to be multiple things on account of the plurality of natures [in him], because things that are predicated of something in oblique [cases][21] do not increase it in number. Therefore, it does not follow from the aforesaid arguments that Christ *is* multiple things, but that he is *of* multiple things—just as it does not follow that a human being is multiple things just because he is a body-soul compound, and the soul is some one thing, and the body is some one thing.

Replies to the objections:

1–3. To the authoritative statements that are used in objections one must reply that they should be understood in the sense of oblique [predication]. Therefore, when it is said that Christ is "one thing and another thing," this must be understood [to mean] "of one and another[22] nature," namely, divine and human. Therefore, the proper sense is that it is the predication of the type "this is of that" that is used here, not of the type "this is that."

4. As for the fourth argument, that is, the objection that "those things are different whose definitions are different," one must reply that this is true where something is predicated of something else in the subject case and formally, not obliquely; however, the consequence does not hold of predication in indirect cases. Hence, the following does not follow: "the definitions of the corporeal and the incorporeal natures are different; however, the human being has both the corporeal and the incorporeal natures; therefore, the human being is different things."

5. The reply to the fifth argument is already clear. Indeed, when we say, "Christ the man is something that is not the Father," the term "something"

---

20. That is, in oblique or indirect cases (lit. "by using cases"). In this and the next two paragraphs, we resolve the abbreviation *câm* found in the manuscripts as *casualem* and not as *causam* as in the edition, which makes little sense.

21. In the genitive, in this case.

22. We resolve the abbreviation *a⁹* found in the manuscripts as *alterius/alterius* instead of the edition's *alius/alius*.

stands for "man," not for the divine essence. However, when we say, "[he] is something that is the Father," [the term "something"] stands for the divine essence. Therefore, it does not follow: "therefore, he is something that is the Father and something that is not the Father," but rather there is a fallacy of the figure of speech here that concludes from multiple "standings for" to a single one, because in the conclusion the term "something" should stand for only one thing; therefore, the conclusion must hold either only for the divine essence or only for "man." . . .

DOES THE UNION TAKE PLACE IN THE PERSON?

SH 3, In un., Tr1, Q4, Ti2, C1 (n. 57), 82–84
The objections are as follows:

1. When something is united or combined [with something else], this does not constitute personal unity: indeed, a *per-son* is something *per se*,[23] and therefore its unity is not one of combination; however, the unity of the Son of God when he is united to the flesh is not a unity of the *per se* kind, but one of combination; therefore, it is not a personal unity. The major premise is clarified by the Master in *Sentences* [3.10.1], where he raises the question "whether Christ, insofar as he is a man, is a person." He says there that "the soul is not a *per-son*," even though it is a "rational substance, because it is not *per se*, but is combined" with the flesh. Therefore, the union of the Son of God with the flesh is not a union [that happens] in the person.

2. Nothing can be both a middle and an extreme in the same sense; but the divine person and the human nature are the extremes of this union; therefore, this union does not happen in the person, because that in which[24] the union of the extremes happens is the middle.

3. Nothing is terminated at itself; therefore, if the [extremes that are] united are terminated at that in which this union happens, it is clear that none of the [extremes that are] united is identical with that in which this union happens; therefore, if in this union the person—namely, the Son of God

---

23. The text here uses a false etymology (which is ancient in origin) of *persona* as if coming from *per se sonans*; the Latin pun is obviously lost in translation.

24. "In which" in this no. 2 as well as in both cases in the next no. 3 renders the reading *in quo* from the variants in the apparatus instead of the *in quod* of the edition.

himself—is one of the [extremes that are] united, this union does not happen in the person.

To the contrary:

a. If this union does not take place in the person, then it happens in a nature: either created or uncreated. If it takes place in the uncreated, that is, divine, nature, then the divine and human natures become one through this union—which is impossible. Similarly, if it takes place in the created nature, the same incongruity will follow, because then, diverse natures will become one. Therefore, this union does not take place in a nature; but it can only be in a nature or in the person; therefore, it takes place in the person.

b. There are two ways in which a union can happen: sometimes it happens in such a way that one [of the united elements] is in a dominant position over the other, and sometimes not. When a union happens in the first way, then the dominant element compels the other to unite with it; and when it happens in the second way, then neither of them compels the other to unite with it, but a third thing comes of the two. Now in this union, the divine nature is the dominant one; therefore, it compels the human nature to unite with it; but it cannot compel it to a unity of nature, where one nature becomes identical with the other; therefore, it compels it to a unity in the person; therefore, this unity takes place in the person, and not in a nature, either created or uncreated.

Solution:

One must reply that, essentially, "one" is used in two senses, unqualified and qualified. There are also two ways of predicating "one" in an unqualified sense: one through unity and one through union. What is one through unity is that in which there is no plurality and which neither exists in many nor [consists] of many; for example, God [is one in this sense]. At the same time, one through union is that which exists in many or [consists] out of many.

What is one in a qualified sense is one by way of placing one next to another. . . . There are three ways of predicating "one" in this sense. In some cases, one is united to another through placing them side by side in such a way that neither acquires a name or a property from the other. In other cases, one is placed next to another in such a way that it acquires from the other a certain property, but not a name. In yet other cases, [one is placed next to another] in such a way that it acquires from the other a name, but not a property. For example, one stone is placed next to another, making a pile, that is, creating something one out of them through aggregation—and yet, one stone acquires neither a name nor a property from another stone. In the second sense of "placing next to each other," an apple or an aromatic herb is united to a hand—for an apple placed into a hand gives it its scent, so that the hand acquires some property from it, but not its name. In the third sense of "placing next to each other," a garment is united with the person who is dressed in it; in this case this person does receive a name from the garment and is called "dressed" but acquires no property from this garment.

As for [the type of] one in an unqualified sense that is one through union, it is also predicated in several ways. One way is when two things are united while the natures of both remain intact, with no change. Another way is when the natures of both do not remain intact. There are two scenarios here as well: either both natures are changed or just one of them is. One of the natures is changed, for example, when one [of the things united] dominates the other and compels the other into unity with it or its nature. An example of this is when a large quantity of wine is united with a little bit of water. An example of both natures changing is when water is united with honey, forming a third thing. Also, there are two ways of achieving a union where both natures remain intact: either their union results in something third, or it does not, but one becomes the other. An example of the first is the union of soul and body, which results in a human being, which is composed of both components: indeed, neither the nature of the soul nor of the body is changed here. An example of the second type of union is when a branch of a pear tree is united to an apple—or some other—tree, on to which it is grafted: indeed, in this case both natures—namely, pear and apple—remain intact, and apples never become pears, nor vice versa—and yet no third entity results from this union—such as a tree that is neither a pear tree nor an apple tree—but one emerges out of the other, namely, a pear tree out of an apple tree, because as a result of the grafting, the dominant [entity] compels the other to unite with itself, so that it grows out of it, but is not it.

The type of union, then, where the other [member] is changed, takes place in the member that compels the other to [unite with] its nature. The type of union where both members are changed takes place in a third thing, namely, in a third nature, and this third emerges or comes into existence from the other two. However, the union where one comes out of the other, as in the example of grafting, takes place in one hypostasis, in such a way that there is one hypostasis of two natures there. Hence, when one grafts a pear branch on to an apple tree stump and they are united through this grafting, the [grafting] results in one hypostasis—that is, one tree—comprising both pear and apple, which have two completely different natures. In this case we have something that is one in hypostasis, not one in nature.

Taking this into consideration, we must reply, to the extent of our abilities (for *we are not worthy to unloose the latchet of his shoes*, that is, to explain this sacred union), that the union of humanity and deity is of the sort where one comes out of the other, and not of the sort where one becomes the other or where the two become a third thing. In this respect we read in James 1:21: "*receive with meekness the engrafted word*," that is, the Son of God united with the human nature. Thus, since the divine person is the dominant element in this union, it compels the human nature to unite with its hypostasis. For this reason humanity is not a part of the divine person, but is *of it* (*de illa*), because both [natures] share only one hypostasis, while at the same time each nature maintains its integrity. It is for this reason that James says: "*receive the engrafted word*." It is clear, then, that this union takes place in one divine hypostasis or person.

Replies to the objections:

1. To the first argument to the contrary, one must reply that one meaning of "*per se*" excludes "being with" something else (in this sense "*per se*" is equivalent to "not being with something else"), and another meaning excludes "dependence on" something else (in this sense "*per se*" is equivalent to "not being dependent on something else"). Therefore, when one states that a "person" is a "*per se* being," this is true in the sense that it does not depend on anything else. However, this does not preclude it from being with something else. Therefore, a person is a "*per se* being" in the sense of not depending on anything else. However, it can be with something else. In the same way, a substance is called a *per se* being despite the fact that it might be conjoined to something else, because it does not depend on that [thing with which it is conjoined]. In this sense an apple [stump] united to a pear [branch, as in grafting,] is a *per se* being, because one does not depend on the other. Similarly, the Son of God is a *per se* being in this union, because his hypostasis or person does not depend on the human nature.

However, one might object: no unity of the "united" type is a personal unity. One must reply to this that something can be united to something else in such a way that the former is compelled into this unity with the latter and participates in it, or in such a way that the former gives its own unity to the latter and compels it into a unity with itself. For example, this is the way that an apple [branch] dominates when it is grafted on to a pear [stump] by compelling the pear [stump] into a unity with its own hypostasis. On the other hand, the pear [stump] is united to [the apple branch] in such a way that it participates in this unity and is drawn toward it. Therefore, the unity of that which is united by way of being drawn into a unity with something else is not a personal unity. However, the unity of that which is united by way of drawing something else [into a unity with itself] is [personal]. This is the way the Son of God is united to the human nature, because he draws it into a unity with his hypostasis, and not vice versa; therefore, his unity is personal.

2. To the second objection, that "nothing can be both a middle and an extreme in the same sense," one must reply that when one says, "this tree [trunk] is united with this graft," we can consider "this tree" insofar as it is an instantiation[25] of nature or insofar as it is an individual, because, as will become clear later, both considerations are acceptable. Now, insofar as it is an instantiation of nature, it does function as an extreme of this union. However, insofar as it is an individual, in this sense it is an intermediary[26] of this union. Indeed, in this sense it is that in which this union takes place, because this thing, namely, a tree, is united with the graft in its individuality or hypostasis. Similarly, if the Son of God is understood as an instantiation of nature, in this sense he is an extreme of this union. However, insofar as he is a person, in this sense he is an intermediary of this union, because the Word is united with the human nature in the person. Thus, [the Son of God] is both an intermediary and an extreme in different [senses].

3. To the third objection, that "nothing is terminated at itself," one must reply that this is true [if the thing in question is taken] in the same sense. But consider the following example: a circle both begins a line and is terminated at it; therefore, one and the same thing can terminate at itself, as long as it is taken in different senses. Similarly, one must reply, insofar as the person that is the Son of God is taken as an instantiation of nature, it

---

25. Literally, "a thing of nature" (*res naturae*).

26. There is no way of translating the Latin term *medium* into English here that would not be awkward; other options are "mean," "middle," or one can leave it as "medium"; the sense, however, is perfectly clear.

functions as an extreme of this union. However, insofar as it is taken as a person, in this sense it is an intermediary and terminates this union—and thus is terminated at itself, as long as it is taken in different senses.

But then there is a further question: that person who you say is the intermediary of this union is united. But in what is it united, then, as a union takes place in something? Similarly, there will be a question about that in which you will say it is united, as to where *that* is united, and thus there will be an infinite regress. One must reply here that one extreme is united with another extreme in a different fashion compared to how an intermediary is united with its extremes. Indeed, extremes are not united with each other [directly], but by means of an intermediary, while an intermediary is itself [directly] united with its extremes. And for this reason it is improper to question where the union of an intermediary is, because it is united by itself, not through some other intermediary. One can give a similar reply about the person. . . .

DOES THIS UNION PRODUCE ANY CHANGE IN WHAT IS SO UNITED?

SH 3, In un., Tr1, Q4, Ti2, C7, Ar1 (n. 63), 92–93

The objections are as follows:

1–2. To be changed means to be in a different state now compared to previously; however, that which is now something different compared to before is in a different state now compared to before; therefore, that which is now something different compared to before has changed. However, the Word through its union with the flesh is something different compared to what it was before; therefore, this union produces a change in the divine nature. Indeed, to be changed means exactly to be in a different state now compared to previously; but to be something now that one was not before is a greater [difference] than to be in a different state now compared to before; therefore, if the latter [difference] amounts to a change, so does the former; however, the Word in this union is something (*aliquid*) that it was not before, because now it is a man and it was not that previously; therefore, it has changed.

3. That which transitions from nonexistence to existence undergoes change; therefore, that which transitions from some [form of] nonexistence to existence [of this sort] undergoes change; however, the Son of God as a result of

the incarnation transitions from not-being-man to being man; therefore, he is changed as a result of this union.

To the contrary:

a. All change implies imperfection; however, the eternal Word is in no way imperfect; therefore, it cannot undergo, nor has it undergone change. Bernard [in *On Consideration* 5.6.17] says in this regard: "God is always one and the same, one with himself, remaining in the same state." Psalms [101:28]: *"but you are the same, and your years shall have no end."*

Solution:

One must note that there are several ways things are united. In one way, both elements of the union are changed, for example, when water is mixed with wine. In another way, only one of the elements is changed: for example, when the sunlight is united with the air, the light in this union does not change nor receive any disposition that it did not have previously. Even though right now it is "illumining" something and previously it was not, this does not create a new disposition in the light, but in the recipient, because now it is "illumined," but previously it was not. Taking this into consideration, one must reply that the union between the Word and flesh produces no change in the Word, but the change is only in the humanity that now receives the light of divinity and previously it did not, and this causes no change in the eternal light.

Replies to the objections:

1. To the first objection, one must reply that "something is in a different state now compared to previously" either on account of a change in this thing itself or on account of a change in something else, which is now related differently to the first thing compared to before. For example, we call the sun "illumining" based on how it acts on the air [now], despite the fact that it did not do so previously—and yet the sun is not changed in itself, but it is only the air that is related to it differently now compared to before, while the sun itself remains the same as it was before. Therefore, I say that the Word is not in a different state now compared to [the state it was in] before, but something—namely, humanity—is related differently to the Word now compared to before.

2. The reply to the second objection is similar.

3. To the third objection, one must reply that as a result of this union, the Son of God does not transition from some form of nonbeing to some form of being, but something that is related to it, namely, the human nature,

transitions from not-being-divine to being divine through a union with the Word in one person [that leads] to one personal existence. . . .

IS CHRIST GOD INSOFAR AS HE IS A MAN?

SH 3, Tr1, Q4, T1, D3, M4, C3, Ar2 (n. 51), 74–75
Objections:

1. Everything that is predicated of something insofar as it is itself, either acts as its *per se* accident, or is its definition, or part of its definition, or its effect; however, God does not relate to Christ insofar as (*secundum quod*) he is a man in any of these ways; therefore, Christ is not God insofar as he is a man.

2. Christ, insofar as he is a man, is a rational mortal animal; however, if these traits are repugnant to divine existence, then Christ insofar as he is man will not be God or the Son of God.

3. The next question is whether Christ is God or the Son of God insofar as he is *this man*. Since human existence according to its definition is repugnant to divine existence, so is the existence of *this man*; therefore, if he is not God insofar as he is a man, nor is he God insofar as he is *this man*. Furthermore, God does not relate to *this man* as his definition, or part of his definition, or as his *per se* accident or effect; therefore, he is not God insofar as he is *this man*.

To the contrary:

a. Christ has the power to remit sins insofar as he is a man, as in Matthew 9:6: "*But that you may know that the Son of man has power on earth to forgive sins, then says he to the sick of the palsy,*" etc. However, only God has the power to remit sins; therefore, Christ is God insofar as he is a man.

Solution:

One must reply that the expression "insofar as" (*secundum*)[27] has multiple meanings. For sometimes it points to a cause, sometimes to a natural condition, and sometimes to the unity of person. In addition, sometimes it points to the efficient cause, as in: "Christ was resurrected insofar as he is God";

---

27. The usual translation of *secundum* is "according to." The English rendition using this expression ("Christ according to that, according to which he is a man") would be too tedious, so the translation and hence the "linguistic" discussion here are approximate.

sometimes to the material cause, as in: "Christ redeemed us insofar as he is a man"; sometimes to the formal cause, as in: "Christ is something insofar as he is God." As for pointing to a natural condition, this happens when one says: "the Son of God remits sins insofar as he is God," that is, "Christ remits sins insofar as he is one having the divine nature." And sometimes it points to the unity of person, as in: "Christ created the stars insofar as he is a man," that is, "Christ created the stars insofar as he is *that one* or *that person*, who is a man." A similar example would be when one says: "[Christ] has the capacity to remit sins insofar as he is a man."

Replies to the objections:

1. In this way, a reply to the first objection is clear. Indeed, if the expression "insofar as" (*secundum*) denotes a cause or natural condition, the statement "Christ is God or the Son of God insofar as he is a man" is false. However, if it denotes the unity of person, it is true. Indeed, if it indicates a natural condition, the meaning is: "Christ is God by reason of his human nature," and this is false. However, insofar as [this expression] denotes the unity of person, the meaning is: "Christ is God insofar as he is one who is a man," and this is true.

2. To the second objection, one must reply that it is natures or essences that receive definitions, not persons or individuals. Hence, natures that are diverse according to their definitions [can] belong to one and the same individual: indeed, the definitions of "white" and "man" are different, but an individual can be both white and man. Similarly, although the definitions of God and man are different, one and the same person can be both God and man.

3. To the third objection, one must reply that one must analyze the expression "Christ is God insofar as he is this man." Indeed, the pronoun "this" can point to an individual man, and in this case, if the expression "insofar as" denotes a cause, the statement is false. But if it denotes personal union, it is true, as is clear from what has been said. Or it can point to the person of the Son of God, with the term "man" being used appositively with it, and in that case the following statement is true in an unqualified sense: "Christ is God insofar as he is the Son of God, who is a man."

CHAPTER 8
FREE CHOICE

DOES FREE CHOICE EXIST?

SH 2.1, In4, Tr1, S2, Q3, Ti3, M1 (n. 389), 466–67

It seems that there is no "free" choice in the sense of "flexibility" [between good and evil]:

1. Jerome [*Letter* 39.2] argues as follows: "God is good as far as his will is concerned, and he made humans in his image." Therefore, he made humans good as far as their wills are concerned. But if this is a [valid] consequence [of the preceding], so is this: "God cannot be not good; he made humans in his image; therefore, he made them in such a way that they cannot be not good; therefore, they possess no flexibility of free choice as regards opposites"; but this is the [kind of] freedom that we speak of; therefore, humans have no freedom.

2. The power of doing good that is not mixed with a power of doing evil is better than the kind that is able to do either, namely, both good and evil; this is evident, because this is the sort of power that God has. Therefore, given that the Greatest Good lacks all envy, and that this sort of power [to do only good] is the most excellent, and that he could impart it, he did impart it to rational creatures that are made in his image; therefore, rational creatures possess the power of doing good that is not mixed with a power of doing evil; therefore, they do not possess freedom of choice, in the sense in which it is flexible with respect to [choosing] either good or evil.

3. If no creature existed in the universe that had such a power, that is, to do good but not evil, the universe of creatures would be incomplete, because God could make such a creature; therefore, such a creature does exist. However, if there is such a creature, only rational creatures fit the bill; therefore, rational creatures have no flexibility as to [choosing] either good or evil; therefore, neither do they have the kind of freedom of choice that we speak of here.

To the contrary:

a. John Damascene [*On the Orthodox Faith* 2.27]: "All that can be generated is subject to change; now animated irrational things change in accordance with bodily change; rational things [change] in accordance with choice; things that possess thinking power [change] in accordance with thought; things capable of action [change] in accordance with decision making." It remains, then, that rational creatures are subject to change in accordance with choice; but choices are made flexible by the freedom of choice; therefore, [rational creatures] possess the flexibility of free choice.

b. St. Bernard [*On Grace and Free Choice* 1.2]: "Remove free choice, and there will be nothing to save; remove grace, and there will be no source of salvation." However, rational creatures are ordained to be rewarded; but in order to be rewarded, one must have merit; but in order to have merit, there has to be some mechanism of earning merit; therefore, if the mechanism of earning merit is free choice, human beings must possess it.

c. Augustine in *83 Questions* [2]: "The person who is good out of [free] will is better than the one who is good of necessity." Therefore, free will must have been given to humans.

Reply:

I concede that rational creatures possess the ability to choose freely in the sense of flexibility to choose either good or evil.

Replies to the objections:

1. To the objection that "God is necessarily good, and humans are made in his image and likeness, and therefore must be necessarily good, and consequently lack the flexibility of choosing freely," etc., one must reply that the comparison does not work in this sense, but as follows: God is good out of his [free] will, and he made humans "in his image" in the sense of making them good out of *their* [free] will.[1] Indeed, since creatures are from nothing, they are changeable and thus represent the opposite of necessity, because only a perfect power possesses necessity—which means only God possesses necessity, not creatures, for there is a deficiency of power in creatures. Therefore, it does not follow that if God is necessarily good, therefore, humans, who are in his image, will be necessarily good as well.

2. To the other objection, one must reply that it is true that God could impart to some creature a power that is bound to do good; however, [he could only do this] by grace, not by nature. For no creature can be given naturally the flexibility to do good, but not evil (unless by "nature" you

---

1. That is, made them capable of choosing to be good.

understand that which is given to a human being from the beginning, even though it does not belong to his or her essence). The reason why such an ability cannot be given to a human being naturally is that creaturely existence by its nature is necessarily accompanied by changeability. Therefore, just as it is impossible to impart to human beings that their nature not be created, in the same way it is impossible to impart to them that it not be changeable. The latter is imparted only to the Son, who proceeds from the Father while remaining identical [to him] in nature. However, whatever creatures cannot have naturally can be imparted to them by grace.

3. To the other objection one must reply that it is not logical that if the ability to be bound to do good is not naturally imparted to the human being, the universe of creatures is incomplete. However, the conclusion would be logical, perhaps, if it were not imparted to human beings in any way, namely, neither by [nature nor by] grace. . . .

IS FREE CHOICE CALLED "FREE" FOR THE REASON THAT IT IS INDIFFERENT TO [CHOOSING] GOOD OR EVIL?

SH 2.1, In4, Tr1, S2, Q3, Ti3, M2, C3, Ar1 (n. 397), 475–76

Arguments in favor [i.e., that free choice is indifferent to good or evil]:[2]

a. Damascene [*On the Orthodox Faith* 2.27]: "rational creatures are changeable as regards their choices." Indeed, [this sort of] choice is "free" precisely because it can either choose or reject. Therefore, since choosing, as well as rejecting, is indifferent to both [good and evil], free choice is called [free for the reason that it is] indifferent to good or evil.

b. Bernard [*On Grace and Free Choice* 10.35]: "[Free] choice is called 'free' because the will in it is equally free as regards either good or evil things." Therefore, etc.

c. Hugh of St. Victor: "The ability to do good belongs to power; the ability to do evil belongs to weakness; however, neither essentially belongs to freedom." Therefore, since freedom is [observed] in those [matters that pertain to both good and evil], it would be indifferent to both.

---

2. See also *Magistri Alexandri de Hales Quaestiones disputatae 'Antequam esset frater'* (Quaracchi: Collegii S Bonaventurae, 1960), Tome 1, q. 33, memb. 3, dist. 3, 592 in 566–608.

d. Augustine in *Hypognosticon* [4]: "free choice (*arbitrium*)³ receives its name from "choosing" (*arbitrare*), namely, because rational creatures deliberate about what to choose and what to reject."

[Objections] that it has a greater tendency toward good:

1. Anselm [*On Free Choice* 1]: "the power to sin is neither freedom nor part of freedom." He proves that it is so [ibid.]:⁴ "if an addition of something [to something else] diminishes [the latter] and its subtraction increases [it]... [then] it is neither freedom nor part of freedom"; but the power to commit sin is of this sort; therefore, etc.

2. As Bernard says [in *On Grace and Free Choice* 9], neither humans nor angels share with God (whose image they carry) the power to commit sin; however, they [all] do share free choice, to the extent that it is a power to act rightly; therefore, free choice in humans rather tends toward the good than toward evil.

3. As [Augustine] puts it in *On Free Choice of the Will* [2.1–2], God gave humans free choice in order that they might use it rightly, not in order that they might not use it rightly; however, it is used rightly in [choosing] good and not rightly in [choosing] evil; therefore, free choice has a greater tendency toward good than toward evil.

4. Augustine says in *On the City of God* [14.11.1]: "the choice of the will is truly free only when it does not serve vices and sins," for such is [the type of choice that is] given by God; therefore, free choice has a greater tendency toward good than toward evil.

Objections that it has a greater tendency toward evil:

5. Bernard [in *On Grace and Free Choice* 10.35]: "No one would think that 'free choice' is so called because a power or faculty makes it oscillate between good and evil, because it can fall by itself, but not get back up." Therefore, it has a greater tendency toward evil than good.

6. Free choice in humans of itself suffices to [choose] evil, but not the good; therefore, it has a greater tendency toward evil than good.

7. The allure and pull of evil is greater than that of the good; therefore, one should say it has a greater tendency toward evil than good.

3. See note 7 on the terminology, specifically on *arbitrium*.
4. For the full argument, without which this objection is incomprehensible, see the section "About Augustine's Definition of Free Will," SH 2.1, In4, Tr1, S2, Q3, Ti3, M2, C2, Ar1 (n. 394), 472.

Reply:

There are three ways of looking at "free choice." The first way is under the aspect of "not being coerced": in this sense it is called "free" because it is indifferent to good or evil. Another way is to look at "free choice" under the aspect of that nature, according to which it is something we share with God, that is, insofar as free choice is ordered to the good. In this sense it has a tendency primarily toward good, and it is in this sense that Anselm [in *On Free Choice* 1 and 3] says that "no ability to commit evil is part of freedom." The third way is to look [at free choice] under the aspect of the deficiency of nature, which it possesses on account of having been created, or in light of the deficiency of the will itself. It is in this sense that it has a greater tendency toward evil than good, because of itself it has a proclivity toward evil, and it is in this sense that Bernard says that "no one would think that 'free choice,'" etc.

Replies to the objections:

Based on this, one can reply to the authoritative statements [a–d]. Indeed, those authoritative statements, which conclude that free choice is indifferent to good or evil, must be understood as speaking of free choice under the aspect of that nature, which prevents it from being coerced.

1–4. As for the other [opinions] that conclude that it tends only toward the good or mostly toward the good, they must be understood as speaking of free choice insofar as it is something we share with God.

5–7. The rest [of the opinions] must be understood as speaking of free choice under the aspect of the deficiency that it has, on account of which deficiency it is called fickle and is more inclined toward evil than toward good. . . .

ABOUT ANSELM'S DEFINITION OF FREE WILL

SH 2.1, In4, Tr1, S2, Q3, Ti3, M2, C2, Ar1, Pr1 (n. 393), 472

The first definition, that of Anselm, goes as follows: "free choice is the power of preserving righteousness for its own sake."

There are objections against it:

1. It doesn't seem that it fits universally, because both God and good and evil angels share [the power of] free choice; however, no "power of preserving righteousness" is present in evil angels, nor in the damned, for no righteousness can be in them; therefore, it cannot be "preserved" in them; therefore, this definition does not fit them.

2. Rational creatures possess the power of either preserving or abandoning righteousness, and the power of free choice is capable of either; but then why is it defined only with reference to one of the two?

3. "Free choice is the power of preserving righteousness for its own sake"; but nothing is ordered to itself as to its own end; therefore, it is odd to refer to the "power of preserving righteousness for the sake of righteousness."

Replies to the objections:

1. One must say that one can take the "power of preserving" in two senses. In one sense this entails the presence of that which can preserve, that which can be preserved, and the means by which it can be preserved. In this sense, there is no "power of preserving righteousness" in the absence of righteousness. This is not how it is taken in Anselm's definition of free choice. However, in another sense the "power of preserving" refers only to that which pertains to the nature of the one who is able. In this sense, there is a "power of preserving righteousness" [even] in the absence of righteousness. Anselm provides an example of this in the power of sight. In one sense, it entails the seer, the object of sight, and the medium [of seeing]. In this sense, if no object of sight is present, or if there is some deficiency on the part of the required disposition of the medium, we say that a human being is not capable of seeing this thing. However, in another sense the power of seeing refers only to the capacity that the seer has. In this sense, one can speak of the power of sight whether the object of vision is present or not, and whether the medium is duly disposed or not.

2. To the question why it is not defined as a "power of abandoning" while it is [clearly] the power of [choosing] opposite things, I say that there are two ways of understanding the "power of [choosing] opposite things." Sometimes both of these opposites [that can be chosen] are taken in an absolute sense (*per se*); sometimes one is taken in an absolute sense, and the other accidentally (*per accidens*); sometimes one is taken in an absolute sense, and the other is not. Free choice, then, is not aimed at [choosing] evil either in an absolute sense or accidentally, but simply [operates with] evil.[5] Therefore, when one speaks of the "power of abandoning," one does not define its end but only that with which [it operates].

3. To the objection that "righteousness is not its own end, and therefore it does not have to be preserved for its own sake," I reply that righteousness

---

5. As one of available options.

is of two kinds: created and uncreated. The second kind is in God, and the first kind—which is [ordered] to the second—is in [the power of] free choice. Therefore, the kind of righteousness, for the sake of which this [i.e., created] righteousness must be preserved, is uncreated. However, free choice is defined as it is common to both God and creatures; therefore, it must take "righteousness" as it befits both: with respect to God [as] the final cause, and with respect to creatures merely [as] a norm (*ratio*),[6] and not the final cause, because [created righteousness] is not its own final cause.

ABOUT AUGUSTINE'S DEFINITION OF FREE WILL

SH 2.1, In4, Tr1, S2, Q3, Ti3, M2, C2, Ar1, Pr2 (*n. 394*), 472–73

The second definition goes as follows: "free choice is the faculty of reason and will, by which the good is chosen when grace is present (*assistens*) and evil [is chosen] when grace is absent (*desistens*)."

There are objections against it, as follows:

1. Anselm says that if an addition of something to something else diminishes the latter and its subtraction increases it, that something is neither that something else nor its part; however, the power to commit sin, as such, diminishes freedom: for the one who is capable of acting rightly and not capable of not acting rightly is freer than the one who is capable of acting rightly or not rightly; therefore, the power of committing sin is not part of freedom; therefore, neither [is it part] of free choice; but then it should not be part of its definition.

2. Diverse powers are not contained in one and the same faculty; but reason and will are diverse powers; therefore, free choice is not the faculty of those powers.

3. If the "faculty of will and reason" denotes the same thing as "free choice," it is superfluous to add "by which the good is chosen," etc.

Replies to the objections:

1. To the first objection, one must reply that freedom is of three kinds: of nature, of grace, and of glory. The natural kind is freedom from coercion; the gracious kind is freedom from sin; and the glorious kind is freedom from misery. When it is said, then, that "if an addition of something to something

---

6. Which allows one to achieve the end.

else diminishes the latter and its subtraction increases it, that something is not a part of that something else," this is not meant to apply to natural freedom, because nature can neither increase nor diminish. (Bernard [says in *On Grace and Free Choice* 8.24]: "The will endures equally in both good and evil.") However, this is meant to apply to [freedom] from sin and misery: indeed, both sin and misery can increase or diminish. Hence, one can be freer only from those [two]. Therefore, the power of choosing evil in the absence of grace is not part of freedom as it is common to both God and creatures, but only as [it exists in] creatures.

2. To the other objection, one must say that "reason" means two different things. For sometimes "reason" stands for the "cognition of truth"—and this type as such does not pertain to free choice. "Reason" also stands for the "cognition of the good," in two senses. There could be a "cognition of the good" [of the type that] simply [tells us] what ought to be done or not done. Again, this type does not form something one with the will, to fit the definition that "free choice is the faculty of reason and will." However, "reason" can also stand for the "cognition of the good," not only [in the sense of telling us] what ought to be done or not done, but [in the sense of the type of] operative knowledge of the good for the purpose of bringing it into being—and this is the proximate disposition to [the exercise of] the will. Therefore, just as the proximate disposition [to a form] and the form [itself] in some way make up something one, in the same way, in this sense, reason and will [form something one], in order to become, as it were, one power. In this sense, there can be one faculty of reason and will: with reason taking the advisory role and the will taking the impelling role.

3. To the third one must say that the addition to the definition "by which the good is chosen" is not superfluous. For even though the "faculty of will and reason" denotes the same thing as "free choice," nevertheless, this [part of the definition] does not yet convey the meaning that this is the power to [choose] opposites. However, this meaning is conveyed in what follows: "by which the good is chosen" etc. In addition, the "faculty of will and reason" is of two kinds. For there is a kind of natural faculty that is determined to one thing only—and this kind is not the same thing as free choice. And then there is another, voluntary, faculty, which is directed at [choosing] opposites—and this type is the same thing as free choice, and it is this type that is defined by the following phrase "by which the good is chosen," etc.

ABOUT BERNARD'S DEFINITION OF FREE WILL

SH 2.1, In4, Tr1, S2, Q3, Ti3, M2, C2, Ar1, Pr3 (n. 395), 473–74

The third definition goes as follows: "free choice is a consensus that involves both the freedom of the will that cannot be lost and the judgment of reason that cannot be swayed."

There are objections against it, as follows:

1. The question arises as to what is meant here by "con-sensus": does it mean to "sense together with" (*consentire cum sensu*) the mind or with the flesh? If it means to "sense together with" the mind, no such consensus would be evil. However, if [it means to "sense together with"] the flesh, no such consensus would be good. It remains, then, that this consensus would be [to "sense together with"] both the mind (and this sort of "sensing together with" would be good) and the flesh (and this sort of "sensing together with" would be evil). However, this sort of consensus down the middle does not seem to pertain to free choice. On this account Bernard says [in *On Grace and Free Choice* 10.35]: "No one would think that 'free choice' is so called because a power or faculty makes it oscillate between good and evil." Therefore, this consensus, to the extent that it is indifferently disposed toward good or evil, does not pertain to free choice.

2. One questions the statement about the "freedom of the will that cannot be lost": it seems that it suggests that the freedom of the will cannot be lost, but this seems to be false. Indeed, Augustine says in *Enchiridion* [30]: "a man who uses free choice badly loses both it [i.e., free choice] and himself." Therefore, free choice can be lost; however, this is not understood to pertain to the capacity or power [itself]; therefore, [it is understood] to pertain to freedom; therefore, freedom can be lost.

3. One questions the statement about the "judgment of reason that cannot be swayed." Indeed, Bernard [in *On Grace and Free Choice* 4.11] distinguishes between free choice (*arbitrium*) and free deliberation (*consilium*); but it is "free deliberation" that seems to fall under this last part of the definition; therefore, it is not only "free choice" that falls under it: for it belongs to the nature of "free deliberation" to choose what is beneficial or not.

4. Bernard says [in *On Grace and Free Choice* 2.4]: "If reason induced necessity in the will, the will would no longer be free." Therefore, the

judgment of reason can only have an advisory (*per modum consilii*) function in relation to the will; therefore, free choice (*arbitrium*) does not seem to be different from free deliberation (*consilium*), nor the other way around; therefore, that consensus would be free deliberation, etc.

5. In the statement about the "judgment of reason that cannot be swayed," the phrase "cannot be swayed" can mean, first, that it cannot be swayed toward nonrighteousness. In that case free choice on the part of reason would always choose rightly, whether the right will would follow or not, because if this were not to happen, reason would be either right or not right (just as the will is either good or evil), and therefore in this sense the expression "cannot be swayed" could not be used.

Or this phrase can mean that the will would never move except based on the judgment of reason. To the contrary, [one observes] that the will sometimes knowingly moves toward evil, and since [in such a case] it moves toward evil knowingly, it moves against the judgment of reason. For as Bernard says [in *On Grace and Free Choice* 2.3], it does many things against the advice or judgment of reason. In this sense, then, the expression "cannot be swayed" cannot be used [either].

In what sense, then, can one say that it "cannot be swayed"?

Replies to the objections:

1. To the first objection, one must reply that the term "consensus," as Bernard says, is given [precisely] on account of being down the middle between the sense of the mind and the sense of the flesh, or the appetite. For sometimes it con-sents to [i.e., senses together with] that, which the sense of the mind dictates, and sometimes to that, which the sense of the flesh dictates. However, by nature it is not equally disposed toward both, but its own tendency is to follow the sense of the mind, namely, the good.

2. To the second objection, one must reply that "natural" freedom cannot be lost, since it is assumed that "nature" is of the essence of those things in which it is. However, insofar as "nature" stands for the "natural" good of innocence that was given at the beginning—according to what is said in the *Sentences* 2.24[.2], [which characterizes this good as] the "freedom of choice that is immune from any ruin or corruption, as well as the righteousness of the will and the liveliness of all powers of the soul"—in this sense it can be lost. Also, it can be lost insofar as "freedom" stands for freedom from sin. Therefore, it can be lost in these ways. However, this is not the sense that is

used in the argument. Instead, [what is meant is] that it was not possible or not fitting for it to be coerced.

3. To the third objection, one must reply that "free choice" (*arbitrium*)[7] is not the same as "free deliberation" (*consilium*), as Bernard says: "judgment (*iudicium*) discerns what is allowed and what is not, and deliberation approves of what is beneficial and what is not." However, the former is not identical with the latter: indeed, by using our judgment, we discern many things to be licit or illicit, and yet we fail to approve of these licit things and to reject the illicit. Based on this, the "judgment" that is meant in the definition of free choice is not the one that is common to "judgment" (*arbitrium*) and "deliberation" (*consilium*).

4. To the fourth objection, one must reply that although reason does not impose necessity on the will, and therefore the "judgment (*iudicium*) of reason" does not seem to be anything other than [its] "deliberation (*consilium*)," nevertheless, it is not "deliberation" in the same sense as in what we mean by "free deliberation": for that sort of "deliberation" results from either [the presence of] grace or its absence. At the same time, "judgment" (*iudicare*) in the first sense proceeds from reason itself taken on its own, while "free deliberation" in the proper sense of the term refers only to the freedom of grace.

5. To the fifth objection, one must reply that judgment is referred to as something that "cannot be swayed" because it cannot be separated,[8] since reason is inseparable from free choice. Bernard in this regard says [in *On Grace and Free Choice* 2.3]: "Rational will, wherever it directs itself, always has reason [with it] as its companion and even, in some way, its attendant: not in order to proceed always based on reason, but in order never to proceed without it." However, "judgment that cannot be swayed" is not taken in the sense of [not departing from] righteousness, just as the objection states.

---

7. The terminology in the English translation may sound confusing here; we have chosen "free choice" to translate *liberum arbitrium* to follow the traditional rendering of this phrase. However, in the Latin the term is actually "judgment," which makes it synonymous with other terms for judgment.

8. The logic here is tenuous, although the source verb *declinare* for the term that we translate as "to be swayed" can mean "to lead astray," and thus "separate" from the previous position.

HOW DO THESE THREE DEFINITIONS DIFFER AMONG THEMSELVES?

SH 2.1, In4, Tr1, S2, Q3, Ti3, M2, C2, Ar2 (n. 396), 474–75
Solution:

One must reply by stating that there are four causes: the cause that is the first mover; the final cause; the material cause or that which acts as the material cause; and the formal cause. When Bernard's definition states that "free choice is consensus," he has in mind the moving cause: indeed, "consensus" refers to the coming together of powers in the direction of the moving cause, for it is up to us whether to consent to God or not. As for Anselm's definition, when it mentions the "power of preserving righteousness for its own sake," he has in mind the final cause: indeed, eternal righteousness is the end to which free choice as such is ordered by means of its own act. As for Augustine's definition of free choice, he has in mind the powers, namely, reason and will, which play the role of the material cause: indeed, they are moved by the prime mover toward the good, and grace is the form, by means of which they are directed toward their end. And the fact that those powers on their own can freely move toward evil does not present an obstacle. Indeed, free choice is not created for this purpose. However, since it is capable of [choosing] evil, it is meritorious for it not to consent to evil, as in Ecclesiasticus 31:10: "*he who could . . . commit evil and did not*," etc. . . .

DO HUMANS POSSESS THE SAME KIND OF FREE CHOICE IN THE STATES OF INNOCENCE, SIN, AND GRACE?

SH 2.1, In4, Tr1, S2, Q3, Ti3, M3, C4 (n. 405), 482
It seems that they do not:

1. *Sentences* 2.24.2: "Free choice is the rectitude of the will and the liveliness of all powers of the soul that is immune from every flaw and corruption." But according to this statement, it is not appropriate [for a human being] in the state of sin, where there is the corruption of sin, crookedness of the will, and a decline and death of the powers [of the soul] due to sin. In addition to that, even in the state of grace, there is a wounding of the powers of the soul through punishment. Therefore, "free choice" is not predicated in the same sense as regards these three states.

2. Augustine in *Enchiridion* [30]: "What sort of freedom can one have who is bound as a slave except when he finds delight in sin? For he who does the will of his master freely, serves freely. This means that he who is slave to sin is free to sin." Therefore, since the human being in the first state [i.e., of innocence] does not have this sort of freedom, humans in the state of innocence and sin do not possess the same kind of free choice.

3. The following statement from the book *On Rules of the Faith* [84] leads to the same conclusion: "Free choice is more free to serve evil and less [free] to do good," and this is observed in the state of sin; however, the opposite is observed in the states of innocence and grace; therefore, free choice is not predicated in the same sense as regards the states of innocence, sin, and grace.

To the contrary:

a. Just as humans could change their choice, which remained flexible in the first state [of innocence], so [they can] in the states of sin and grace; but possessing the same ability—namely, to change one's choice—amounts to possessing the same kind of free choice; therefore, in all three states free choice is of the same kind.

b. Free choice was given to humans in the state of innocence—nor have they lost it through sin to the extent of not being able to either correct sin through penance or persist in sin. Augustine [i.e., Gennadius, in this context] says in *On Church Dogmas* [21]: "After humans had fallen through the seduction of Eve by the snake, they lost the goodness of their nature and the strength of judgment, but not [the ability to make a] choice, in order that they may not lose the ability to correct sin, and in order that that, which they had not resolved by free choice, might not be indulged meritoriously." Therefore, humans possess the same kind of free choice in the states of innocence and sin.

Solution:

One must reply to this that humans do possess the same kind of free choice in these states.

Replies to the objections:

1. The first objection does not contradict this, because [humans] possess that first characteristic of freedom in the state of innocence. And what is meant by that natural freedom is not that which makes humans free from coercion, but that which gives humans that original natural rectitude, which God has freely given humans and which enables humans to persist in the state of goodness, should they wish to do so.

2. To the second objection, one must reply that the servitude of sin is not compatible with the freedom of grace, but it is compatible with natural freedom. For this reason humans do possess the kind of free choice that stems from natural freedom in both states, that is, of grace and sin.

3. The reply to the statement from *On Seven Day Cycles* [i.e., *On Rules of the Faith*] is similar. Since it is said [here] that free choice is freer to do evil, and it is said elsewhere that it is freer to do good, one must reply that what is intended here is not natural freedom—because it is indifferent to both good and evil, as Bernard says [in *On Grace and Free Choice* 8.24]—but freedom of grace in [doing] good, or the proclivity of the will itself toward evil. . . .

DO THOSE TO WHOM FREE CHOICE IS APPROPRIATE HAVE IT IN EQUAL DEGREE?

SH 2.1, In4, Tr1, S2, Q3, Ti3, M4, C1 (n. 407), 484–85
It seems that they do not:

1. One type of freedom is self-sufficient; it is neither created nor received, and it is appropriate only to God. Another type is created and received; this type is shared by angels and humans. Of the created variety, one type possesses rectitude, which it preserves, and another type lacks it. Of the variety that possesses rectitude, one type possesses it separably, and another inseparably. Now, the type that possesses it separably had belonged to angels before good angels affirmed [their goodness] and bad angels fell, and it belongs to all humans before their death, who possess the same rectitude. The type that possesses rectitude inseparably, however, belongs to good angels and humans, except that [good] angels possess it after they affirm [their goodness] and good humans possess it after their death. Of the variety that lacks rectitude, one type lacks it in a way that it cannot be recovered, and another in a way that it can be recovered. The type that lacks rectitude in a way that it can be recovered belongs only to humans in this life who lack rectitude, even though many will not recover it. And the type that lacks it in a way that it cannot be recovered belongs to wicked humans and angels, except that it belongs to angels after their fall, and to wicked humans after their death. Therefore, since these ways of possessing free choice are not equal, those to whom free choice is appropriate do not have it in equal degree.

2. The freedom that is less mixed with servitude is not equal to the freedom that is more mixed with servitude; for this reason, neither will free choice be equal in these two states, but it is less mixed [with servitude] where natural servitude is absent, e.g., in God. Also, [it is less mixed with servitude] where no servitude to sin or punishment is present—for example, in good angels, in whom neither [type of] servitude is present—compared to where it is present, for example, in good humans in this life, in whom there is servitude of punishment. And yet [free choice] is less [mixed with servitude] in the latter compared to the damned or to evil humans presently [living]. Therefore, free choice is not predicated of all of those equally.

3. Not even every state of human existence is equal [as regards free choice]. For this reason Augustine, *On the City of God* [22.30.3]: "Just as the first [type of] immortality, which Adam lost by sinning, consisted in being able not to die, and the last [type of] immortality will consist in not being able to die, in the same way the first [type of] free choice consisted in being able not to sin, but the last [type of] free choice [will consist in] not being able to sin." Therefore, in the state of innocence [humans] did not possess free choice to the same degree as they will in the state of glory.

To the contrary:

a. Bernard [*On Grace and Free Choice* 4.9]: "Of necessity, freedom equally pertains to both God and all rational creatures." Therefore, free choice is predicated equally of all those who have it.

b. Bernard [ibid.]: "Freedom of the will remains equally functional in both evil and good persons even in the presence of the captivity of the mind." Therefore, it is not diminished due to the servitude to sin or misery; therefore, free choice is equally present [in all states].

c. Bernard [ibid., 9.28]: "It is free choice alone that does not undergo any diminution or decrease of its [capacity], because it seems that it is in free choice that some substantive image of eternal and unchangeable divinity is impressed most powerfully. For even though it did have a beginning, it knows no decline nevertheless, in the sense of receiving any increase on account of justice or glory, or suffering decrease on account of sin or misery." Therefore, free choice would be predicated equally of those of whom it is predicated.

Replies to the objections:

1. Free choice is predicated equally of those of whom it is predicated in the sense of not being coerced in anyone. Indeed, although God can do

anything he wants with his creations endowed with reason, he does not coerce their wills nevertheless, but allows them to remain free. Therefore, insofar as "equally" implies "not more or less," free choice—in the sense of being free from natural servitude—is predicated equally of all intellectual substances. However, if "equally" implies "not in a prior or posterior way" (by this, I mean greater or lesser participation in the likeness of God) free choice is not equally predicated in this sense of all rational creatures—nor is it [equally predicated] of [freedom] that lacks rectitude versus the one that has it, and the same holds of other types.

2. One should use the same [line of argument] to reply to the second objection, the one about freedom being more or less mixed [with servitude].

3. As for the third objection, one must reply that all states share an equal degree of free choice insofar as freedom from coercion is concerned, which, as it were, is called essential freedom. However, freedom is not predicated equally [of all states] insofar as it is [freedom that is] ordered in relation to grace, for in this sense it is predicated to a lesser or greater degree. . . .

IS FREE CHOICE REASON OR WILL, OR SOME POWER THAT IS NEITHER REASON NOR WILL?

SH 2.1, In4, Tr1, S2, Q3, Ti3, M2, C1, Ar3 (n. 392), 470–71

That it is will:

1. Damascene asserts [in *On the Orthodox Faith* 3.14]: "Free choice, in my opinion, is nothing but the will."

2. Augustine [*On Free Choice* 3.3.7]: "Our power extends to our will, which cannot be coerced, more than to anything else"; but free choice is of this sort; therefore, etc.

3. Our merit mainly depends on our will and on our free choice; therefore, one is the other.

4. Bernard [*On Grace and Free Choice* 8.24]: "It is not unfitting to describe free choice as free consent through the will."

5. Bernard [ibid., 2.4]: "Free choice everywhere follows the will, to the extent that the will always has free choice for as long as it operates." Indeed, just as the will endures in [making] good and bad [decisions], so does free choice.

That it is reason:

6. Augustine, *On Five Replies* [i.e., *Hypognosticon* 3.4.4]: "Free choice (*arbitrium*) received its name from deliberating (*arbitrando*), by [using] the rational power, [to determine] what it would choose or reject."[9]

7. Bernard [ibid., 4.11] makes a distinction between free choice, free contentment, and free deliberation, and says: "choice is judgment, for just as it is the prerogative of judgment to determine what is allowed and what isn't, so it is the prerogative of deliberation to approve what is practical and what isn't, and so it is the prerogative of contentment to test what pleases one and what doesn't." Therefore, since it is the prerogative of free choice to determine what is allowed and what isn't, and this belongs only to reason, it seems that free choice belongs only to reason.

8. Psalms 38:7: "*the human being walks in the image*"; [but it is] reason [that is] the "image" of God; however, free choice is a way for humans to uphold the image of God; for this reason Richard [in *On the State of the Inner Human Being* 1.3] says: "free choice approaches God more closely and upholds his image." Therefore, free choice is reason.

That it is neither reason nor will, but some power that is different from either reason or will:

a. The image of the Trinity in the soul is represented in the cognitive part by memory, intellect, and will, and correspondingly in the motive part, as Augustine says [in *On the Trinity* 10.11 and 11.3], by free choice, reason, and will. So the will corresponds to the will; reason to the intellect; and therefore free choice to memory; therefore, just as mind or memory represents the image in the cognitive part, in the same way, free choice [represents it] in the motive part; but then it seems that this power is different from both reason and will.

b. Reason is a particular power for knowing, and the will is [a particular power] for desiring; however, free choice is not a particular power, because Augustine says [in *Hypognosticon* 3.5.7]: "When we speak of free choice, we speak not of a part of the soul, but of the whole." Therefore, if particular powers are distinguished from universal ones, free choice is different from either reason or will.

---

9. The sense of the quotation, which is lost in the corrupt syntax, has been restored from the original passage.

c. Damascene [in *On the Orthodox Faith* 2.22] considers free choice a universal mover in the soul, for which reason he says: "it wishes freely, it judges freely, it desires freely, it deliberates freely," etc.; but a universal mover is different from a particular one, which leads to the same conclusion as previously.

d. Bernard [*On Grace and Free Choice* 10.33]: "There is a correspondence: the image has the same role in the body as form in the [material] world: it moves most powerfully, orders, administers, and is not coerced by any necessity." Therefore, if it is "most powerful," it is not a particular power, but one that universally governs.

Reply:

I concede that free choice "universally governs," just like the mover, which presides over the entire [physical] world, universally governs. However, note that [the term] "free choice" has the same range as "mind." Indeed, sometimes "mind" encompasses the entire cognitive faculty, in which sense Augustine [in *The Spirit and the Soul* 39] says that "mind" encompasses the "image" as far as the cognitive power is concerned, and "likeness" as far as the affective power is concerned. And in this sense, the Master says in the *Sentences* I[.3.2] that these three—namely, memory, intelligence, and will—constitute one mind. In another sense, however, "mind" comprises [only] part of the image, and in this sense "mind" refers to preserving the likeness, "intelligence" refers to cognition, and "will" to desiring the highest truth. Similarly, if one takes the motive part [of the soul], "free choice" sometimes is used in a specific sense, and sometimes nonspecifically: nonspecifically, when it refers to the general power of the soul, while the soul's acts belong to other [powers of the soul]; in this sense, it is nothing other than the rational power [to choose] opposites. It is in this sense that Augustine says: "When we speak of free choice, we speak not of a part of the soul, but of the whole." For in this sense [free choice] comprises the entire image as far as the motive part [of the soul] is concerned. "Free choice" can also have another specific sense, signifying "acting as one wishes." "Free choice" in this sense is common to both rational creatures and the Creator. Or [if it means] "to obey God," it is appropriate for a rational creature that is good. Or [if it means] "to elect," this act is executed by both reason and will and is common to all rational creatures. However, in this sense, insofar as it is accepted as a specific power, it is distinct from either reason or will. In this sense, in the motive part [of the soul, free choice] represents the image of the Father, reason [represents the image] of the Son, and will [the image of] of the Holy Spirit.

Replies to the objections:

1–5. Therefore, to those authoritative statements of the saints that seem to conclude that free choice is the will, one must reply that the saints do not intend to say that free choice is essentially the will, but that freedom mostly has to do with the will, and free choice is called will for this reason alone.

6–7. To the objection that it is reason, one must reply that it is understood that way on account of "choice" in the sense of "judgment": for just as *free choice* is sometimes called the will on account of what is *free* in it, so is it sometimes called reason on account of the *choice* (in the sense of "judgment") in it; subsequent arguments [a–d] indicate that.

8. To the objection that "it is reason that is the image of God, and it is also free choice that is a way for humans to uphold the image of God" I reply that there are two senses of "reason": in a common sense, it stands for the entire higher motive part [of the soul], and in this sense, it is the same as "free choice" in its nonspecific sense; in a specific sense, it stands for the act of discernment, and in this sense, free choice in its specific meaning is different from reason. . . .

IS MERIT OR DEMERIT ESTIMATED BASED ON THE POWER OF FREE CHOICE?

SH 2.1, In4, Tr1, S2, Q3, Ti3, M7 (n. 416), 490

It seems that it is:

a. 1 John 3:3: "*sanctifies himself*"; the Gloss: "Does not take away free choice"; therefore, it is that in which merit resides.

b. In *On Seven Day Cycles* [i.e., *On Rules of the Faith* 90]: "The motive power toward the good resides in free choice."

c. Bernard [*On Grace and Free Choice* 14.46]: "The entire and only function of free choice—its merit—is that it consents"; for this reason, merit consists in consenting, and demerit in not consenting; therefore, free choice is where merit or demerit resides.

Alternatively, it seems that [merit or demerit] must reside in the will:

d. [Pseudo-]Bernard, in *On the State of Virtues* [2.17]: the sense is: "the reason for merit or demerit resides in the will." And the reason for this is: "nothing is in our power to the same extent as our will" [Augustine, *On Free*

Choice 3.3.7]. Therefore, it is the will that primarily exhibits order toward God: indeed, the highest will of the Father and the Son is the ultimate thing in the Trinity, and [our] created will is the first thing in us. Therefore, merit and demerit must be estimated based on the will.

e. Bernard says [in *On Grace and Free Choice* 3.6]: "Because the will alone, on account of its innate freedom, is not coerced to consent or dissent by any force or necessity, one can rightfully say that it is capable of either justice or injustice." Therefore, it is the power in which merit resides.

It also seems that the power [that determines merit or demerit] is reason:

f. Children and insane people cannot earn merit, even though they possess the will, because they lack the ability to use reason; therefore, the power of [earning] merit resides in reason.

g. This [power to earn merit] is associated with the image of God; but the image of God in the mind is the power of cognition.

Solution:

One must reply to this that that which is capable of [earning] merit, resides [in all three:] in free choice, reason, and will. Indeed, merit is [earned] when the rational soul, which is "in the image," is in conformity with the uncreated image through a free act as far as its motive part is concerned. For this reason the conformity of free choice [with the image] consists in being able; [the conformity] of reason [with the image consists] in judging or deciding; and [the conformity] of the will [with the image consists] in willing or choosing. And if any of the above is removed, so is the capacity to earn merit. Indeed, if on account of determined necessity one lacks the ability, where would merit come from? Again, if one acted or desired without judging, there would be no merit: otherwise, irrational beings that act on impulse would earn merit. Again, if one did judge, but lacked the will to [implement] this [judgment], there would be no merit. It remains, therefore, that merit is estimated on the basis of all three of these, in order that in this way the created trinity might conform with the uncreated Trinity in action.

CHAPTER 9
MORAL THEOLOGY

WHAT IS ETERNAL LAW?

SH 3, P2, In1, Q un., C3 (n. 226), 316–19
Multiple definitions exist.

I. Augustine, in the book *On Free Choice of the Will* [1.6.15], gives this definition of the eternal law: "The notion of eternal law can be explained briefly as follows, as that by which it is just for all things to be supremely well ordered."

One could object to this definition that it is not just for all things to be as good as they can be, even by the goodness that they are meant to have by nature. Therefore, it is not just for all things to be supremely well ordered. This conclusion is clear because "goodness" and "order" are similar. For as evil and disorder fall under one category, so goodness and order fall under another, while what is best and supremely ordered falls under yet another. And it is clear that it is not just for all things to be as good as they can be, because if this were just, all things would be best, even by the goodness they are meant to have by nature, but this is not the case. Therefore, it is not just for all things to be supremely well ordered.

II. Augustine gives another definition of the eternal law in his book, *On True Religion* [30.56]: "there appears to be a law above our mind which is called truth. This truth is unchangeable, which is the law of all arts, and the law of the omnipotent craftsman."

The objections against this definition are as follows:

1. The first objection concerns the statement that "it is the law of all arts." Now, as Augustine says in *City of God* [8.19], one can also encounter magical and malicious arts. If therefore the eternal law is not a law of evil, then it is not a law of evil arts. For this reason, it is wrongly said that it is "the law of all arts"; one would need to say that it is [only] the law of good arts.

2. Similarly, an objection can be raised against this definition's claim that the "law is that of an omnipotent craftsman," because the liberty of God is such that "it is not subjected to any law or any judgment," as Anselm says in his book, *Why God Became Man* [1.12].

III. The third definition of the eternal law is posited by Augustine in *On the Free Choice of the Will* [1.6.15]: "the eternal law is the highest principle, which must always be obeyed; through it the evil merit a miserable life, the good merit a good life, and through it the temporal [law] is rightly promulgated and rightly changed."

Against this definition, it can be objected:

1. The first objection is against the part [of the definition] which states that, "[the eternal law] must always be obeyed," because it is the same as the will of God, as the highest principle is the will of God. But Augustine says [*Enchiridion* 101] that "a good son by a good will, wills that his father live, whom God wills to be dead." That the father might die is according to the eternal law or will of God. Therefore, the good son is able to will rightly but contrary to the eternal law. Thus, [that law] must not always be obeyed.

2. It can be objected as follows, against that part of the definition which states that "through it, the evil merit a miserable life and the good merit a good life": because merit and demerit stem from our will, but the prize or punishment from the law. Thus, we are not deserving or undeserving through the law. Further, we ask whether these denotations of "eternal law" operate at equal [levels of abstraction] in regard to its substance, or if one is more general than another; and also how they relate to this [law].

Solution:

The notion of divine law can be considered in three ways, just as an eternal law can. For the eternal law can be considered with reference to good and evil or to the good only. As regards the good only, it can be considered either so far as it concerns goods generally or goods specifically, which are the goods of rational creatures only. In the first sense, it is fitting to say that "the eternal law is that by which it is just for all things to be supremely well ordered." For in its arranging capacity, the eternal law concerns both good and evil, because God makes and arranges what is good, and although he does not do evil, he arranges it. Thus, to arrange is a common act of this law with respect to [both] good and evil, and this is the way we should understand it in relation to good and evil. As regards the law as it concerns the good in general, whether it concern goods of rational or irrational creatures, this definition is fitting: "the eternal law is the law of all crafts and the law of the omnipotent craftsman." For insofar as the law is the art of an omnipotent artificer, it concerns the divine cause, which is the art and cause of all good things. As regards the law as it concerns the good that pertains to the rational creature only, this definition is fitting: "the eternal law is the highest reason, which must always be obeyed." For the rational creature must be ordered through laws; thus, the temporal law is promulgated by humans to govern them. And so, as it befits this [eternal law] to produce temporal laws, as stated in the definition, it is clear that this [i.e., the production of temporal laws] concerns a rational creature. Similarly, the clause "that which must always be obeyed" pertains to it with respect to the rational creature, because the act of obedience pertains only to the rational creature.

Replies to the objections:

1. We reply to the objection to the first definition according to Augustine, who says in *On Genesis* [3.24.37], commenting on the passage "*God saw all that he had made, and it was very good*," that while he said of singular things that they were good, he said of the whole that it was very good, because anything is good in itself, but is very good in terms of the whole. We must therefore draw a distinction between what we are able to understand about singular things, and in this way, it is said that all [singular] things are good; or in the context of the whole, which is twofold: either concerning the current order or the order in an unqualified sense, as it contains the whole succession of the order of present, past, and future things, because a thing which is present has also an order to a thing in the past and to another thing in the future. Now, if we speak of the order of the universe as understood in terms of the current order, we cannot say that all things are very good in the universe, because they could be better. But when we understand the whole succession of the present, past, and future order, then all things are very good in the universe, in such a way that they cannot be better. And therefore, just as it is good that all things may be as good as they can be, not separately but in the universal order, as already stated, so in the same way it must be said that, "it is just that all things should be supremely ordered," and this is how we understand that definition. Or it can be said that all things in principle are supremely ordered in the universe, as Augustine says in *On Genesis* 8.[23], where he says, "the divine will subjected all things first of all to itself, then corporeal creatures to spiritual ones, then irrational to rational, earthly to heavenly." However, we could say that in this train of thought there is a fallacy of the figure of speech, because in this statement, the phrase "all things" does not have an actual referent; therefore, it does not refer to actually existing things, but this statement could be made in relation to all eternity; however, when it is later said "it is not just for all things to be the best," the phrase "all

things" in that case does have an actual referent, for here it refers to actually and presently existing things.

II. 1. Regarding the first objection to the second definition, it must be said that as strictly speaking a law that is bad or that suggests something bad is no law at all, so strictly speaking an art that is bad is no art; for art, virtue, and law fall under the category of the good, while evil, vice, and artlessness fall under the category of evil. Thus, it must be said that the magical arts, insofar as there is truth in them, are from the eternal law; however, insofar as there is falsity and evil in them, they are not. Neither are they properly called arts, and thus the eternal law is not their law. For the deception of the demons is the beginning of all magical arts, and in this regard there is falsity, evil, and inordinateness in them, so that in this sense they are strictly speaking not arts.

2. To the second, it must be said according to Augustine in the *Confessions* [2.5.10], that "your law, Lord, is the law of laws, and your law is you, and you are the law itself." Therefore, we should understand "the law of the omnipotent artificer" appositively (or in terms of identity) and not possessively. Hence, Augustine says [in *On True Religion* 30.56] that this [law] is the highest truth, and it is clear that the highest truth is God. However, the argument [in the objection] proceeds as if the statement had a possessive sense through non-identity.[1] The eternal law, then, is there [in the second definition] defined in relation to all goods generally, which are derived from the first eternal art, which is the first cause. But certain goods are from it immediately, as those which come from divine operation; certain mediately, such as those that come from human operation. Therefore, the law is said to be "of all the arts," in the sense of being the rule of good operations of rational creatures. However, it is called the "law of the omnipotent artificer" insofar as it is the rule of those goods which are immediately from the creator.

III. 1. To the first objection to the third definition, it must be said that this definition befits the eternal law as it relates to rational creatures, for this law is the principle of order for rational creatures, as has been noted. But rational creatures have a threefold order: to God, to the self, and to the neighbor. Insofar as the eternal law is the principle of the order of the rational creature to God, to whom [this creature] is subject and obedient, it is described as

---

1. That is, "the law of God" where "law" is different from "God" and is a "law for God."

"that with which one must comply." Insofar as it is the principle of order of rational creatures to themselves, it is said to be "that through which the evil [merit] a miserable and the good, [a happy life]," and so on, because the human being merits or demerits punishment or glory of their own accord. Insofar as it is the principle of order of the human to the neighbor, it is described as "that through which the temporal [law] is rightly promulgated." Therefore, in order to demonstrate that it is the universal principle of order in rational creatures, that definition consists of that many [i.e., this particular number of] elements. To the objection that it is not "that with which one must comply," it must be said that the rectitude of our will is not always achieved through conformity to the divine will with respect to what is willed, but with respect to the one willing. For the movement of the will is related to the one willing and to what is willed; therefore, the conformity of my will to God should always pertain to the one willing, but not always to what is willed. Thus, I should conform myself to him in such a way that I may will what God wills me to will, not that I may always will what he wills. On this, the Gloss comments on [the words] of the Psalms [31:1], "*praise adorns the righteous*": for it is fitting that whatever God wills you to will, you also will. It does not say that you must will whatever God wills. And so the good son, willing that the father should live, whom God wills to die, conforms his will to and complies with the divine, because he wills what God wills him to will, namely, that his father live. This is what Augustine says in the *Enchiridion* [101]: [God] wants "the son to will for his father to live" from natural piety "whom God wills to die" from his judgment.

2. To the second, it must be said that "merit" signifies in one way the act worthy of beatitude or of misery, or the good or evil act. In another sense, merit signifies the order of an act to the reward, whether it be beatitude or punishment. While an act itself is from free choice, the order of the act toward a reward is from the eternal law. According to the first sense, it is true that merit and demerit stem from our will. But this is not the case in the second sense, because to order a good or evil act to beatitude or punishment is not from free choice. Thus, Augustine implies that the eternal law orders the good act to beatitude and the evil to punishment, saying: the eternal law has affirmed the following by its unchangeable stability, that merit [should consist] in the will, and the reward in beatitude or misery. And so it is clear that the order to a reward is from it [the eternal law]. . . .

IS THE NATURAL LAW UNIVERSALLY DERIVED FROM THE ETERNAL LAW?

SH 3, P2, In1, Q un., C7, Ar4 (n. 233), 328–29

1. The derivation of laws from the eternal law is through reason which understands the eternal law; but only the rational creature is allowed to see and to consult the eternal law, as Augustine says in his book, *On True Religion* [31.58]. Therefore, the natural law is derived from the eternal law only insofar as the former exists in rational creatures. Since therefore there is a natural law in rational and irrational creatures, as Isidore says, in *Etymologies* II, that the natural law is "the one nature taught to all animals," it is not derived universally from the eternal law. The major proposition is made clear by Augustine in *On Free Choice of the Will* [1.6.15]: "nothing is just or legitimate except what humans have derived for themselves from the eternal law," but this derivation is through understanding.

2. The second reason. There is no derivation from the law except according to the act and power of the law; but the act or power of the law, as has been said, and as it is held in the *Canon* [i.e., Gratian's *Decretum* 1.3.4], is: to order, to prohibit, to permit, to counsel, to punish, and to assign reward. But all these acts only pertain to the rational creature, because neither precept nor prohibition, nor reward nor counsel, is made through the law except [as it pertains] to the rational creature. Therefore, the law is derived from the eternal law only insofar as the former exists in rational creatures.

Some might say to this that these are the proper acts of the law, not that laws are derived according to them; moreover, there is an act common to [all laws], namely, to constrain, according to which the [laws] are derived, and this befits the eternal law with respect to both rational and irrational creatures, because it constrains insofar as it sets limits on the power of rational and irrational creatures indiscriminately, and so [the law] is derived according to the principle of constraint. Thus, Augustine says in *On Genesis* [9.17.32]: "the most normal course of every nature has certain natural laws, which impose certain limits on the acts of the vital spirit, which is created, which even an evil will is not able to surpass." Similarly, of the elements, he says: "and the corporeal elements of this world have a definite power and certain qualities, which [determine what] each one is able or not able [to do]." From this, it is clear that constraint applies to all creatures. But against this, it is objected that irrational creatures are limited by necessity and rational creatures are not, since they have free choice; therefore, the term "constraint" is equivocal in these and not [applied] according to a common meaning. From which the same consequence as before follows.

On the other hand:

a. Every good is universally from the eternal goodness; therefore, every natural law, because it is good, is in every case from the eternal law.

Solution:

Every natural law is derived from the eternal law, on the basis of how near to or remote from God the natures are, in which this law is. For the natural law is threefold. First, it concerns the order of rational creatures, which is described in Romans 2:14: *"those who do not have the law, naturally do those things that pertain to the law."* And this is even said in the Gloss on this passage: "the law of nature, by which anyone understands and is conscious of what is good and what is evil." Likewise, there is a natural law concerning the order of irrational, sensible creatures, of which Isidore speaks: the natural law "is that which nature has taught to all animals," such as males [being] with females. Likewise, there is a natural law concerning the order of all other creatures, namely, irrational and insensible, of which Augustine speaks in the *Soliloquies* [1.1.4]: "God, whose laws determine the rotation of the axis [of the world] and the course of the stars." According to these differences, the natural law is universally from the eternal law. Nevertheless, the first [type of law] is nearer than the second and the third, and the second nearer than the third, insofar as rational creatures remain closer to God than sensible ones and sensible ones [closer] than insensible and irrational ones.

Replies to the objections:

1. To the first, it must be said that the notion of the eternal law is twofold, according to Augustine. First, there is an eternal law, by which "it is just that all things are supremely well ordered." Then there is an eternal law, which is the "highest reason, to which all must comply, by which the evil lead a miserable life and the good lead a good life." From this it is clear that the eternal law signifies the divine art and wisdom, insofar as it ordains creatures and the movement of creatures, and that order according to the law in all creatures is from it [the divine wisdom] and the law equally. But the order is twofold: for a certain creature, namely, the rational one, is the lord of its own acts, but others are not, namely, irrational creatures. Therefore, the eternal law orders

by a necessary order the acts of irrational creatures; the acts of rational creatures, however, are not ordered by a necessary order but remain in them a free choice. To the objection that the derivation [of the natural law] from the eternal law is according to understanding, it must be said that this is said with respect to the temporal law and not the natural law. Thus, Augustine speaks of the temporal law when he says, "nothing just or legitimate," etc. The reason for this is that the natural law is in us without our cooperation, but is imparted and impressed by God: for he impresses the power of natural order in both rational and irrational creatures. But in the temporal law, we cooperate so that we contribute to this law's observance by ourselves. This cooperation is through rational understanding, however, and therefore [such understanding] is implied when thinking about that law.

2. To the second, it must be said that just as heating describes the essential (*per se*) and principal act of fire, and the hardening [of clay] the consequent and not the principal act, so constraint describes a consequent effect of the law. But the principal act that applies to all and according to which [other laws] are derived is to order, because the eternal law is that by which "it is just for all things to be supremely well ordered," and this act persists in precepts, prohibitions, and in other acts of the law, and latterly concerns irrational creatures and their acts, because the order runs through all acts. Thus, Augustine says in *On Genesis* 8.[23]: "the divine will first of all subjects all things to itself, then corporeal creatures to spiritual ones, then irrational to rational, terrestrial to celestial," and so order runs through all things. It can even be said that, if we extend the meaning of "precept" in the same way that we extend the meaning of "obedience," that derivation [of laws from the eternal law] can follow the logic of a precept. For we extend the term obedience to both rational and irrational creatures when we say that all things obey God, and this is a natural subjection. Thus Psalm 148:5 says: "*he commanded and [all things] were created; he established a precept, which shall not pass.*" And the Gloss: "The precept, that is the law and the circumstance." And similarly, Anselm in *Why God Became Man* [1.4]: "Any creature, when it naturally serves the order prescribed (*praeceptum*) for it, is said to obey God, and most of all the rational creature, to which it is given to understand what one should do." And so, extending [the meaning of] a precept, it can be said that this derivation proceeds according to the logic of a precept. . . .

IS THE NATURAL LAW A COGNITIVE OR MOTIVE HABIT?

SH 3, P2, In2, Q2, C2 (n. 244), 343-44

1. Romans 3:20: "*the cognition of sin comes through the law.*" Therefore, the effect of the law as such is cognition, even though this [passage] refers to the written law. Therefore, as the "law" part is common to the natural and the written law, the natural law is also a cognitive habit, because it shares in common with the written law its effect, which is cognition.

2. Gloss on Romans 2:14: "the natural law is that by which anyone understands," etc. Therefore, its effect is to understand, and it is a cognitive habit.

3. Romans 2:15: "*the requirements of the law are written,*" and the Gloss: "that is, it is firmly infixed in reason." But a habit infixed in reason is cognitive.

On the other hand:

1. No cognitive habit binds the will to do or not to do anything, because cognition is not binding. But the law is called that which binds[2] one to do or not to do something. Therefore, it is an operative or motive habit and not a cognitive one.

Solution:

As free choice is "the faculty of will and reason," it is clear that free choice entails three things, namely, the faculty, reason, and the will. Therefore, there are three acts of the natural law which correspond to these three aspects of free choice. The first involves binding, which it has with respect to "faculty," because the faculty in itself is freely flexible, and therefore in relation to it, the natural law binds. The second act of the natural law is to show, which correlates to "reason," and this according to the interpretation by which the law (*lex*) derives its name because it involves reading (*legere*), as Isidore says in *Etymologies* [5.3.2], "the term 'law' (*lex*) is derived from 'reading' (*legendum*)." The third of its acts is to instigate or motivate one to do good and to shun evil, which matches "will," as Isidore says in *Etymologies* [5.4.1], "the natural law is common to all, for the reason that we universally have it by natural instinct, not by any constitution."

Therefore, the natural law is defined with respect to a faculty as that which binds and restrains; with respect to reason as what illumines reason; with respect to the will as what instigates to the good. And so it participates in

---

2. In Latin the word for "law" (*lex*, from *leg-s*) and that for "bind" (*lig-are*) are cognates.

the nature of both habits, namely, cognitive and motive, and the [aforesaid] arguments are based on its diverse acts. . . .

CAN THE NATURAL LAW BE ERASED?

SH 3, P2, In2, Q3, C1 (n. 246), 346–47

1. The first objection: the Gloss on Romans 2:14, "*For when the gentiles,*" etc., says, "As was stated, it is not that grace is negated through the word 'nature,' but rather nature is repaired through grace. When this grace has renewed the interior person, it writes [on the heart] the law of justice, which has been deleted by guilt." And here "nature" stands for "natural law." Therefore, it is deleted through guilt and is erasable.

2. Second, Malachi 2:15: "*Guard your spirit and do not despise the wife of your youth.*" The Gloss: "a wife, that is the natural law written on the heart, by which even unbelievers are compelled to say: may God judge, may God see, and I permit him to judge all things between you and me. This wife is something that resides in our spirit, because she is always coupled to our spirit, and if she recedes from us, we immediately offend God." The [natural law] therefore recedes and therefore is erasable from the soul.

3. Third, that which is able to [act on] something greater is also able to affect something lesser. If therefore guilt can erase the law of grace, which is greater than the law of nature, then it can also erase the law of nature, which is therefore erasable.

On the other hand:

Augustine in *Confessions* 2.[4]: "Your law, Lord, and the law written on the hearts of human beings, which iniquity cannot erase, punishes theft. For what thief suffers another thief with equanimity?" From this it is clear that [the natural law] is not erasable, because if it were erasable, this would be on account of a certain iniquity.

Solution:

Something can be erased in two ways, either as regards its essence or as regards its effect, as is clear in the eclipse of the sun: for the light of the sun is not lacking in this case as regards its essence but only as regards the effect it has on us, which is to illumine, although it always shines in itself. In the same way, the natural law, which is as the sun in the soul, as regards its essence, is never erased from [the soul], but always shines in it in itself. Nevertheless, it is sometimes erased in its effect, namely, because it does not always illumine the soul itself, as when the soul turns away from God and is darkened through sin. Thus, the shadow of sin, interposed between the soul and God, prevents the effect of the law. Thus, the Gloss on Romans 2:14 says, "*For when the gentiles,*" etc.: "the image of God is not so rubbed away in the soul [on account] of the temporal effects of the fall, that none of its features remain there [in the soul]. What was impressed there through the image of God when it was created is not entirely destroyed." Thus, the natural law always remains written in the soul. For that law itself is impressed through the image, and on this account, even if the ability to read that law is destroyed by earthly effects, nevertheless, the essence [of the law] is not [destroyed]. And this is how one can interpret the reason given in the Gloss on Malachi 2:15, which says that the natural law "*is always joined with our spirit*"; therefore, it cannot be erased from it. And this is understood insofar as it pertains to the essence of the natural law.

Replies to the objections:

1. To the first objection, which shows that [the natural law] is erasable without qualification, it must be said that there is a writing of the law in terms of essence and in terms of manifestation. When therefore it is said that "the natural law of justice is inscribed" [in us], this is not the case as regards essence, but as regards manifestation, so that what was darkened through sin might be enlightened.

2. To the second objection, it must be said that the natural law may recede as regards operation or effect, but nevertheless not according to essence, as a lord is said to have receded when he does not have rulership in his home.

3. To the third objection, it must be said that it does not follow that if grace which is greater [than nature] can be erased, then what is lesser can be erased also. For it does not follow that "grace erases mortal sin, which is greater; therefore, it also erases venial sin, which is lesser." Similarly, it does not follow that "guilt erases the law of grace, which is greater; therefore, it also [deletes] the natural law, which is lesser." For guilt is naturally opposed to the law of grace and not to the law of nature, and therefore it deletes this and not that [one], except as regards effect. And likewise, although the law of grace is more powerful than the law of nature, nevertheless, it is not as durable in the subject, because that law [of nature] is naturally inserted in the soul and is therefore not erasable from it through sin as is the other one [i.e., law of grace]. . . .

DOES THE NATURAL LAW ORDAIN US TO GOD?

SH 3, P2, In2, Q4, M2, C1 (n. 250), 353

a. Ecclesiasticus 17:9: "*he teaches them discipline*" and the Gloss: "he has given discipline and the natural law to human beings, that they may be subjected to their creator and may honor him with good works." Therefore, the natural law entails that humans be subjected to the creator and that they should be ordained to him through obedience.

b. Cicero in the *Rhetoric* [2.54] says that the natural law "is not that which opinion generates but which a certain innate power instills, such as religion, piety, etc." And he says that "religion offers ceremony and worship of a certain superior nature, which is called divine." Therefore, religion consists in the worship of the divine nature. If therefore religion is a part of the natural law, the natural law ordains us to God and to his worship.

On the other hand:

1. Hugh of St. Victor [*On the Sacraments* 1.12.4]: "There are only two precepts in the natural law, namely, that you not do to others what you would not want done to yourself" (Tobias 4:16), and "*whatever you will to be done to you*, etc." (Matthew 7:12). But through this precept, the rational creature is only ordained to the neighbor and not to God. Therefore, either Hugh's distinction is insufficient or the law does not ordain us to God.

2. The Gloss on Romans 2:14, "*For when the gentiles,*" says: "the natural law [holds that] one should not inflict injury on anyone, and should not shortchange another, but abstain from fraud and perjury and such things, and, to put this briefly, should not wish to do to another what you would not wish to be done to yourself, which concords with evangelical doctrine," as in Matthew 7:12. From this it is clear that the precepts of the natural law are reduced to this: "*whatever you will that others do to you*," etc. If therefore that law ordains us to the neighbor and not to God, it is clear that the natural law does not have a precept ordaining us to God.

Solution:

As the Gloss on Romans 2:14 says, insofar as human beings are in the image and likeness of God, "they have a law by which they understand and are conscious in themselves of what is good and what is evil." For insofar as humans are in the image, they have a cognition of the first truth, which is God, because, as Augustine says [in *De spiritu et anima* 10], the image is located in the power of understanding. However, insofar as human beings are in the likeness of God, they have the power and obligation to love the highest good, because the likeness consists in the power of loving, according to Augustine, and because of this, the law does prescribe that humans be ordained both to God and to the neighbor.

Replies to the objections:

1. To the first argument to the contrary, it must be said that these mandates[3] do presuppose the order of the human being to God. For just as in the mandate to love the neighbor we understand the love of the self (which is clear when it is said, "do not steal," etc., which is reduced to the mandate, "don't do to others, etc.," and the latter to this one: do to others what you would want done to yourself, that is, do to others the good that you would want your neighbor to do to you, and what is presupposed here is the love of the self) so one must reduce the mandate of the natural law to the love of one's self. . . . Indeed, the mandate "do what you would want done to yourself" is reduced to the love of one's self, as was shown, and so the mandate to love the self is the foundation of the mandates of the natural law. But the love of self, insofar as a person loves themselves ordinately and for a good end, implies the love of God and the love of neighbor. For if I love myself and my own existence, I naturally love the origin of my own being and of its conservation. This [origin], however, is God and so the love of God is naturally founded in [one's love for oneself]. Likewise, any thing whatsoever naturally loves something similar to it in species, because nature desires its own likeness, which implies the love of the neighbor. For loving myself means loving naturally my own species and what is similar to me in species. Nevertheless, in another mode, love of self is said to be the foundation of the city of the devil, namely, insofar as it is not ordained to the right end, but this is not the type [of love] that we are speaking of here. Thus, the precept of nature, insofar as it is "of nature," is founded on the love of the self. From this it is clear by what mode it ordains the self to God and to the neighbor, because in the love of self is understood the love of God and neighbor. And from this it follows: do to others what you would wish to have done to yourself. However, the law of grace elevates nature, because it posits the love of God as the foundation of everything, and thus the reply is clear. . . .

3. That is, that "you do not do unto others," etc.

DOES THE NATURAL LAW INSTRUCT US TO LOVE GOD ABOVE ALL THINGS?

SH 3, P2, In2, Q4, M2, C3 (n. 252), 357–58

1. The Gloss on Ecclesiasticus 17:9, "*he teaches them discipline,*" says: "natural and written law suggest that we must love God with our whole heart, soul, and power, and we must guard his mandate to love God and neighbor." Therefore, in the natural law we are able to read that God must be loved above all things, because this is what it means to love him with the whole heart.

2. Through nature, anyone loves his or her own being above all else; but loving one's own being, one naturally loves the origin of one's being [which is supernatural]. But the love, by which one loves the origin of one's being, is equal to that by which one loves oneself or even something greater. If therefore the ultimate principle of the being of human creatures is God, therefore, one naturally loves him above all things, because there is no difference between this love and that of the self.

3. To love is to will the good of another. But from the natural law, I love God. Therefore, from the natural law I will him the good that is appropriate for him. Therefore, since his own good is the highest, I naturally will him the highest good. But loving myself, I do not will myself the highest good because my proper good is the highest. Therefore, I naturally will a greater good for God than for myself; therefore, the natural law prescribes to me to love God above me and above all else.

On the other hand:

a. It is impossible that the knowing agent should naturally understand something greater than itself. But love does not extend itself above understanding, because the good is not loved unless known. Therefore, it is impossible that someone naturally love another more than the self. Therefore, through the natural law, no rational creature can love God above the self and all things. The major premise is clear, because certain things are understood through their likenesses in the soul, others, however, through themselves as being in the soul, such as things that are directly present in the soul; in the latter way, the soul understands itself and its justice and its affections, because the soul is present to itself, and similarly so are those [affections]. If therefore this [latter] cognition is greater than that which is through likenesses, as nothing is more present to the soul than itself, it is impossible that the soul can know something else better than itself; neither even can it know God [in this way] because he is not as present to the soul as it is present to itself, because the soul understands him through likenesses and *"through a mirror, darkly"* [1 Corinthians 13:12].

b. In order for the intellect to know God as he is, it is necessary that it [the intellect] strip itself of its form, because as long as it uses itself [i.e., its natural form as intellect], by this very act it sees God through a likeness, and so not as he is. Therefore, it is necessary for the intellect to go beyond itself or above itself in order to understand God as he is. Similarly, in order for our affection to love God more than itself, it must go beyond itself; if therefore naturally the soul is not able to go beyond itself or to choose anything above itself, then it is not naturally capable of loving God above itself, and so it is not naturally capable of loving him charitably.

Solution:

To love God above all things and above oneself and for the sake of himself is, as it were, instigated and insinuated in the natural law, though not in the sense of making us [love] or leading us [to this love]. For the natural law, insofar as it is a law, shows and suggests to the soul that it should love God in this way. Insofar as it is natural, however, its relation to the soul involves instigating it to this love. And therefore the Gloss on Ecclesiasticus 17:9 says: "this natural law suggests that we should love God with the whole heart." Thus, it says that [the natural law] insinuates and instigates to this love but does not lead to it, which is why the law of grace is necessary, which leads to this [love]. It is also true that, in addition to that, after sin the law of Moses is necessary.

Replies to the objections:

1. To the first objection, it must be said that the Gloss does not say that the law makes us love, but only that it suggests that we do so. Thus, it is described according to insinuation and not according to leading to it.

2. To the second objection, that "everyone naturally loves their own being and their own origin," it must be said that the love of one's origin is twofold, because there is a love of one's origin insofar as it is an origin and love for the origin in an absolute sense, not insofar as it is one's origin: for example, I can love God as he is in himself or as my origin. The natural law, therefore, does not prescribe that we love the origin in itself and absolutely above all things but that we love it insofar as it is our origin; this is clearly there [in the law]. But in that case the love of self and of one's origin are the same, because the soul does not love its origin, insofar as it is its origin, except

because it associates it with its own being, which is what it loves, and not the converse. And in this sense the soul cannot naturally love God more than itself because nature does not extend beyond itself.

3. To the third objection, it must be said that this argument does not stand, namely, "I wish the highest good for God but not for myself; therefore, I love God more than myself." However, from this it follows: "therefore, I will a greater good for him than for myself." Indeed, there is the "willing" and the "good" there. Therefore, this adverb "more" can modify either that "willing" or that which I call "good." If it is taken to go with the "good," that argument would not follow. But if it goes with the "willing," then it does follow, because loving comes from the will and not from the good that is willed. By nature, however, I will more strongly for myself my own good, which is lesser, than for God his own good, which is greater, as soldiers desire for themselves their own small patch of land more than they desire for the king to obtain his great kingdom. . . .

IS THE LAW OF MOSES NECESSARY FOR SALVATION?

SH 3, P2, In3, Tr1, Q1, C2 (n. 260), 369–70

1. Hugh of St. Victor, in *On the Sacraments* [1.6.7], says that in the natural law there are three things, namely, the precept, which concerns what is necessary; prohibition, which concerns what is harmful; and concession, which concerns matters of indifference. But no sin so blinds humans as to prevent them from knowing through a natural judgment of the natural law what is to be done and what to be avoided. As Augustine says in the *Questions on the Old and New Testament* [4]: "Who is ignorant of what is appropriate for good life or that one ought not inflict on another something that they do not want to happen to themselves?" Therefore, without the law of Moses, humans are able to know what is necessary for their salvation. Thus, the law is not necessary for their salvation.

2. In us there is an adjudicative power concerning those things which are necessary for salvation, namely, synderesis. Similarly, in us there is a power that is desirous of salvation. Therefore, without the law humans are able to see or know and desire what is necessary for their salvation and the law is not necessary for it.

3. Augustine [*On Grace and Free Will* 3]: "Ignorance excuses no one to the extent of saving them from burning in perpetual fire." And this is

understood to pertain to the ignorance of those things which are necessary for salvation; but ignorance of the law of Moses does serve as an excuse that saves one from an eternal fire, as is clear as regards the blessed Job and other saints, who did not know the law in the time of the law and were not of the Jews. Therefore, the law of Moses was not necessary for salvation.

On the other hand:

a. The knowledge of things that should be believed and the performance of things that should be done is necessary for salvation. But the law of Moses, in a figurative[4] way, does give knowledge of things to be believed and does pertain to salvation; as far as moral precepts are concerned, however, it pertains to the performance of things that should be done and even to the knowledge of these things. Therefore, it is necessary for salvation.

Solution:

The law of Moses includes the natural law through the explanation of morals, and it includes the law of grace in a figurative way in the ceremonial precepts. Therefore, it should be called necessary for salvation as regards moral things that pertain to the natural law, useful for salvation to those people who were not of the Jews as regards ceremonials and symbols before the promulgation [of the law], but necessary [for salvation] after its promulgation for those who belonged to the Jews, to whom the law was given. And from this the reply to the objections is clear. . . .

IS THE LAW OF THE GOSPEL THE SAME AS THE NATURAL LAW?

SH 3, P2, In4, Tr1, Q4 (n. 546), 843–45

1. Romans 2:14: *"If the gentiles not having the law naturally do what the law requires, they are a law to themselves, because they show that the work of the law is written in their hearts."* From this it is accepted that the natural law is written into the heart and conscience of humans. Thus, the Gloss on this passage says that the natural law is that "by which anyone understands and is conscious in themselves of what is good and what is evil." If therefore the law of the gospel is the law which is inscribed in the human heart, by which we understand and are conscious of what is good, and what is evil (whence Jeremiah 31:33: *"I will give my law in their visceral parts, and I will write it in*

---

4. That is, symbolic, allegorical; not direct.

their hearts," which statement is understood to be about the law of the gospel), the law of the gospel is the same as the law of nature.

2. Whatever the law of nature dictates, the law of the gospel dictates, but not the converse. Therefore, the natural law is integral to the law of the gospel.

3. The law of the gospel is the universal law, which is always applicable for all. However, every law which is always and for all is the natural law, because what is natural, is always and for all, and is not acquired or received later. Therefore, it remains that the law of the gospel is the same as the natural law.

4. Also, that which is such by nature, is also such of itself, to a greater degree. Therefore, if the gospel by nature is the law to the greatest degree, it would also be the law of itself; therefore the gospel will be the same as the natural law. Gratian says in the beginning of the *Decretum* [1.1]: "the natural law is what is contained in the Law and the gospel," siding with Isidore in *Etymologies* [5.2.1]: "all laws are either divine or human; divine [laws] are known naturally, and human [laws] from customs." Also, if one were to say, with Gratian [*Decretum* 5.6.3], that "the natural law is contained in the law and in the gospel, nevertheless, not everything that is found in the law and in the gospel can be proved to cohere in the natural law. For there are certain morals and certain mystical aspects in the law. Moral mandates pertain to the natural law and therefore demonstrably are not susceptible to any change. However, the mystical on the surface is proved alien to the natural law, [although] insofar as its moral import is concerned, one could find a link to it [i.e., natural law]."

On the other hand:

a. In the gospel and even in the law there are moral principles, which are according to the suppositions of faith, such as the worship of the assumed humanity of Christ and so forth; but those things which are according to the supposition of faith transcend the dictates of reason and nature. Therefore, the moral principles of the gospel or the law generally are not contained in the natural law.

b. Nature and grace are not the same but differ essentially. Nor are the order of nature and of grace [the same]. Therefore, neither are the rule or the law that is according to the order of nature [the same as] the law that is according to the order of grace. But then neither will the law of the gospel, which is the law of grace, be the same as the natural law, which is according to the order of nature.

c. Natural powers are not the same as the powers given by grace. Therefore, neither will the natural law be the same as the law of grace.

d. It is one thing to be obliged to do something by reason of the exigencies of nature and another by reason of the exigencies of grace. For example, from the exigencies of nature there is an obligation to love the benefactor and the friend, not, however, the evildoer or those who harm you. From the exigencies of grace, however, there is an obligation to love those who harm you and do you evil. Luke 6:32: *"if you love those who love you, what grace is that to you? Love your enemies, do good to those who hate you."* If therefore differences between laws amount to differences between what ought to be done, because the law is nothing other than a description of what ought to be done or the evil to be avoided, the law of the gospel will be other than the law of nature.

Reply:

As nature is ordered to grace, so the law of nature is ordered to the law of the gospel, but the natural law is not the same as the law of the gospel. Nevertheless, the natural law is not abolished through the gospel but perfected. For example, the natural law says that God must be loved, because he is our benefactor and creator. The law of the gospel says that he is to be loved, because he is good and the redeemer. Likewise, the natural law says that we must love our neighbors because they are human and conform to us in species and because we are made by the same creator. The law of grace, however, dictates that the neighbor must be loved because they are a child of God or can be and because they are made in the image of God and we are redeemed by the same one. Therefore, the obligation to love God and neighbor in the natural law and the law of the gospel stem from different causes, although the former is ordained to and perfected through the latter. From this it is clear that the natural law is not the same as the law of the gospel; nevertheless, the natural law is ordained to the [law of the gospel] as to its perfection. And thus Isidore says that the divine law is evident naturally, and for this reason it is true that "the natural law is contained in the law and the gospel."

Replies to the objections:

1. To the first objection, that the law of the gospel is written in the heart like the natural law, it must be said that this is true, but in different ways. For there is an inscription of what should be done according to the dictate of what is written in the conscience and which is the same in all from creation,

and there is an inscription according to a dictate impressed on conscience which is from faith or justification in those who believe. The first inscription is from nature and the second is from the law of the gospel. The first is inserted by nature and the second is given or superadded by grace. And therefore it is figuratively said in Jeremiah 31:33: "*I will give my law*" and in Romans 1:16, "*the gospel is the power of God for the salvation of all who believe*," because as the natural law is the same for all humans, so the law of the gospel is the same for all believers.

2. To the second objection, it must be said that the natural law is not a part of the law of the gospel, but it is nevertheless its foundation, as nature is the subject of grace. Therefore, whatever the natural law dictates, the law of the gospel also dictates, but by a higher reason. For example, according to the law of nature matrimony is prescribed for the generation of the human race and the multiplication of the species. According to the prescription of grace, however, it is so that human children can be regenerated as children of God and offspring can be multiplied for the worship of God.

3. To the third objection, I respond that the law of the gospel is universal and "always and for all" in one way and the natural law is so in another way. For the law of the gospel is universal and applies to all in a causal sense; according to its effect, however, it is universal for believers, for although grace is offered to all according to the way of causality, nevertheless, according to effect it is only shown to those who are disposed and receive it. However, the natural law is universal and applies to all according to cause and effect: for all persons are naturally imprinted with it and it follows human nature inseparably. The law of the gospel, however, is universal and "always for all" in itself or as regards the grace of the one giving, not nevertheless as regards the effect in the one receiving, while the natural law is "always and for all" according to its effect in the recipient.

4. To the last objection, I respond that that rule of the philosopher, "what is such by nature," etc., applies to the comparison of a natural habit to an acquired habit, not to the comparison of a [natural to a] gratuitous habit; rather, what is gratuitous is greater than what is natural, that is, more noble and worthy, although not as long-lasting. Nevertheless, both the natural law and the law of the gospel are called eternal and perpetual, but in different ways: for the former is perpetual as regards all and in effect, and the latter is perpetual of itself and as regards believers.

IS THE LAW OF THE GOSPEL THE SAME AS THE LAW OF MOSES?

SH 3, P2, In4, Tr1, Q5 (n. 547), 845-46

1. The faith of the New and Old Testaments is one, and it is not essentially different; therefore, the law of the New and Old Testaments will be one and the same. For if there is unity on the part of the cognition of truth through faith, then there should be unity on the part of the order to the good through the law.

2. Matthew 5:17: "*I did not come to destroy the law but to fulfill it*"; as the Gloss says: "the gospel is the recapitulation of the old law." If therefore the recapitulation of the law does not make the law different, then the law of the gospel and the law of Moses are not different.

3. The gospel is the fulfillment of the law; therefore, the full law is the law of Moses plus the gospel. Therefore, there is not a difference between the law of the gospel and the law of Moses.

4. The same law in its initial stage and in its complete stage are not two different laws; but this is how the law is related to the gospel, Matthew 5:20: "*Unless your righteousness abounds*," etc. The Gloss: "The precepts that are given at the initial stage (i.e., in the Law) are more abundant than those that are added at the final stage (i.e., in the gospel)."

On the other hand:

a. The letter of the law and the spirit of the law are not the same; but the law of Moses is the letter of the law and the law of the gospel or Christ is the spirit, according to Romans 7:6.

b. The law that concerns actions and the law that concerns faith are not the same; but the law of Moses concerns actions and the law of the gospel concerns faith, according to Romans 3:27.

c. The law of signs and shadows is not the same as the law of truth and demonstration; but the law of Moses is the law of shadows and signs, according to Hebrews 10:1: "*the law is the shadow of future things, not their image.*" However, the law of the gospel is the law of truth and demonstration. Therefore, the law of Moses and the law of the gospel are not the same.

d. The laws that have diverse ends are therefore diverse; but the end of the law is the fear of God (Ecclesiastes 12:13), while the end of the gospel is the love of God (1 Timothy 1:5). Thus, Augustine says [in *Against Adimantus*

17:2], "In brief, the difference between the law and gospel is between fear and love."

e. Temporal and eternal laws are not the same; but the law of Moses is temporal, as Galatians 3:19 says, "*What therefore is the Law? It was posited on account of our transgressions, to restrain them, until the seed [Christ] comes.*" However, the gospel is the eternal law, Revelation 14:6: "*I saw the angel holding the eternal gospel,*" and Matthew 24:35, "*heaven and earth will pass away, but my word will not pass away.*"

Reply:

One must reply that the law of Moses and the law of the gospel are one law in terms of their universal import but different in terms of their proper meanings. Thus, Augustine says in *Against the Adversaries of the Law and the Prophets* [1.17.34], "the ones who rightly worship God, find one God in both testaments, and they love the goodness of one and the same God in both testaments, and fear his severity in both." However, there are multiple ways of defining "universal" or "common": in relation to an efficient cause, in relation to an end, and in relation to sense. The universal legislator of the law and the gospel is the one God, James 4:12: "*there is one legislator and judge.*" There is one end, namely, Christ. Thus, Augustine writes in *Against the Adversaries of the Law and the Prophets* 2 [7.26], "Who is the end of the law? To this, not I but the apostle himself responds: '*The end of the law,*' he says, '*is Christ for the justice of all who believe*' (Romans 10:4), [and it is] the perfecting end, not the one that kills. He is surely called that 'end,' at which are aimed all actions that derive from any obligation. Now the difference between an obligation and an end is that an obligation consists in those things which we ought to do, and an end is that for the sake of which we do them." [Finally,] there is one sense, because [there is] one universal truth. Thus, Gregory says in [*Homilies* 1.6.4] commenting on Ezekiel 1:16, where it is said that there were "*wheels within wheels,*" "what the law proclaims, the gospel displays," and likewise, the same author, "divine statements, even if they are made at separate points in time, are united by sense."

Similarly, "proper" can be understood in multiple ways: in relation to an efficient [cause] and a final [cause] and a sense. In relation to the efficient cause, the law and the gospel differ, because the law is given through a mere human being, but the gospel through Christ. John 1:17, "*The law was given through Moses.*" In relation to the end they also differ: for the end of the law is to deflect evil through fear, but the end of the gospel is principally to do good through love. Thus, Augustine in *Against the Adversaries of the Law and the Prophets* [2.7.25], "The New Testament differs from the Old, because in the latter, humans were constrained by fear, and in the former, they are given the latitude of charity." In relation to the sense, however, they differ because in one, truth is presented figuratively, and in the other, the truth is presented clearly, as far as symbolism is concerned. Thus, Augustine says, in *The Harmony of the Evangelists* [1.1]: "What the law and prophets have announced, is presented as delivered and completed in the gospel." Likewise, in the law there is inchoate truth, and here there is perfect truth, as far as morals are concerned. Thus Matthew 5:20, "*unless your righteousness surpasses,*" etc., and Augustine says in this respect: "The precepts that are given at the initial stage are more ample than those that are added at the stage of completion."

Therefore, it must be said that the law of Moses and of the gospel are one law in terms of their universal import but different in their proper implications, and this is because one was given to carnal people, and another to spiritual ones, one to children and the other to those who are perfected. Thus, as Augustine says in *On True Religion* [17.34], the wise doctor gives one mandate to the sick person through his ministers and another through himself. In this way, God gave one law through Moses and another through himself in the gospel. As Augustine says in *To Marcellinus* [*Ep.* 138.2]: "The teacher usually prescribes something different to an adolescent than to a child by changing the requirement but not changing the doctrine, [however, the doctrine] remained the same, although [the way of instruction] changed." In the same way, the Creator intentionally prescribed different ways of teaching one and the same truth in the law and in the gospel, in the former case [teaching] the children and in the latter adults. And this distinction allows one to address the objections.

LYDIA SCHUMACHER is Reader in Historical and Philosophical Theology at King's College London, Department of Theology and Religious Studies, and Principal Investigator of the European Research Council project on Authority and Innovation in Early Franciscan Thought. She has published four monographs: *Divine Illumination: The History and Future of Augustine's Theory of Knowledge*, *Rationality as Virtue*, *Theological Philosophy*, and *Early Franciscan Theology*.

OLEG BYCHKOV is Professor of Theology at Saint Bonaventure University, New York. The most recent of his books are the edition/translation *John Duns Scotus: The Report of the Paris Lecture* and the collection of essays *Aesthetic Theology in the Franciscan Tradition: The Senses and the Experience of God in Art*, co-edited with Xavier Seubert.

MEDIEVAL PHILOSOPHY: TEXTS AND STUDIES

Ronald E. Pepin, *The Vatican Mythographers*
Paul Thom, *The Logic of the Trinity: Augustine to Ockham*
Charles Bolyard and Rondo Keele, eds., *Later Medieval Metaphysics: Ontology, Language, and Logic*
Daniel D. Novotný, *Ens rationis from Suárez to Caramuel: A Study in Scholasticism of the Baroque Era*
John Buridan, *Treatise on Consequences*. Translated by Stephen Read, Introduction by Hubert Hubien
Gyula Klima, ed., *Intentionality, Cognition, and Mental Representation in Medieval Philosophy*
John Duns Scotus, *On Being and Cognition: "Ordinatio" 1.3*. Edited and translated by John van den Bercken
Claude Panaccio, *Mental Language: From Plato to William of Ockham*. Translated by Joshua P. Hochschild and Meredith K. Ziebart
Andrew LaZella, *The Singular Voice of Being: John Duns Scotus and Ultimate Difference*
Lydia Schumacher and Oleg Bychkov, eds. and trans., *A Reader in Early Franciscan Theology: The "Summa Halensis"*

www.ingramcontent.com/pod-product-compliance
Lightning Source LLC
Chambersburg PA
CBHW032030290426
44110CB00012B/744